SMALL BUSINESS INTERNET FOR DUMMIES®

by Greg Holden
with Stylus Media

IDG Books Worldwide, Inc.
An International Data Group Company

Foster City, CA ◆ Chicago, IL ◆ Indianapolis, IN ◆ Southlake, TX

Small Business Internet For Dummies®

Published by
IDG Books Worldwide, Inc.
An International Data Group Company
919 E. Hillsdale Blvd.
Suite 400
Foster City, CA 94404
www.idgbooks.com (IDG Books Worldwide Web site)
www.dummies.com (Dummies Press Web site)

Library of Congress Catalog Card No.: 97-81222

ISBN: 0-7645-0288-3

Printed in the United States of America

10 9 8 7 6 5 4 3 2 1

1O/QZ/QS/ZY/IN

Distributed in the United States by IDG Books Worldwide, Inc.

Distributed by Macmillan Canada for Canada; by Transworld Publishers Limited in the United Kingdom; by IDG Norge Books for Norway; by IDG Sweden Books for Sweden; by Woodslane Pty. Ltd. for Australia; by Woodslane Enterprises Ltd. for New Zealand; by Longman Singapore Publishers Ltd. for Singapore, Malaysia, Thailand, and Indonesia; by Simron Pty. Ltd. for South Africa; by Toppan Company Ltd. for Japan; by Distribuidora Cuspide for Argentina; by Livraria Cultura for Brazil; by Ediciencia S.A. for Ecuador; by Addison-Wesley Publishing Company for Korea; by Ediciones ZETA S.C.R. Ltda. for Peru; by WS Computer Publishing Corporation, Inc., for the Philippines; by Unalis Corporation for Taiwan; by Contemporanea de Ediciones for Venezuela; by Computer Book & Magazine Store for Puerto Rico; by Express Computer Distributors for the Caribbean and West Indies. Authorized Sales Agent: Anthony Rudkin Associates for the Middle East and North Africa.

For general information on IDG Books Worldwide's books in the U.S., please call our Consumer Customer Service department at 800-762-2974. For reseller information, including discounts and premium sales, please call our Reseller Customer Service department at 800-434-3422.

For information on where to purchase IDG Books Worldwide's books outside the U.S., please contact our International Sales department at 650-655-3200 or fax 650-655-3295.

For information on foreign language translations, please contact our Foreign & Subsidiary Rights department at 650-655-3021 or fax 650-655-3281.

For sales inquiries and special prices for bulk quantities, please contact our Sales department at 650-655-3200 or write to the address above.

For information on using IDG Books Worldwide's books in the classroom or for ordering examination copies, please contact our Educational Sales department at 800-434-2086 or fax 817-251-8174.

For press review copies, author interviews, or other publicity information, please contact our Public Relations department at 650-655-3000 or fax 650-655-3299.

For authorization to photocopy items for corporate, personal, or educational use, please contact Copyright Clearance Center, 222 Rosewood Drive, Danvers, MA 01923, or fax 978-750-4470.

is a trademark under exclusive license to IDG Books Worldwide, Inc., from International Data Group, Inc.

About the Author

Greg Holden is founder and president of Stylus Media, a group of editorial, design, and computer professionals who produce both print and electronic publications. The company gets its name from a recording stylus, which reads the traces left on a disk by voices or instruments and translates those signals into electronic data that can be amplified and enjoyed by many.

One of the ways Greg enjoys communicating is through explaining technical subjects in non-technical language by writing computer books, which help other people use the Web to share their own personal and professional interests. *Small Business Internet For Dummies* is his sixth book.

Greg describes himself as a lover of literature. He received a M.A. in English from the University of Illinois at Chicago, but that only gave him an official credential for what he had been doing since he was a tiny tot. As a preschooler, he was displayed by his proud but rather puzzled parents as the kid who read from the encyclopedia to impress his relatives at family gatherings. You can read about some of his triumphs and traumas in the poetry and short stories that he scribbles down at odd moments.

After graduating from college, Greg became a reporter for his hometown newspaper, first covering sewers and school boards and then working his way up to having his own column (called "So It Goes") in which he voiced his perspective on the world. Working at the publications office at the University of Chicago was his next job, and it was there that he started to use computers. He discovered that he loved desktop publishing (with the Macintosh and LaserWriter) and, later on, the World Wide Web.

Greg loves to travel, but since his two daughters were born he hasn't been able to get around much. He lives with his two kids and his wife in an old house in Chicago that he has been rehabbing for — well, for many years now. He is a collector of objects such as pens, cameras, radios, and hats. He is always looking for things to take them apart so that he can see how they work and fix them up. Many of the same skills prove useful in creating and maintaining Web pages. He is an active member of Jewel Heart, a Tibetan Buddhist meditation and study group based in Ann Arbor, MI. Not surprisingly, he also produces a newsletter and a Web site for Jewel Heart.

He met John Casler at the University of Chicago, where John was a computer and technical specialist in the publications office and was the supervisor of the instructional laboratory in the Department of Computer Science. They discovered many common interests, not the least of which is that they are both the father of two girls. Now they are partners in Stylus Media, and continue to be good friends. John has a day job at Lucent Technologies and is a successful fine artist whose work is frequently shown at Chicago-area galleries. John's artwork is displayed in the "clip art" that accompanies the Web Page Workshop exercises on the CD.

ABOUT IDG BOOKS WORLDWIDE

Welcome to the world of IDG Books Worldwide.

IDG Books Worldwide, Inc., is a subsidiary of International Data Group, the world's largest publisher of computer-related information and the leading global provider of information services on information technology. IDG was founded more than 25 years ago and now employs more than 8,500 people worldwide. IDG publishes more than 275 computer publications in over 75 countries (see listing below). More than 60 million people read one or more IDG publications each month.

Launched in 1990, IDG Books Worldwide is today the #1 publisher of best-selling computer books in the United States. We are proud to have received eight awards from the Computer Press Association in recognition of editorial excellence and three from *Computer Currents'* First Annual Readers' Choice Awards. Our best-selling *...For Dummies*® series has more than 30 million copies in print with translations in 30 languages. IDG Books Worldwide, through a joint venture with IDG's Hi-Tech Beijing, became the first U.S. publisher to publish a computer book in the People's Republic of China. In record time, IDG Books Worldwide has become the first choice for millions of readers around the world who want to learn how to better manage their businesses.

Our mission is simple: Every one of our books is designed to bring extra value and skill-building instructions to the reader. Our books are written by experts who understand and care about our readers. The knowledge base of our editorial staff comes from years of experience in publishing, education, and journalism — experience we use to produce books for the '90s. In short, we care about books, so we attract the best people. We devote special attention to details such as audience, interior design, use of icons, and illustrations. And because we use an efficient process of authoring, editing, and desktop publishing our books electronically, we can spend more time ensuring superior content and spend less time on the technicalities of making books.

You can count on our commitment to deliver high-quality books at competitive prices on topics you want to read about. At IDG Books Worldwide, we continue in the IDG tradition of delivering quality for more than 25 years. You'll find no better book on a subject than one from IDG Books Worldwide.

IDG BOOKS WORLDWIDE

John J. Kilcullen
John Kilcullen
CEO
IDG Books Worldwide, Inc.

Steven Berkowitz
Steven Berkowitz
President and Publisher
IDG Books Worldwide, Inc.

WINNER

Eighth Annual Computer Press Awards ≥ 1992

IX WINNER

Ninth Annual Computer Press Awards ≥ 1993

Tenth Annual Computer Press Awards ≥ 1994

X WINNER

XI WINNER

Eleventh Annual Computer Press Awards ≥ 1995

IDG Books Worldwide, Inc., is a subsidiary of International Data Group, the world's largest publisher of computer-related information and the leading global provider of information services on information technology. International Data Group publishes over 275 computer publications in over 75 countries. Sixty million people read one or more International Data Group publications each month. International Data Group's publications include: **ARGENTINA:** Buyer's Guide, Computerworld Argentina, PC World Argentina; **AUSTRALIA:** Australian Macworld, Australian PC World, Australian Reseller News, Computerworld, IT Casebook, Network World, Publish, Webmaster; **AUSTRIA:** Computerwelt Osterreich, Networks Austria, PC Tip Austria; **BANGLADESH:** PC World Bangladesh; **BELARUS:** PC World Belarus; **BELGIUM:** Data News; **BRAZIL:** Annuário de Informática, Computerworld, Connections, Macworld, PC Player, PC World, Publish, Reseller News, Supergamepower; **BULGARIA:** Computerworld Bulgaria, Network World Bulgaria, PC & MacWorld Bulgaria; **CANADA:** CIO Canada, Client/Server World, ComputerWorld Canada, InfoWorld Canada, NetworkWorld Canada, WebWorld; **CHILE:** Computerworld Chile, PC World Chile; **COLOMBIA:** Computerworld Colombia, PC World Colombia; **COSTA RICA:** PC World Centro America; **THE CZECH AND SLOVAK REPUBLICS:** Computerworld Czechoslovakia, Macworld Czech Republic, PC World Czechoslovakia; **DENMARK:** Communications World Danmark, Computerworld Danmark, Macworld Danmark, PC World Danmark, Techworld Denmark; **DOMINICAN REPUBLIC:** PC World Republica Dominicana; **ECUADOR:** PC World Ecuador; **EGYPT:** Computerworld Middle East, PC World Middle East; **EL SALVADOR:** PC World Centro America; **FINLAND:** MikroPC, Tietoverkko, Tietoviikko; **FRANCE:** Distributique, Hebdo, Info PC, Le Monde Informatique, Macworld, Reseaux & Telecoms; **GERMANY:** Computer Partner, Computerwoche, Computerwoche Extra, Computerwoche FOCUS, Global Online, Macwelt, PC Welt; **GREECE:** Amiga Computing, GamePro Greece, Multimedia World; **GUATEMALA:** PC World Centro America; **HONDURAS:** PC World Centro America; **HONG KONG:** Computerworld Hong Kong, PC World Hong Kong, Publish in Asia; **HUNGARY:** ABCD CD-ROM, Computerworld Szamitastechnika, Internetto online Magazine, PC World Hungary, PC-X Magazin Hungary; **ICELAND:** Tolvuheimur PC World Island; **INDIA:** Information Communications World, Information Systems Computerworld, PC World India, Publish in Asia; **INDONESIA:** InfoKomputer PC World, Komputek Computerworld, Publish in Asia; **IRELAND:** ComputerScope, PC Live!; **ISRAEL:** Macworld Israel, People & Computers/Computerworld; **ITALY:** Computerworld Italia, Macworld Italia, Networking Italia, PC World Italia; **JAPAN:** DTP World, Macworld Japan, Nikkei Personal Computing, OS/2 World Japan, SunWorld Japan, Windows NT World, Windows World Japan; **KENYA:** PC World East African; **KOREA:** Hi-Tech Information, Macworld Korea, PC World Korea, Publish in Asia; **MACEDONIA:** PC World Macedonia; **MALAYSIA:** Computerworld Malaysia, PC World Malaysia, Publish in Asia; **MALTA:** PC World Malta; **MEXICO:** Computerworld Mexico, PC World Mexico; **MYANMAR:** PC World Myanmar; **NETHERLANDS:** Computer! Totaal, LAN Internetworking Magazine, LAN World Buyers Guide, Macworld Netherlands, Net, WebWereld; **NEW ZEALAND:** Absolute Beginners Guide and Plain & Simple Series, Computer Buyer, Computer Industry Directory, Computerworld New Zealand, MTB, Network World, PC World New Zealand; **NICARAGUA:** PC World Centro America; **NORWAY:** Computerworld Norge, CW Rapport, Datamagasinet, Financial Rapport, Kursguide Norge, Macworld Norge, Multimediaworld Norge, PC World Ekspress Norge, PC World Nettverk, PC World Norge, PC World ProduktGuide Norge; **PAKISTAN:** Computerworld Pakistan; **PANAMA:** PC World Panama; **PEOPLE'S REPUBLIC OF CHINA:** China Computer Users, China Computerworld, China InfoWorld, China Telecom World Weekly, Computer & Communication, Electronic Design China, Electronics Today, Electronics Weekly, Game Software, PC World China, Popular Computer Week, Software Weekly, Software World, Telecom World; **PERU:** Computerworld Peru, PC World Profesional Peru, PC World SoHo Peru; **PHILIPPINES:** Click!, Cerebro/PC World, Computerworld/Correio Informático, Dealer World Portugal, Mac*In/PC*In Portugal, Multimedia World; **PUERTO RICO:** PC World Puerto Rico; **ROMANIA:** Computerworld Romania, PC World Romania, Computerworld Philippines, PC World Philippines, Publish in Asia; **POLAND:** Computerworld Poland, Computerworld Special Report Poland, Cyber, Macworld Poland, Networld Poland, PC World Komputer; **PORTUGAL:** Telecom Romania; **RUSSIA:** Computerworld Russia, Mir PK, Publish, Seti; **SINGAPORE:** Computerworld Singapore, PC World Singapore, Publish in Asia; **SLOVENIA:** Monitor; **SOUTH AFRICA:** Computing SA, Network World SA, Software World SA; **SPAIN:** Communicaciones World España, Computerworld España, Dealer World España, Macworld España, PC World España; **SRI LANKA:** Infolink PC World; **SWEDEN:** CAP&Design, Computer Sweden, Corporate Computing Sweden, Internetworld Sweden, it.branschen, Macworld Sweden, MaxiData Sweden, PC World Sweden, PCaktiv, Windows World Sweden; **SWITZERLAND:** Computerworld Schweiz, Macworld Schweiz, PCtip; **TAIWAN:** Computerworld Taiwan, Macworld Taiwan, NEW ViSiON/Publish, PC World Taiwan, Windows World Taiwan; **THAILAND:** Publish in Asia, Thai Computerworld; **TURKEY:** Computerworld Turkiye, Macworld Turkiye, Network World Turkiye, PC World Turkiye; **UKRAINE:** Computerworld Kiev, Multimedia World Ukraine, PC World Ukraine; **UNITED KINGDOM:** Acorn User UK, Amiga Action UK, Amiga Computing UK, Apple Talk UK, Computing, Macworld, Parents and Computers UK, PC Advisor, PC Home, PSX Pro, The WEB; **UNITED STATES:** Cable in the Classroom, CIO Magazine, Computerworld, DOS World, Federal Computer Week, GamePro Magazine, InfoWorld, I-Way, Macworld, Network World, PC Games, PC World, Publish, Video Event, THE WEB Magazine, and WebMaster; online webzines: JavaWorld, NetscapeWorld, and SunWorld Online; **URUGUAY:** InfoWorld Uruguay; **VENEZUELA:** Computerworld Venezuela, PC World Venezuela; and **VIETNAM:** PC World Vietnam.   3/24/97

Dedication

To my mother and father, who were my first teachers, and who continue to help me learn every day about myself and relating to others, both online and offline.

Acknowledgments

One of the things I like best about this book is that it's a teaching tool that gives me a chance to share my knowledge about computers, the Internet, and communicating your message to others in an interactive way. As any businessperson knows, most large-scale projects are a team effort.

In the course of writing this book, I met a lot of businesspeople. I was struck by the fact that the most successful entrepreneurs also tended to be the ones who were the most generous with their time and experience. They taught me that the more helpful you are, the more successful you'll be in return.

I want to thank all those who were profiled as Case Studies, particularly Joshua Baer of SkyWeyr Technologies, Scott Bernberg of Graphic Expectations, Bill Cameta of Cameta Camera, Dennis Dori of Charter Sailing Unlimited, Jan Gilder of Sense and Nonsense, Mike LeBlanc of the INKBOX Company, Leigh McLean of Customer Service Review, Debbie Levitt of As Was, Joel MacIntosh of Ranchweb, Claire Marino of Marino & Co., Doug Mummenhoff of DayMen Photo Marketing, Chris Phillipo of Tread Publications, Nicholas Raftis of Dymaxeon Engineering, Cliff Sharples of Garden Escape, David Shumate of Lakeville Engineering, Inc., and Paul Whalen, Jr. of The Image Connection.

I would also like to acknowledge some of my own colleagues who helped prepare and review the text and graphics of this book, and who have supported and encouraged me in other lessons of life.

Thanks to my friend and Stylus Media partner John Casler (jcasler@ paranet.com), who taught me multitasking, shared his real-world knowledge of intranets and the Web, and contributed the JavaScript goodies mentioned in Chapter 17.

Madonna Gauding (madonna@interaccess.com) gave me a refresher course on how valuable it is to have a right hand person who cheerfully and competently responds to many requests, such as for lists of URLs and other resources for businesspeople.

Ann Lindner's teaching experience proved valuable in suggesting ways to make the text more clear.

For editing and technical assignments, I was lucky to be in the capable hands of the folks at IDG Books Worldwide: project editor Pat O'Brien, technical editor Allen Wyatt, CD guru Kevin Spencer, and Heather Dismore and her permissions staff.

Thanks also to Brian Gill and David Rogelberg of Studio B, and to Jill Pisoni of IDG Books for helping me to add this book to the list of those I've authored and, in the process, broaden my expertise as a writer.

I met my wife, Mary, in a creative writing class and am grateful to have her by my side as we continue to be students together, especially in parenting and traveling. And, ultimately, the future is in the hands of the generation of my two daughters, Zosia and Lucy, who allow me to learn from the curiosity and joy with which they approach life.

Publisher's Acknowledgments

We're proud of this book; please register your comments through our IDG Books Worldwide Online Registration Form located at http://my2cents.dummies.com.

Some of the people who helped bring this book to market include the following:

Acquisitions, Development, and Editorial

Project Editor: Pat O'Brien

Acquisitions Editor: Jill Pisoni

Media Development Manager: Joyce Pepple

Associate Permissions Editor: Heather H. Dismore

Copy Editor: Linda Stark

Technical Editor: Allen Wyatt

Editorial Manager: Mary C. Corder

Editorial Assistant: Michael D. Sullivan

Production

Project Coordinator: Valery Bourke

Layout and Graphics: Steve Arany, Lou Boudreau, Linda M. Boyer, Angela F. Hunckler, Drew R. Moore, Brent Savage, Janet Seib

Proofreaders: Christine Berman, Kelli Botta, Laura L. Bowman, Michelle Croninger, Joel K. Draper, Rachel Garvey, Nancy Price, Janet M. Withers

Indexer: David Heiret

General and Administrative

IDG Books Worldwide, Inc.: John Kilcullen, CEO; Steven Berkowitz, President and Publisher

IDG Books Technology Publishing: Brenda McLaughlin, Senior Vice President and Group Publisher

Dummies Technology Press and Dummies Editorial: Diane Graves Steele, Vice President and Associate Publisher; Mary Bednarek, Acquisitions and Product Development Director; Kristin A. Cocks, Editorial Director

Dummies Trade Press: Kathleen A. Welton, Vice President and Publisher; Kevin Thornton, Acquisitions Manager; Maureen F. Kelly, Editorial Coordinator

IDG Books Production for Dummies Press: Beth Jenkins Roberts, Production Director; Cindy L. Phipps, Manager of Project Coordination, Production Proofreading, and Indexing; Kathie S. Schutte, Supervisor of Page Layout; Shelley Lea, Supervisor of Graphics and Design; Debbie J. Gates, Production Systems Specialist; Robert Springer, Supervisor of Proofreading; Debbie Stailey, Special Projects Coordinator; Tony Augsburger, Supervisor of Reprints and Bluelines; Leslie Popplewell, Media Archive Coordinator

Dummies Packaging and Book Design: Patti Crane, Packaging Specialist; Kavish + Kavish, Cover Design

◆

The publisher would like to give special thanks to Patrick J. McGovern, without whom this book would not have been possible.

◆

Contents at a Glance

Cartoons at a Glance

By Rich Tennant

page 85

page 7

page 111

page 219

page 181

page 345

page 327

Fax: 978-546-7747 • E-mail: the5wave@tiac.net

Table of Contents

Introduction

∙∙∙

*T*his is a roll-up-your-sleeves kind of a book. With easy-to-understand vocabulary and easy-to-follow instructions, you will soon master exciting new technologies that will benefit your small business. The goals of getting connected and setting up shop on the Internet are within your grasp. Whether you are starting up a new business or expanding an existing organization, you will learn what you need to know to grow and flourish in the new medium of cyberspace.

Almost all entrepreneurs are familiar with the concepts of stocking a new storefront, holding promotions, and marketing successful companies in the "real world." This book will direct that same drive to get ahead to get you on the Internet or, if you are on the Net already, help you use it more effectively.

You've probably spent thousands of dollars on signage, advertising, and computerized cash register systems. A relatively small investment is required to purchase a modem, get a connection, and develop a Web site. With the help of this book, you will soon be publicizing your business before millions of potential clients.

A Little Pep Talk

If you have been reluctant to join the World Wide Web, let me entice you with the promise that the Internet is not only profitable but also fun. Once you are on it and have used it for even a short time, you will be comfortable with it, especially if you use a friendly Web browser to navigate the online universe.

Small business owners who confess their cold feet to me, usually mention the following factors:

- ✔ **Computers.** Many of the business owners who should be online but aren't seem uncomfortable with using computers and don't understand how networks work. They need someone to guide them along — and *Small Business Internet For Dummies* is intended to do just that.

- ✔ **Uncertain results.** Nothing is guaranteed, and I'm not going to say that every single business is certain to reap huge benefits from the Internet. Because they don't know ahead of time how many of their customers and clients are on the Net, some proprietors don't want to invest the energy in the unknown. This book provides the bridge you need to get the best possible results with the least investment of time and money.

If you're the type who still needs to test the waters before you do business on the Internet, this book gently leads you up the learning curve. Once you're online, you'll also master techniques to improve your presence.

Where This Book Is Coming From

With each month that goes by, the number of Internet users increases exponentially. Whether you believe the surveys that count 40 million users or the ones that provide a "conservative" estimate of 20 million users, there are a lot of people out there in cyberspace. Before long, the Internet will reach that critical mass where *most* people begin to use the Internet regularly for everyday shopping and other financial activities. When that happens, look out: the Internet will be a powerhouse for small businesses.

So, why wait to fall behind your competition? The goal of this book is to help you connect your small business to the Internet and use it effectively now, while the Net is still new and cutting edge. This book guides you through the following steps:

- Purchasing software and hardware you need to get online
- Recognizing what separates a "dud" Web page from a successful one
- Getting your catalog online and allowing customers to make secure online purchases
- Staying ahead of bigger competitors by designing and organizing a professional and effective Web site

How to Use This Book

Want to get on the Internet for less than $100 — or even for free? Zip ahead to Chapter 1 and get some tips on low-cost Internet connections. Want to connect your office network and set up your own e-mail or Web surfers? You find out about that, too. Feel free to skip back and forth to chapters that interest you. I made this book into an easy-to-use reference tool that you will be comfortable with, no matter what your level of experience with computers and networking. You don't have to scour each chapter methodically from beginning to end to find what you want. The Net doesn't work that way and this book doesn't, either!

What This Book Assumes

This book assumes you have a small business of perhaps eight employees or less (that includes those of you who work alone or at home), or you are interested in starting a new business on the Internet.

It also assumes you have or are ready to get the following:

✔ **A computer and a modem.**

✔ **Instructions on what to buy or obtain and how to use it.** Some small business owners do it all themselves, and like it that way. You find plenty of suggestions and practical, step-by-step exercises to guide you along.

✔ **Just enough technical know-how.** If you don't want to do your own networking and Web site design, don't worry. You don't have to feel that you are stranded all by yourself. This book helps you understand your options and gives you a basic vocabulary so you can work productively with consultants you hire.

What's Where in This Book

This book is divided into seven parts, and each part contains chapters that discuss a stage in the process of Web publishing. In each chapter you find step-by-step instructions and icons that present short bits of useful information. Here are the parts of the book and what they contain:

Part I: Getting Started

If you're an absolute computer novice or have only been using computers and the Internet for a short time, this is the place to start.

Part II: Bringing the Internet to Your Employees

This part describes how your employees can use the Net — both the worldwide Internet, and the miniature Internet you can set up for you and your staff, which is called an _intranet_. You learn about using Internet technologies for training and communication, and how to provide consultants and suppliers with access to your internal network.

Part III: Improving Communication

Effective communication is a key to business success. The Internet can provide the small business owner with many new ways to communicate: with employees, with customers, or with other businesspeople. This part discusses the best business uses of Internet communication tools like electronic mail, discussion groups, and conferencing.

Part IV: Securing Your Business

Along with all the new communications and marketing opportunities the Internet provides, there's also an increased security risk. This part discusses potential problems and describes ways to prevent trouble. You learn about general security methods on the Internet, and specific ways to conduct business transactions securely online.

Part V: Selling Your Products

The information in Part V is for those small business owners who want to reach out to potential customers using the Internet's limitless resources. You learn how to advertise and get attention for your online business. You also get an introduction to creating a Web site and obtaining a unique domain name. You discover ways to encourage "hits" or visits to your site, and how to provide customer support online.

Part VI: The Part of Tens

Filled with tips, cautions, suggestions, and examples, The Part of Tens presents many kinds of information that help you plan and create your own business presence on the Internet.

Part VII: Appendixes

You find a grab bag of information in the appendixes that are part of this book.

Conventions Used in This Book

Important bits of information are formatted in special ways in this book to make sure you notice them right away. Here they are:

"In This Chapter" lists: Let's start at the very beginning, with the lists at the start of every chapter. They represent a kind of table of contents in miniature form. They tell you the topics covered and the software that's examined in that chapter.

Numbered lists: When you see a numbered list, you should follow the steps in a specific order.

Bulleted lists: Bulleted lists, however, indicate things that you can do in any order or include special descriptive information.

Web addresses: When I describe activities or sites of interest on the World Wide Web, I include the address or Uniform Resource Locator (URL) in a special typeface often like this: www.idgbooks.com.

Keep in mind that the newer versions of popular Web browsers, such as Netscape Navigator and Microsoft Internet Explorer, don't require you to enter the entire URL. For instance, if you want to connect to the IDG Books Worldwide site mentioned in the preceding example, you can get there by simply entering the following in your browser's Go To box:

idgbooks

Icons Used in This Book

Small Business Internet For Dummies also uses special graphical elements to get your attention. These are called icons. Here's what they look like and what they mean:

Provides you with reasons to master the material in the chapter, and encourages you to focus on what you want your Web site to accomplish.

Just as it's good business practice to set clear goals, it's also important to evaluate how well you have achieved those goals. You can then revise what you've done so you can be even more successful.

Points out some technical details that you may find to be of interest but that are optional to understand. Non-techies are welcome to skip them altogether.

 Indicates that the CD-ROM at the back of this book contains a demo version of the software.

 Flags practical advice about particular software programs or about issues of importance to businesses.

 Points out things that can develop into problems if you're not careful.

 Alerts you to important facts and figures to keep in mind.

Feedback!

The whole point of this book is to help you express yourself and communicate in the exciting new medium of the Internet. For example, I hope that you'll let us know what you think about this book by contacting us online or by *snail mail* at:

IDG Books Worldwide Inc.
7260 Shadeland Station, Suite 100
Indianapolis, IN 46256

Or you can e-mail us at feedback/dummies@idgbooks.com. And remember to check out the *...For Dummies* Web site at www.dummies.com.

If you want to reach the author directly, you're welcome to do that, too. Send e-mail to Greg Holden at gholden@interaccess.com.

Part I
Getting Started

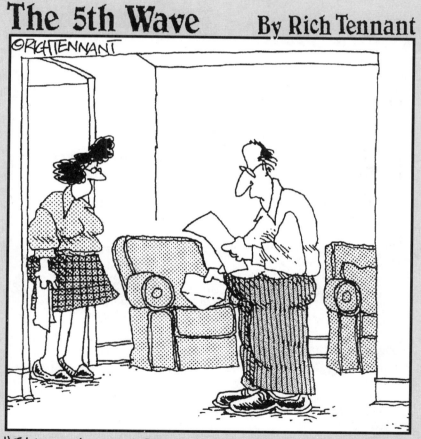

The 5th Wave — By Rich Tennant

"It's a letter from the company that installed our in-ground sprinkler system. They're offering Internet access now."

In this part . . .

Get ready to turn on the lights, put up the Grand Opening sign, and throw open your doors to your customers. The first part of this book will lead you through the process of starting up a new business on the Internet or expanding an existing company to go online.

Chapter 1

Making a Splash on the Internet

In This Chapter

▶ Jumping on the fast track to the Internet: Low-cost and no-cost solutions

▶ Understanding how the Net works and benefits small businesses

▶ Avoiding the fallacies and pitfalls of doing business online

▶ Measuring the success of your Internet and World Wide Web presence

*A*s a famous man said years ago: You ain't heard nothin' yet.

That illustrious character was Al Jolson. Seventy years after the jazz singer reached his peak of show-business fame in the 1920s, his well-known statement can be applied to the Internet, which has helped to bring him back to life. When a British theatrical producer named Paul Elliott wondered if people had an interest in paying money to see a new musical about Jolson, he used the Internet to find out. His company put out a page of information about Jolson on the World Wide Web, and instantly connected with the legions of fans who still admire the singer, even 50 years after his death. The musical opened in London in 1995, played for more than a year, and went on to become a hit in Toronto as well.

The official Web site for the London production of *Jolson* is at www.idm.co.uk/jolson.

Nope, I ain't heard nothin' yet about the Internet — its impact on small businesses, startups, and individual entrepreneurs is only beginning to be felt.

International Data Corp. (www.idc.com) estimates that the dollar value of goods and services purchased over the Web will increase dramatically, from $2.6 billion in 1996 to more than $220 billion during 2001.

Small Business Success Stories

A bankrupt auto dealer named Pete Ellis started an Internet auto purchasing service called Auto-By-Tel (ABT) on the online service Prodigy in 1995. Today, his Web site (as shown in Figure 1-1) gets 3 million *hits* (the Internet's term for visits) and 40,000 serious inquiries each month. ABT has forged strategic partnerships with Chase Manhattan Bank and other big players, and has projected revenues for 1997 of between $25 million and $30 million.

Auto-By-Tel's Web site is at `www.autobytel.com`.

The media is full of stories about companies, whether big or small, that are making lots of money on the Internet. But what about small companies of, say, eight employees or less, or the lone entrepreneur whose only computer is a borrowed laptop? Internet small business success stories aren't always dramatic, but they're not hard to find, either.

For small businesses like Charter Sailing Unlimited, a one-person charter yacht broker based in Chicago, even a moderate amount of success can make a big difference. Not long after Charter Sailing Unlimited dramatically redesigned its site on the Web (`www.sail-csu.com`), owner Dennis Dori received a flurry of business, including a $14,000 reservation that more than paid for the costs of getting online and revamping his site, which is shown in Figure 1-2.

Figure 1-1: Auto-By-Tel: An Internet small business and a big success.

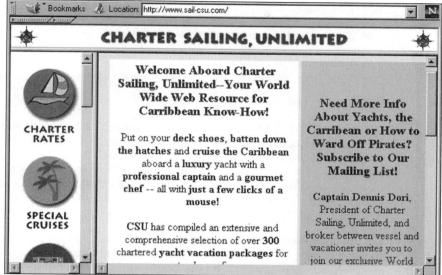

Figure 1-2:
A one-person business that's finding success through the Internet.

Dori's experience is typical of many small businesses. Although he's been in business for years, he's far from a computer expert. "People ask me what kind of computer I own, I tell them 'beige,'" he jokes. Dori depends on two computer consultants, Karl Peterson and Serena FitzSimons of the Argus Company (www.argus.com), to design the site, get it online, and publicize it.

Dori's success on the Internet hasn't been dramatic, and hasn't been without setbacks. In the seven months after the site's debut, Dori received 225 serious inquiries, which yielded only eight reservations for charter yacht trips. He receives many inquiries from children and others who aren't seriously interested in chartering a boat and who just waste his time. And he has to follow up initial contacts on the Web with phone and fax conversations. But Dori knows that without his Internet connections, he may miss some of his orders from faraway countries like Monaco. He emphasizes patience and the importance of promoting your site on an ongoing basis. "I can't totally depend on the Net to make a sale, but it makes a great introduction," Dori says.

Grab that brass ring

If you think that your company may be too small to be a successful player on the Internet, think again. Now's the time to get on the Net, and this book shows you how to do it.

You're probably asking yourself some basic questions like:

- Why should I connect my business to the Internet?
- What can I do after I get online?
- What is the Internet, anyway? Who runs it, and how does it work?
- How do I go about connecting my business to the Internet?

I'm going to skip the first three questions for the moment and leap ahead to the fourth. After all, if you purchased this book, or are sitting in one of the megabookstores sipping latte and leafing through it, you already know that you want to get on the Net. You want to know how to do it, easily and economically. You can do it. There's no doubt about that. You just need to define your goals in concrete form and have a clear idea of what you want to do, and what you *can* do, online.

Lots of people think that the Web *is* the Internet, and that getting online means creating a Web page. Being online doesn't necessarily mean you need to create a Web page and sell your goods and services online — if you *want* to make money selling on the Net, a Web page is the way to go.

The Internet is much more than the Web. Your Internet presence can perform lots of other useful support functions that can help a business succeed. Here are just a few examples of how the Net can be of value to small businesses, and the chapters in which the topics are discussed:

- Do research on clients, competitors, and new opportunities (see Chapter 16).
- Find employees, suppliers, and consultants (see Chapter 6).
- Communicate and transfer files with workers outside the office (see Chapter 9).
- Research markets, check stock prices, and get late-breaking news (see Chapter 16).
- Save money on long-distance phone calls (see Chapter 9).
- Publicize a business and gain credibility (see Chapter 12).
- Create communities by giving your customers a place to discuss common interests with discussion groups (see Chapter 8).
- Conduct personalized and efficient customer support (see Chapter 14).

If you already have a general idea of what the Internet is and you simply want to know what you need to do to get online right away, the next few sections provide you with some quick, low-cost options.

Jump Right In, the Water's Fine!

Small business managers don't have time to do lots of research. You may be interested in the history of the Internet and related technical details, but you're also concerned about the practical aspects of getting your business online right *now*. Whether you are a lone entrepreneur or a member of a small office, the Internet can help you do it.

Here's one possible scenario for how the Internet can help a self-employed person: You work alone, you only have one computer, and you have a great idea for a new company. You don't have much money to spend, and you have to do most, if not all, of the work yourself. You want to know how to economically connect to the Internet so that you can boost your company off the ground. Later on, when you've had some success, you can learn additional details about the Net and spend time setting up a more elaborate network.

Here's another scenario that involves a group of employees: You run a small business and employ less than eight people. You're doing okay, but you want to find new customers and save money on postage, long-distance phone calls, and delivery services. You don't have a big budget for computers, and can't even afford to hire a consultant to get you started. In other words, you're ready to do a little *bootstrapping*.

Step-by-step Internet for bootstrappers

Most small businesses contract with designers to create Web pages and put them online. (See Chapter 6 for information on what such consultants do and how much their services can cost.) If you don't have the means to hire the help, however, you can climb the learning curve and do the work yourself. Just follow these steps:

1. **Check your memory.** Internet software is easy to obtain, and many programs come in versions for different computer platforms. However, the newer Web browsers and Web page editors are memory-hungry. Be sure that you have enough food to feed them. You really need at least 16MB of RAM to run a Web browser and other programs; 24MB or 32MB is better if you have it. RAM stands for Random Access Memory, which is the built-in memory your computer uses to run programs on your computer. You can designate some of the memory available on your hard disk (or hard drive) to serve as *virtual memory* but you'll be robbed of disk storage space.

2. **Check your processor.** Your computer's processor determines how fast you can perform basic tasks like saving files and launching programs, not to mention Internet-related tasks like sending and receiving electronic mail messages, transferring files, downloading data, and so on. If you're using Windows 95 or NT, you need a 486 or Pentium PC processor to run most Web browsers or other Internet programs; on a Macintosh, it's best to have a PowerMac, Performa, or a Quadra computer, running Mac System 7.1 or later.

PCs and Macintoshes both allow you to set aside some of the space on your hard disk to serve as virtual memory. Here's how to designate virtual memory on either system: You can check your Windows 95 PC's processor speed and available memory by selecting Start⇨Settings and then choosing Control Panel from the pop-up menu that appears. The Control Panel window opens. Double-click on the System icon. The System Properties dialog box opens. The processor type and amount of RAM are listed under Computer at the bottom of the dialog box. If you have a Macintosh, while the Finder is active, select About This Macintosh . . . from the Apple menu. The About This Macintosh window appears. This window tells you the type of Macintosh you have, what version of the System you're running, and how much memory is available.

3. **Get a connection.** Virtually any company, from the biggest corporation to the smallest startup, that connects to the Internet pays a fee to either a commercial online service such as America Online or to an Internet Service Provider (ISP).

An ISP is a company whose business is providing individuals and companies with access to the Internet. When you sign up with an ISP, you're assigned an e-mail address and space on a server where you can publish *Web pages,* the documents that everyone can access on the World Wide Web. Service providers offer many different types of connections, which vary in bandwidth — the amount of data that can be transmitted along the line being used. The fastest connections (that is, the ones with the highest bandwidths) are provided by dedicated lines that run directly to your home or business. Higher bandwidth connections can be expensive (see Chapter 3). The least expensive connections rely on ordinary telephone lines; you use your computer and a modem to call a modem at an ISP. You're then temporarily connected to one of the ISP's computers, which is connected to the Net all the time.

Check out Chapters 2 and 3 for a more detailed rundown of the hardware you need to place your business on the Net; Chapter 3 describes the different kinds of Internet connections that you can use. Before you buy a modem, find out if you have cable modem or ADSL service in your area.

4. Get a modem. A modem is computer hardware that converts digital signals for transport along ordinary phone lines. Most individuals and small businesses use modems to connect temporarily to the Net. Many computers come with modems built into them. If you don't have a built-in model, you need to purchase a modem at a computer store. Use a modem that transfers at least 28.8Kbps (that's kilobits per second, or thousands of bits per second) of data. A slightly faster modem that works at 33.6Kbps can also be found easily, and 56Kbps modems are becoming common, although not all Internet Service Providers have the necessary hardware to work with them.

5. Create a Web page. The best place to publicize your business and provide contact information is on a Web page. The process for creating the page is described in more detail in Chapter 13. All Web pages are created using a set of instructions called HTML (HyperText Markup Language). However, you don't need to learn HTML in order to design a simple Web page. Instead, you can download and/or purchase one of the Web page programs mentioned in Chapter 4. These programs enable you to format Web pages with headings, body text, lists, and images by clicking on buttons or choosing menu items rather than entering HTML code.

One of the things that makes the Web unique among Internet services is its ability to convey color and images on users' computer screens. To add images to your Web pages, you can:

- Copy clip art from creators who offer the images for free use.

- Draw your own images using a computer graphics program.

- Process photos into digital data by putting them through a scanner.

- Capture images to a computer disk using a digital camera.

6. Publish your pages. Publishing means that you can move your Web page documents from your computer to the directory set aside for you on AOL or provided by an ISP. Your provider usually gives you the software needed to get your files online.

7. Test your pages. Visit your own pages by connecting to the Net and visiting your site with your Web browser. Proofread your pages and correct any errors. Be sure to update your pages for accuracy as well.

After you're online, the key to success is marketing and publicizing your site using all of the Internet's business tools: e-mail, discussion groups, real-time conferencing, interactive forms, and tools for transferring files. The Internet is ideally suited to one-to-one marketing that reaches customers who really want what you have to offer. See Chapter 12 for suggestions on how to get the word out about your site.

Table 1-1 gives you some estimates on the cost of connecting to the Internet and developing a simple Web presence for your business if you do the work yourself.

Table 1-1	Estimated Do-It-Yourself Internet Costs
Item	*Estimated Cost*
ISP account for basic access	$9.95 to $19.95 per month
Web space for business	$29.95 to $50 per month
Modem	$79 to $259
Memory upgrade	$29 to $249
Web page software	$20 to $139
Scanner	$199 to $499
Digital camera	$499 to $989

These estimated costs and other dollar figures given in this book are provided only as guidelines because prices change all the time. Check your local computer store and Internet Service Provider or commercial online service for current rates. You can also purchase computer equipment on the Internet itself, either through discussion groups where users post items for sale, or through Web sites like the ONSALE online auction house (www.onsale.com).

Low-cost Internet access

What's that? You say that your company's boots don't even have straps so you can pull them up, and you need an even cheaper way to get online? Here are some suggestions:

1. **Sign up with America Online.** You can pay a fee for several hours of access each month, plus an hourly fee thereafter. Or, you can pay a single flat monthly charge for unlimited access.

2. **Use AOL's own Web page software.** In my opinion, one compelling reason to sign up with AOL is the potential for creating a dirt-cheap Web site. AOL provides each individual user with 2MB of space, which is plenty of room to publish a full Web site. AOL also provides lots of documentation and support designed to help beginning Internet users (who are often called *newbies*) get on the Web. You can use AOL's Personal Publisher (see Chapter 13) to set up a Web page and publish it. Although you may still have to buy a modem, you potentially end up

paying only $10 to $20 per month to have your business site on the Web. AOL also has a more expensive option called PrimeHost that gives businesses more Web space and a special Internet address, called a URL (Uniform Resource Locator) that's easy to remember. But if you're just starting out, the 2MB option is a good way to test the waters.

AOL, by the way, also provides each user with five screen names, each of which can have its own e-mail address. In effect, you can have up to five e-mail addresses for one account. Multiple e-mail addresses can serve a business in a number of ways. You can designate one e-mail address for your personal mail and another for your company corre-spondence. If your small office has one computer connected to AOL, you can set aside one e-mail address for each of your employees using the single AOL account.

A no-cost Internet presence

What's that? You say that your business doesn't even have any boots? In other words, you're *really* strapped for money and still want to create a Web page and enjoy the benefits of e-mail service. Can you get on the Net without spending any money at all? Finding a way to connect may take a little extra work and may be inconvenient, but it can happen. Here's how:

1. Borrow someone's computer, or use one at your local public library that's set up for Internet access.

2. Start up the Web browser that's supplied with the computer that you're using.

3. Go to the Web site operated by an organization called GeoCities. This site has the URL www.geocities.com. GeoCities is a site that enables users to obtain free memberships. As a GeoCities member, you're entitled to your own e-mail address and the opportunity to create your own Web page, which GeoCities publishes on the Web. The services are all free, as long as you have a way to reach GeoCities.

4. Fill out the electronic membership form and become a member of GeoCities with a unique username and password.

5. Locate a GeoCities neighborhood where you can set up your Web site. One area, called Eureka, is set aside for small business owners and home office workers (as shown in Figure 1-3).

6. Create your Web page using a software program called the Basic HTML Editor, which is provided by GeoCities. This is not software that you have to download to your computer. You can access and use the software with your Web browser.

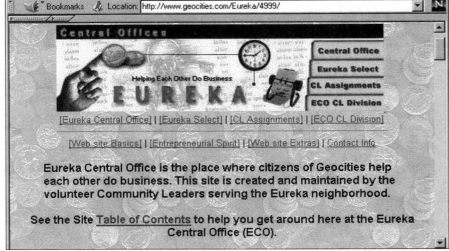

Figure 1-3:
A GeoCities
neighborhood
for small
business
users.

7. Publish your Web page on the GeoCities site by using software (also provided by GeoCities) called EZ File Upload.

You then have to check the page by coming back on a regular basis to the library or to the borrowed computer. Actually, you can use any computer, as long as you connect to the same site and enter a username and password.

The Study, Report, Propose Approach

Jumping right on the Internet is great if you have the authority and the will to do it. But it's also a good idea to find out what the Internet is and how it works before you set out to launch your company online.

Often, it's someone who has a computer and knowledge of the Web who proposes that the company consider connecting to the Internet or developing its own Web site. Such a person may have middle management experience and the ability to estimate expenses and project benefits of a Web presence, making an easier sale to those people in the organization who hold the purse strings.

Get a partner business to help you

You don't have to do it all yourself when you want to get on the Net. Some businesses strike alliances with larger businesses that already have their own Web sites. The best partner is one who does not compete with you directly, but who sells a related product and is happy to host your Web page for you. If you're lucky, like Gempler's (see Chapter 15), you can find a company like Meredith Corporation, which operates a Web site called @griculture Online (`www.agriculture.com`). The creators of @griculture Online eagerly agreed to help Gempler's create a Web site and host it as well. The host then is able to list Gempler's as one of its Web Partners on its own home page.

You can make your Web site more content-rich, and thus more valuable, by including links to related organizations. @griculture Online does this by including hypertext links to the Gempler's site and other related companies like NK Seeds and CNA Agriculture. If you can find an organization that's already online and who may want to promote what you have to sell, your costs and obstacles to getting on the Net are dramatically reduced. The other company benefits by having more content to offer, which increases the number of visitors to the host's own site.

Even if you're in charge and have the authority to approve such expenses yourself, it's a good idea to spell out to your staff exactly what your goals are in getting online, and to explain the proper use of Internet technologies. An Internet connection that no one understands or knows how to use may not reach its full potential in usefulness to your organization.

Whatever your situation, the next few sections provide you with a crash course in Internet 101. You discover what the Internet is, how you can connect to it, and how your company can benefit, with emphasis on the particular needs of small organizations, as well as the personnel and budget constraints that every small business manager has to face.

What's behind the Internet hype?

You hear about it on TV, on the radio, and over lunch: Talk of the Internet is in the air, and everyone seems to be suggesting that businesses need to be on the Net. So, what does it mean to be on the Internet, and what does the Internet mean for small businesses in particular?

The Internet is a network of interconnected computers used by as many as 40 million individuals all over the world. That fact alone means that any business that connects to the Net can consider the impact of attracting international clients or customers. The Net is ideally suited to goods and services that appeal to people across the country or around the world, rather than just those potential customers in a local neighborhood.

Who's in charge?

Although it may not appear obvious, the Internet does have an organization. One of the frequently asked questions about the Net is, who runs it? No single group is in charge of everything, but some of the more important Internet groups include:

- ✔ **The Internet Society.** This group of nonprofit organizations, government agencies, corporations, and other volunteers coordinates the development of Internet technologies and applications (www.isoc.org).

- ✔ **The Internet Architecture Board.** These volunteers (www.iab.org/iab) manage standards and address allocation, as well as other aspects of the Internet.

- ✔ **The Internet Engineering Task Force.** The IETF (www.ietf.cnri.reston.va.us/) designs Internet architecture and makes sure that the Internet operates smoothly. Comprised of network engineers, designers, operators, vendors, and researchers around the world, the IETF conducts its work through working groups and mailing lists.

- ✔ **The W3 Organization.** This group of organizations (www.w3.org/pub/WWW) funds the design and coordination of standards for developing the World Wide Web. The W3 comes up with reference codes and specifications for the Web infrastructure, such as electronic commerce, security, and the evolution of HTML.

These groups establish policies that affects the Net or the Web as a whole; for this reason, the ISP or commercial online service that you use for business or personal access to the Net can be considered an important policy-setter. Many groups of users such as discussion groups or mailing lists are self-policing and have their own set of rules, called Netiquette, that you should understand before you participate in them (see Chapters 7 and 8).

Internet services

Thanks to the World Wide Web, the Internet is becoming a great place to do business, as well as share information, communicate with each other, and use software. But the Internet is much more than just the Web. Successful businesses take advantage of as many of these *Internet services* as they can.

Each of the Internet services enables individual computers to copy, present, and transfer data. Each is accessed with its own client software, and each presents information in its own way:

- **The World Wide Web** adds color, images, and animations to plain text, and links files to one another by means of hypertext.

- **Electronic mail (e-mail)** enables you to send plain-text messages as well as transfer attached files and applications, and even display graphics and colors. E-mail is a fast and efficient way for business-people to converse with customers, employees, suppliers, or colleagues.

- **Usenet** discussion groups enable groups of users to exchange messages about topics of mutual interest. Businesses can do some great market research through Usenet.

- **File Transfer Protocol** can enable companies to transfer applications and complex graphics files easily.

- **Gopher** presents information in a list-based, window-oriented format.

- **Wide Area Information Servers (WAIS)** can be used to find information quickly.

- **Telnet** is a bare-bones, old-fashioned way of connecting a computer to the Internet as a dumb terminal, and can be used to search library catalogs and other databases.

All the Internet services are explained in more detail in Chapter 4.

CNET, one of the better news organizations on the Internet, published 20 often-asked questions about the Internet. You may find some of your own questions answered there (www.cnet.com/Content/Features/Techno/Networks/index.html).

Commercial online services

If you sign up with America Online, Prodigy, or the Microsoft Network, you're online. If you sign up with an Internet Service Provider like EarthLink, you're online too. So what's the difference?

Commercial online services are businesses that aren't really part of the Internet, but that give their customers access to the Net.

The big difference between an ISP and a company like America Online (AOL) is in content. An ISP only exists to get you online or to host your Web site. It's up to you to find the content you're looking for. AOL not only gives you access to an online network, but also provides you with its own content as well. If you're on AOL, you have access to online versions of magazines and other publications that pay a fee to AOL to provide that information to you. You also have access to many bulletin boards, clubs, chat rooms, live forums, and other places to meet people.

Online services such as AOL and Prodigy started out by only providing their own content to their members. As the Internet became more popular, the commercial online services all switched this policy. As long as members first connected to their services, the providers granted their customers access to the Internet through a gateway (as shown in Figure 1-4).

Figure 1-4:
AOL's
Internet
Connection
provides its
users with a
way to
access the
entire Net.

The division between the two online worlds is further blurred because some information resources can be found both on the Web and AOL (such as the wildly successful investment resource called The Motley Fool, which is described in Chapter 8).

The big advantage of a service such as AOL is support. If you work alone and are inexperienced with computers, you can find an easy-to-use interface, plenty of tutorials, and lots of other online users to talk about problems and common interests. On the other hand, if you're serious about running a business on the Internet and becoming an information provider yourself, the freedom of the Internet is generally preferable.

Connecting to the Net

Getting connected to the Net means one of two things: You either have a direct line to your business or you dial up with a modem and have a temporary connection.

A business can, conceivably, have a presence on the Internet without actually having an Internet connection. You can hire someone to create a Web page for your company and publish it on a Web server, without actually being able to dial up the Net yourself. But such a Web page is unlikely to help your business significantly because you don't have the chance to publicize and market your company on the Net, and you don't provide visitors with a way to contact you directly via an e-mail message.

Clients and servers

The Internet uses the *client-server system*. Servers are computers that provide information on a network, and clients are programs that individuals use to access the information. These days, the best known type of client on the Internet is a Web browser, which retrieves image and text files from Web servers.

The word *server* can be confusing because it's used to describe not only a computer that serves files, but also the special software that makes data available to computers that connect to it. Servers on the Net provide huge amounts of information to users around the world. E-mail servers route and store e-mail messages, news servers gather and organize newsgroup communications, and so on.

Internet versus intranet

There are actually two types of networks that use Internet technology: the external Internet and an internal *intranet*. Each can have a significant impact on your business.

An intranet is a network or set of networks that exists within a single organization and that uses Internet software to enable employees to share information and communicate. Intranets are taking the corporate world by storm because they're easy to set up and use, and they're *cross-platform compatible,* meaning they can work with the Macintosh as well as the Windows 95 environment. Intranets also provide a company's employees with a seamless connection to the wider Internet, as long as security measures like a firewall are used, as explained in Chapter 10.

Domains and dot coms

The term *dot com* is becoming part of our modern computer language. I hear the words used in disc jockey's "stage names," as well as in commercials. Dot com is a part of Internet addresses that are assigned to commercial business sites as part of the Domain Name Service, or DNS for short. The DNS is a system of organizing the addresses of computers that provide information across the Internet.

Here's a quick overview of how the DNS works: Every computer that is connected to the Internet is assigned an *IP address,* a series of four numbers separated by dots, such as 128.135.87.0. You can imagine how difficult it would be to find a Web site quickly if you had to remember its IP address. To make Internet addresses easier to find, they are assigned aliases called *domain names* that correspond to the DNS. Distributing Internet sites in this way helps organize sites on the worldwide network so that no single computer, person, or organization has to keep track of everyone else.

When your business connects to the Internet, you can apply for your own virtual *domain name*. A domain name is assigned to any organization that's connected to the Internet, and is used to identify each computer that serves information on the Net. A computer that is connected to the Net all the time and that makes Web pages and other documents available for others to read is called a *server*. Businesses are commercial entities, so their domain names end with *.com,* which is a standard suffix used to identify computers based on their organizations' purposes. Other suffixes are

- *.edu* for educational institutions
- *.org* for nonprofit or other organizations
- *.mil* for military agencies
- *.net* for networks such as Internet providers
- *.gov* for government offices

The other part of a domain name is the one that identifies a company, such as

```
idgbooks.com
uchicago.edu
npr.org
```

Each of these domains can have subdomains that are used to identify computers that serve information to different parts of the organization, such as

```
alumni.uchicago.edu
admin.uchicago.edu
```

A company that connects to the Internet through an Internet Service Provider and that publishes its Web site in a directory located on one of the service provider's computers does not own the domain through which its documents are served. The ISP owns the domain name. However, such a business can have a *virtual* domain that looks like a real domain name (`www.mycompany.com`), but is only an alias for a directory on the service provider's computer. The actual domain is held by the ISP.

What's my URL?

The domain name `www.mycompany.com` is part of an Internet address, otherwise known as a Uniform Resource Locator (URL). A URL is an address that enables you to locate virtually any object that's available on the Internet, from a single graphic image to an entire software archive.

A URL consists of three parts: a *protocol,* a *server name* or *virtual domain name,* and a *filename.* All three are shown in this example:

```
http://www.mycompany.com/PressReleases/release1.html
```

Here's the anatomy of this sample URL:

- ✔ **Protocol.** The protocol is the first part of a URL, in this case `http://`. The protocol tells you what part of the Internet contains the file. Each service of the Internet has its own protocol, or set of standard instructions used to send and receive data. HTTP stands for HyperText Transfer Protocol and is used on the Web; FTP is used for File Transfer Protocol, and so on. The protocol is separated from the rest of the URL by a colon and two slashes.

- ✔ **Server name/virtual domain name.** This is the name of the computer that contains what you're looking for. The computer's actual name in this case is `www`. The server name is followed by the domain name of the organization that owns the computer: `mycompany.com`. Alternatively, this can also be a virtual domain name, if an individual or business has been assigned one.

- ✔ **Filename.** This part of the URL describes the path leading through various directories on the server and pointing to the exact document or object that you want. Each directory in the path is separated from the others by a single slash. In this case the full filename is `PressReleases/release1.html`. The actual document that you want to be displayed by a Web browser is `release1.html`.

This nickel tour of the Internet is just a brief introduction designed to help you impress your bosses and coworkers with quick explanations. For a more detailed description of the structure and workings of the Internet, get a copy of *The Internet For Dummies,* 4th Edition, by John R. Levine et al, published by IDG Books Worldwide, Inc.

To host, or not to host?

There's a big difference between letting someone host your site on the Internet and running your own Internet site. If you do the former, you don't need to have an expensive quick connection or a fast computer that's connected to the Net all the time. You sign an agreement with an ISP, pay a monthly fee, and publish your files on one of the ISP's computers. It's up to the ISP's technical support staff to keep the machines running and maintain the network connection.

On the other hand, operating your own computer to function as an Internet server gives you more control over what goes online. You're in charge of not only what's served, but also which server software programs are used to serve them. You have to designate a computer that functions as a server, and then install software that provides files on the Web or route e-mail messages.

You can either run your server in your own office or at your ISP's facility. The latter alternative is called co-location and it's used by Garden Escape, the garden supply resource whose extensive Web site is described in Chapters 10 and 14. The big advantage of co-location is that you can have the benefit of your ISP's fast, direct connection to the Internet without having to install a direct line to your office.

If you want to run your own server in-house, you need a direct Internet connection. The extra work you invest returns benefits: You can put as much material online as you want, and generally you control the whole operation without having to depend on anyone else.

The need for security

The Net is not a good place to do business in private. If you want to provide *secure commerce* so that people can purchase your goods and services online with a credit card, or if you just have sensitive information that you don't want competitors or unwanted visitors to access, you need to set up some sort of security measures for your business. Safeguards can be as simple as downloading a shareware virus protection program, or as complex as setting up firewalls, routers, and proxies, which are described in Chapter 10.

Why get on the Net?

Lots of businesses think that they *need* to get on the Net. Accordingly, they hire consultants to create Web sites without even knowing what they expect to gain. With so little prior knowledge or goal-setting, it's no surprise that their Web pages turn out to be duds: No one visits, no one sends e-mail, and the page lies in a server gradually becoming a *cobweb site* — one whose contents practically never change.

While writing this book, I spoke to several businesses that offer goods or services on the Net. They all enjoy success in one way or another: They either make money or they're happy with savings or supplementing their other promotional publications. Here are some reasons why *they* got online. Consider these voices of experience as you determine how you may make your Internet business a success.

The Internet can't do it all. To be blunt, it can't dig you out of debt or save you from bankruptcy. Businesses do well on the Net for the same reasons they do well in the real world: Their owners work hard, are committed to success, energetically promote themselves, put a premium on customer service, and have good products and services to sell in the first place. For some businesses that rely on personal contact, such as recruiters and travel agencies, the Internet always acts as a supplement to personal meetings and phone calls. The Internet can be a very *useful* supplement, though, and you may decide that such a role is good enough for you: See the profiles of the small companies Travel Spirit in Chapter 7 and Sense and Nonsense in Chapter 16.

Leveling the playing field

A big and often-cited reason for developing a Web page, getting e-mail, and becoming a presence on the Internet is that the online world enables small companies and large ones to compete more or less equally. Although large organizations may have better access to programmers and technical geniuses who can create a great Web site, it's content that really makes Web sites successful.

A tiny operation with a product that people really need can easily be more popular than a huge organization that puts out an information-poor Web page.

Making the bottom line

Although the costs involved with upgrading computers and getting on the Net are real, you can save money by going online, too. One great savings can be a reduction in printing costs. By publishing employee manuals and newsletters online, you can conserve lots of cash. Another economical approach to business is collaboration by audio- or videoconferencing rather than traveling to remote locations. Then, too, transferring files by e-mail or FTP can save in courier costs. By putting training materials online, you can also spend less valuable staff time in formal classroom-type settings or in having employees tutor one another (see Chapter 5).

Case study: TicketWeb

TicketWeb (www.ticketweb.com) used the Web to test the market and discover whether the company could compete with larger, well-established organizations. TicketWeb's site provides an online place for Web surfers to purchase tickets to music, art, and other events. Being on the Internet allows TicketWeb to reduce its overhead, cut ticket price margins, and thus compete with much bigger competitors. TicketWeb was started in 1995 by partners Rick Tyler and Andrew Dreskin, and now has four full-time and five part-time employees. Customers can order tickets through the Web, by sending an e-mail, or calling the company's toll-free number. In its first year on the Web, TicketWeb grossed over $250,000 in ticket sales. The company is planning to expand beyond the Web to an automated ticket service.

Standardized software

A big advantage of the Internet is that people who use PCs, Macs, or other kinds of computers can all use the same kinds of software. All the programs use a set of standard rules and procedures called TCP and IP. TCP stands for *Transport Control Protocol* and IP stands for *Internet Protocol*. Together, as TCP/IP, these two protocols enable servers and clients to communicate.

TCP/IP support is built into the latest operating systems, such as Windows 95 and the Mac System 7.5 and MacOS 8. Software that uses TCP/IP is widespread on the Internet. You don't have to go to a computer store and purchase it. Some useful programs (notably, StuffIt Expander, which is described in Chapter 4) are provided by their manufacturers on the Net and can be downloaded by anyone as freeware. Other programs are made available as *shareware:* Their creators share them with you for a 30-day or other trial period, and then ask you to purchase the program if you decide to keep it.

Keeping up with the competition

Have you checked to see who among your competitors is on the Net already? You probably can find companies online that are participating in your chosen field. That doesn't mean that you're too late: The other organizations may cover a different aspect of the field than you do. But take a tip: Get going now. If you can get online before your primary competitors, you have an advantage.

As an example, consider Amazon.com. This well-known online bookstore started with only a handful of employees long before the giant bookstore chains like Barnes & Noble ever thought of selling through the Web. The company has since built up a huge customer base, and its bigger competitors like Barnes & Noble are forced to play catch-up, at least when it comes to selling books through the Internet.

To market, to market

The Internet is a great place to conduct market research, whether you're trying to produce a big-time musical about Al Jolson or trying to sell ads on a site devoted to mountain bikes. The Net provides you with preselected communities of users who are all interested in a common topic. Your research can take the forms of mailing lists (see Chapter 7) and discussion groups (see Chapter 8). By participating in these groups' discussions, or by simply "listening in," you can learn a lot about these individuals' concerns and preferences. If you sell computer software, for instance, you can turn to the many discussion groups devoted to computer operating systems or individual programs. The questions, answers, complaints, and topics that come up in the discussions can tell you what programs are used most often, which programs are most popular, and what kinds of software features users need.

The Internet is perfectly suited to businesses whose reach is nationwide or even worldwide. If you own a card shop and only expect to attract business from your town, the Internet may not be the best place for you. On the other hand, if you sell products that appeal to consumers around the country or the world, the Net is the place to sell it.

There's a downside to making your business available to all the Internet users in the world. You may well receive lots of inquiries from people who aren't serious about using your services, but who ask you for information or quotes and then go elsewhere to actually make the purchase. Provide as much information as you can on your site to tell people how much your services cost. You can also provide a Web page form that requires visitors to tell you something about themselves to gauge their levels of interest. You may have to follow up with a phone call in order to separate the tire-kickers who are just casually browsing from those who are serious about making a purchase.

Case study: Image Connection

The Image Connection, a four-person graphic design firm in Cornish, New Hampshire, is on the Web for lots of reasons. The original reason was not to make money but to *save* money.

"Because of our rural setting, nearby towns we do business in are toll calls," says owner Paul Whalen, Jr. "During winter months, travel can be a major factor. We greatly rely on e-mail for both reducing phone costs and transferring files, thus reducing courier and time costs."

After creating its Web site in 1995 and getting e-mail addresses from its local Internet Service Provider, CyberPort, LLC, the Image Connection began to receive inquiries from far beyond its local customer base.

"These days, the first question we get from a new client is, 'Do you have a Web site?'" says Whalen. "Through the Web we are doing business with companies as far away as California; they, in turn, have distributors in Europe."

The Image Connection uses digital imaging to create catalogs, brochures, and greeting cards. They now, by client request, also develop Web sites. They have simple dial-up connections to the Net using 33.6Kbps modems. They have established a good relationship with CyberPort, which has paid off in technical support and assistance.

"The Web allows our clients to investigate our company without having to ask us directly, or spend a great amount of time. It is a comfortable feeling to sit in your office and look into ours. We, in turn, do research for new resources, see what's out there, build credibility, and finish our homework through the Web."

Selling on the Net

Until recently, the majority of Internet users were reluctant to give their credit card numbers out to an online store such as a CD music outlet or a software company in order to make a purchase. Lately though, surveys that track Internet usage trends indicate that added security measures are helping people feel more confident and comfortable with purchasing through the Net. A company can set up secure methods for making purchases by asking customers to fill out a Web page form and submit their credit card numbers and other information to the business (see Chapter 11).

Because many customers are still squeamish about Internet security, you're wise to provide other ways for people to contact you, such as a toll-free number or fax number.

Connecting across the miles

Having an Internet connection means that your business is reachable through e-mail on the World Wide Web. You can contact the office while you're are on the road, in order to retrieve files and get e-mail messages. You can also connect with consultants who work outside the office, such as my colleague John Casler (see Chapter 14), or consultants who can create and market a Web site for you. Give suppliers access to your files so that they can update inventories, as Garden Escape does (see Chapter 14).

How to succeed in business (online) without even crying

Here are a series of steps that you can follow if you want to connect to the Net in a measured, reasoned way so that you can present your colleagues with a full report about the potential benefits of going online.

Dig into the details

Read everything you can about the Internet. The best place to find out about it is by surfing the Net itself. You can find some suggestions for online tutorials in Chapter 5.

Determine the best goals for your organization

You may not want to sell online, and you may not even be interested in promoting yourself because you have enough business already. An Internet connection can supplement your existing advertising or your promotional brochures. Or, creating an internal intranet can help your employees collaborate more efficiently.

Convince your boss (es)

Use the hardware and software suggestions in Chapters 2 and 3 to come up with some cost figures for getting on the Net. Remember to provide a range rather than a definite figure, to cover unexpected expenses you may encounter, such as hardware or software you don't yet know you're going to need.

One good thing about the costs associated with getting on the Net is that they tend to go down instead of up as time goes by, as older technologies are supplanted by newer and less expensive alternatives. Tell your superiors about this in order to reassure them that the Internet tends to be less expensive rather than more expensive after the initial investment is made.

Step-by-step Internet

The first step to launching an online business is either purchasing or finding access to the necessary computer equipment: at the barest minimum, one computer and a modem, or a group of computers that can be networked if you want. After you locate the right hardware, follow these steps.

Making connections with e-mail

Electronic mail is a powerful tool for any business. E-mail enables employees to communicate with each other, helps you send files from one location to another, and chalk up other benefits too numerous to mention here — but they're noted in Chapter 7.

Rolling out a Web page welcome mat

To many people, getting online means creating either a Web page or, more likely, a full-fledged Web site that consists of many Web pages connected by hypertext links: In other words, clicking on a highlighted word or phrase on one page takes you to another page on the same site.

If you decide to connect your company to the Net, it's almost obligatory to create, at the very least, a colorful, informative _welcome page_ or _home page_ that tells visitors who you are, what you do, how to contact you, and why your products are worth looking into.

Taking the on-ramp to an Internet connection

The next step is to get an account with a company that can give you an on-ramp to the Internet through either a wire run to your business, which is called a dedicated connection, or via dial-up to the company's servers with one of your modems. Your connection comes with software as well as technical support.

Putting your office computers in the loop

If your office has an existing network, that is, if two or more of your computers are connected so that you can share files using networking software such as Microsoft Windows NT, you can install server software that enables you to serve documents on an intranet or to the wider Internet.

Become an Internet resource

The most successful business Web pages are ones that visitors visit again and again because the information they publish is so useful and is updated on a regular basis. The way to become a resource that visitors turn to repeatedly is to provide useful information like your product catalog or a periodic newsletter. See Chapter 15 for some options on how to do this.

Protect your company against intruders

After your computer is connected to the global network, you open the doors to potential viruses and other programs that can harm your files. If you want to conduct secure commerce, or if your business has several connected computers, it's important to protect your investment. Playing it safe can be as simple as installing some virus protection software and picking complicated passwords to your Internet Service Provider and other accounts. Or you can go as elaborate as setting up a "perimeter network" outside your local area network that performs IP filtering and uses proxy servers to provide access into and from the wider Internet. See Chapter 10 for more on security options that you can consider for your small business.

Working Smart: Avoiding Internet Fallacies

Sometimes, the difference between achieving your goals on the Internet and falling short is simply knowing what mistakes to avoid. You may have some preconceived notions about getting on the Net — perhaps as a result of hearing casual talk about the process. Here are a few fallacies that you need to consider.

Fallacy #1: You have to advertise

Getting your business on the Web does *not* mean you have to spend thousands of dollars to place display ads on popular Web pages. Some of the large and frequently-visited sites (such as Yahoo!) do charge high rates for their most prominent ad spaces. But that's not what marketing online is about. Rather, the Net is ideally suited to one-to-one marketing that delivers useful content to individuals who want it or who have even specifically requested it. In contrast, traditional marketing is a matter of saturating large numbers of viewers with ads that say little about a product or company in order to tease them into finding out more.

Find your niche audience on the Web — the group(s) most likely to give you business — and communicate directly to those likely customers through e-mail, discussion groups, or Web pages, as described in Chapter 12.

Fallacy #2: You need a home page

Although it's certainly true that a Web page is the central piece in any Internet marketing campaign, it's by no means the only reason to get on the Net. Having e-mail service is just as important to many businesses as putting their catalog on the Web or publishing the ubiquitous Message from the President.

Lots of businesses get on the Web mainly in order to have e-mail service. Some only go online to do research. Some mainly need to transfer files with designers, suppliers, and clients. Don't feel obligated to create a Web page right away; take your time and see what's out there and create the page that suits your business identity.

Fallacy #3: You can expect to rake in the cash

Although stories about businesses that find financial success by being on the Net are plentiful, you don't hear about the far greater number of businesses that get on the Net and don't make lots of money right away, or that don't meet with major gains at all.

First of all, it can take a lot of time for a business on the Net to break even, just as it can for any new company. You may lose money for a year before breaking even. In an article published on *Inc. Magazine's* Web site (`www.inc.com`), Jeffrey Bezos, the founder of the online bookseller Amazon.com (`www.amazon.com`), says he *expects* to lose money in the foreseeable future while he builds his brand name and generates value for his company.

Don't expect to make money right away: Diversify your goals, and be patient.

One of the great things about getting connected to the Net is the accessibility to lots of magazines and Web sites directed at small businesses. See Chapter 16 for more suggestions.

Fallacy #4: This is gonna break the bank

Sure, it can cost tens of thousands of dollars to develop a Web site, buy lots of computers, and hook up the entire office. But it doesn't *have* to cost lots of money, either. The only things you really have to invest in are a computer, a modem, and an account with an Internet Service Provider. After that, you can download software and do it all yourself.

Fallacy #5: The Net has no rules

It's dangerous to start out on the Web and assume that you can do anything you want either because the technology is so new or because the Net is so loosely organized. First of all, the Internet does have an organization — it's run by groups like the Internet Architecture Board and the Internet Society. (See the section entitled "Who's in charge?" earlier in this chapter.)

Second, the Net does have its own set of rules, which is called Netiquette. Netiquette is a set of rules of behavior for those who communicate using e-mail or discussion groups.

Among the more important rules for businesses are the ones that apply to unsolicited advertising on the Net. Basically, don't send advertising messages to groups that don't want them. (In case you're wondering, there *is* solicited advertising on the Net, in the form of newsgroups that exist primarily to announce new Web sites, lists of Cool Sites, and indexes like Yahoo! that want businesses to contribute short ads.)

Just because the rules aren't handed out to everyone who joins up doesn't mean that standards don't exist. The rules are enforced, by users who can retaliate by flooding a server with e-mail. (See Chapter 8 for more about Netiquette and what can happen if you run afoul of it.)

How Do You Spell Success?

Every business needs a way to measure success. On the Internet, businesses can use both qualitative and quantitative means to determine how closely their desired goals are met. The following sections describe some of the more common methods used by Internet businesses to gauge results.

After you go online, don't just let your Web page or other information sit idle. Along with keeping your data current, a key to creating a successful Web site is evaluating results to see if your goals are being met — and improving your Internet information in order to help achieve those goals. Here are a few goals worth considering that are specific to the Internet.

Getting hits

Probably the most obvious way to judge the success of your Web site, and the way that most companies use it, is to count the visits their site receives.

A *hit* to a Web site is a different matter than a visit to a Web site. A hit results when an individual file is accessed on your site. This can be a text file, a graphic image, or another object such as a computer program. Many hits can result from a single visit.

Your ISP may give you a *hit counter*. This is a utility that displays a graphic image in the Web browser window of anyone who accesses your page. This graphic may look like the odometer in your car. There's a hit counter on the Image Connection's welcome page shown in Figure 1-5. (Other hit counters aren't nearly as subtle and tasteful-looking as this one.)

Figure 1-5:
The bottom of Image Connection's home page includes contact information and a hit counter.

Every time someone connects to a page that's held on a Web server, that server counts that visit and records it in a *log file*. You can ask your ISP to provide you with a copy of this file. Interpreting the file can be difficult because some log files count every file access on every Web page. If a page includes a text file and three images, it can count as four hits. Some Internet providers use software called *log analyzers* to count the number of distinct visitors in a given day. Some analyzers can even keep track of *referrals:* the sites that your visitors visit before they come to *your* site. Ask your Internet Service Provider about available programs for counting hits. However, if you want to install your own software, you can find a list at `union.ncsa.uiuc.edu/HyperNews/get/www/log-analyzers.html`.

E-mail inquiries

Your messages on your office's e-mail server can be counted as a measure of how frequently people in the office are using your e-mail service.

Orders

An easy way to quantify your success on the Web is to count the orders that come through your Web site, through your toll-free number, or by e-mail.

Employee satisfaction

Other benefits of being connected to the Internet are harder to measure in quantitative terms. But the advantages are still important.

E-mail gives your staff a place to discuss issues without having to congregate in the hallways or by the water cooler. You may find that training improves because instructions are available on your company's intranet.

Important clients may be happier to contact you by e-mail, because they can always leave you a message, no matter how long or short, any time of the day or night.

Increased productivity

Another way to measure whether your Internet connection is paying off is in the efficiency and speed with which your employees are able to work together and get projects done. You may find that the staff talks to one another more, exchanging ideas more quickly. The Internet helps those workers share ideas and files, and generally improves the climate in which you conduct business.

Chapter 2

Getting What You Need without Seeing Red

In This Chapter

▶ Making up your shopping list for Internet hardware and software

▶ Tailoring your equipment setup to your business needs and goals

▶ Getting the essentials and adding optional tools

▶ Understanding routers, gateways, firewalls, and servers

*G*etting connected to the Internet and surfing the World Wide Web is a pretty simple matter. As long as you have a relatively fast computer, a modem, and an available phone line, you can set yourself up and be surfing the Web in less than a single afternoon.

Using the Internet to help your business grow is more complicated, but still doable. The key is having a clear idea of what sort of *business presence* you want to have on the Net. A business presence means having a Web site, of course, and incorporating into your presentation as much useful and well-organized information as you can provide about your company and your products and services. You may also include an internal version of the Internet, an intranet, that you set up for your employees. Ideally, your Internet business presence reflects a well-prepared marketing strategy and answers to questions like whether you're going to conduct online sales or provide samples of your work online, or whether you're going to do customer service on the Net.

For many small businesses that lack technical support, the obstacle to moving from surfing the Net to providing information and becoming a useful resource online is determining exactly what software and hardware you need. This chapter can help answer your basic questions: What do I need to buy, and how do I prepare a budget for it?

The answers to the need/costs concerns depend on exactly what kind of Internet presence best suits your business needs. A good place to start is by asking yourself questions, such as the following examples, that help you focus your goals for connecting to the Internet:

- ✔ Do I want to connect a single computer to the Internet or provide Internet access to a whole network of computers?

- ✔ Do I want to dial up the Net intermittently or do I really need to be connected 24 hours a day?

- ✔ Do I want to run my own e-mail server so that everyone in the office can have an e-mail address and exchange messages?

- ✔ Do I simply want to surf the Net and publish a small-scale Web site with an Internet provider, or do I want to run my own Web site or FTP site?

You don't need to have the answers to all of these questions before you pursue getting connected to the Net. You can start with a simple Internet connection and then build up as you define your business needs. Before you begin dropping lots of money on hardware, you need to have a good idea of what you want to do. This chapter presents you with some options.

Scenarios for Conducting Business Online

There are as many ways to have an Internet presence as there are businesses. Here are some real-world examples taken from businesses I know personally, some of which are profiled later in this book:

Scenario 1: The owner of a small business works at home. He has two computers in his home office, one Mac and one PC. He uses each computer, and uses e-mail extensively.

Solution: Each computer has software installed so that it can dial up the owner's Internet Service Provider. Each computer also has its own modem so that he can dial up the Net separately or simultaneously. The owner has a simple Web site and a single e-mail address.

Scenario 2: A small company of five employees needs to go online to do research. Only one employee needs to be connected to the Net during working hours. The company does not require a Web site.

Solution: The owner signed up for an account with America Online that gives her unlimited access to AOL and the Internet for a monthly fee. AOL sent her installation disks, and she equipped two computers with AOL access software contained on the disks. She purchased two external modems. Employees dial up AOL on one or both of the computers so that they can search AOL or the Net as needed.

Scenario 3: A restaurant wants to spend as little as possible to get on the Net; the establishment wants to post a Web page that serves as an advertisement and that's included in a directory of local businesses.

Solution: A consultant creates a Web page that tells local visitors the business's address, phone number, and hours of operation and a list of some menu items. The page is visible on the Net 24 hours a day, although the business has no connection to the Net at all; it's only a virtual storefront on the Net.

Scenario 4: Another food service business — a candy supplier — has a Web page and e-mail address, but it wants to be able to sell its items by mail order to a nationwide or even a worldwide audience.

Solution: The candy supplier paid extra to an ISP to publish its Web site on a secure server. The business became a member of CyberCash, which handles the processing of credit card numbers supplied over a consultant-created Web page form.

Scenario 5: A small company has eight employees who are connected via a local area network (LAN) that uses Windows NT for file-sharing. All the employees need to get on the Net from time to time and send and receive e-mail. The company has a Web site and wants to give suppliers access to its files, as well as provide a connection to two employees who are in a satellite office in a nearby town.

Solution: The company signed up with an Internet provider for a direct PRI ISDN (Primary ISDN — see Chapter 3) connection to the Net. This is a direct connection, so the company is accessible on the Net all the time by e-mail or the Web. The company paid an application fee to an organization called InterNIC (see Chapter 13) in order to obtain a virtual domain name for its Web site. In this case, since employees working in other offices need to access the company's network, security measures are also needed to make sure only users with the proper access privileges gain entry. A *perimeter network* consisting of two routers and a computer was set up in order to serve as a *firewall* between the internal office network and the wider Internet. Each employee was issued an approved username and password that they enter each time they access the company's internal network from a remote site.

There are many more ways in which small businesses can use the Internet to attract new clients or customers, communicate more quickly, or market their services. Find the scenario that fits your situation most closely, and begin to develop a shopping list and a budget so that you can get what you need without breaking the bank.

Your Internet Shopping List

Now it's time to come up with a shopping list for what you need. These are just suggestions; your specific situation may be different.

Table 2-1 lists the Internet must-haves:

Table 2-1	**Must-Haves for Internet Access**	
Item	*Description*	*Cost*
Computer	See "Best Bets for Net Hardware" for suggestions on what kind of machine may work best.	You can probably get a PC with a Pentium processor and 16MB of RAM for less than $1,000.
Modem	Your computer may have one built-in. Otherwise you have to buy an external modem, a small device that connects to your computer and to a phone jack.	Modems can cost anywhere from $200 to $500.
Internet software	A Web browser, a program that enables you to view Web page text and images, as well as download files and send and receive e-mail, is a bare-bones basic.	Microsoft Internet Explorer 4.0 is absolutely free; Netscape Communicator can be downloaded for free, but to be an official user and expect technical support you need to purchase the product (a single-user license costs $59).

If you want to connect several computers that are wired together in an office network, things get a little more complicated. In addition to the must-haves, you need the items listed in Table 2-2:

Table 2-2	**If You Need to Connect Your Network**	
Item	*Description*	*Cost*
A LAN-to-Internet gateway	The gateway may be a router, one of the all-in-one Internet solutions described at the end of this chapter.	Costs of routers vary widely, WebRamp routers and Internet gateway devices by Trancell Systems, Inc. range from $500 to $1,000 but more complex routers that permit direct Internet connections can cost much more.

Item	Description	Cost
Security	After you open your internal network to the Internet, you need to make sure unwanted visitors don't invade your system. You may need to designate a computer to serve as a firewall. Some routers provide authentication security as well.	
E-mail server	Plan to equip one of your networked computers with e-mail server software so that your employees can send messages to one another and to visitors on the wider Internet.	Less than $1,000
Modem sharing software	Some programs are available that enable all networked computers to share a single dial-up modem connection to the Internet. That way, you don't have to install an e-mail server.	Less than $500

You can always have your customers call you on the phone to place orders, but it's much more immediate and convenient for your customers to make purchases by submitting a credit card number or other payments online. In that case, you need the items in Table 2-3:

Table 2-3	If You Want to Sell on the Net	
Item	**Description**	**Cost**
A secure commerce server	This is software that can either reside on one of your own office computers or on an ISP's computer. Most ISP's provide their clients with the option of publishing data entry forms and other sales pages on a secure server for an extra monthly fee.	$50 to $100 per month
Payment processing software	This is software put out by CyberCash or First Virtual that enables customers to pay you with a credit card or by Internet checks (see Chapter 10).	Less than $2,000

If you're just starting out and don't have access to a Webmaster, or if you don't have lots of technical expertise yourself, you can publish your files with a Web hosting company or an ISP. However, you may want to follow a more independent path and run your own Internet or intranet servers instead. In that case you need the additional goodies listed in Table 2-4:

Table 2-4	If You Want to Host Your Own Internet Site	
Item	*Description*	*Cost*
A fast computer	Servers have to be able to accommodate many requests for information at the same time. Server software requires lots of memory; 64 or even 128MB of RAM isn't excessive.	Memory costs vary widely, and they differ depending on what sort of computer you have. You should be able to get an extra 16MB of RAM for $35 to $100. Hopefully, you can designate an existing computer to function as your server. If not, you'll have to buy one.
A direct connection	Servers are generally accessible to visitors on the Internet 24 hours a day.	See Chapter 3 for connection costs.
Server software	These are programs that enable you to present files to visitors on the Internet or on an intranet. Depending on the kinds of content you want to serve on the network, you may need a Web server, FTP server, e-mail server, chat server, or discussion group server. The all-in-one solutions described at the end of this chapter have this software pre-installed for you.	Free server software like Microsoft IIS does exist; commercial software can cost $1,000 and up.

You may also need some of the optional hardware, software, or other items listed in Table 2-5 if you want to create your own Web pages:

Table 2-5	Optional Goodies	
Item	*Description*	*Cost*
Webmaster	If you want to connect your office to the Net or host your own Internet site, you may find it useful to have someone in-house not only set up the hardware but also install software on everyone's computers, do troubleshooting and training, and answer questions as they come up. See Chapter 5.	Webmasters are in demand and command good salaries. Be prepared to pay handsomely for someone with programming and networking skills.
Extra phone line	If you have a dial-up modem connection to the Net, you use up a phone line while you're online. Incoming callers may get a busy signal, or they may break your connection suddenly. Investing in another line prevents tying up a phone or fax machine.	Ask your telephone provider.
Scanner or digital camera	If you want to publish photos of your products online, you need one of these input devices. Each one captures an image and converts it to a digital format called a *bitmap* that can be saved as a computer file. The computer file can then be opened in a graphics program and converted to Graphics Interchange Format (GIF) or Joint Photographic Experts Group (JPEG) format in order to be added to a Web page.	Scanners can be found for less than $500, digital cameras for less than $1,000.
Printer	You may want to print out your own Web pages or other documents that you find on the Net and hand them to your customers. Web browsers give you the option of including on the printout details like the URL of the page, the name of the document, and the date.	Laser printers can be purchased for less than $1,000.
Service contracts	When you start adding hardware to your existing setup, it's a good idea to provide for maintenance in case anything goes wrong.	Ask your computer supplier.

(continued)

Table 2-5 (continued)

Item	Description	Cost
Domain name registration fee	A virtual domain name is the short and easy-to-remember URL that's assigned to a Web site, such as www.mycompany.com.	The fee costs about $150 for the first year and $50 to renew annually.
Magazine subscriptions	As stated in Chapter 5, books and magazines about the Internet can help you and your staff keep up-to-date with the latest technology.	Depends on the magazine.
Advertising fees	A banner ad is a small graphic on a Web page that's linked to one of the owner's own Web pages. A viewer who's interested in the ad can click on the graphic and go to the owner's site to find out more about the product or company being advertised. If you want to take out banner ads on the most popular Web sites, you probably have to pay an advertising fee.	Depending on the site, you may be charged by the week, by the month, or by the *impression,* which adds up to each time someone visits the Web page and views your site.
Web site-development costs	Although you can learn how to create your own Web pages, making them look professional and cutting-edge is another matter. Many companies hire consultants to set up a good-looking Web site for them. Consultants can advise on hardware and software, get you an account with an ISP, and update your pages on a regular basis, too.	Cost varies widely, depending on the size of the Web site you want and how much work you are willing to do yourself.

 An article on the Smalloffice.com Web site (`www.smalloffice.com/miser/ mmmattrs.htm`) presents readers with an online form that helps you calculate the cost of starting a business, whether it's going to exist solely on the Internet or if you're going to have an office where you and your employees can work.

The following sections go into more detail on your shopping list essentials.

Best Bets for Net Hardware

The one piece of equipment that you can't do without, when it comes to getting on the Internet, is a computer. You don't have to purchase a new computer, and you don't need every single multimedia bell and whistle; however, you're wise to buy the machine with the fastest processor and the most RAM (Random Access Memory) that you can afford.

The processor is the computer chip, such as a Pentium or 486, that determines how fast your computer carries out its computing functions. The speed at which a processor performs these functions is commonly called its *clock speed,* which is expressed in megahertz (MHz). The higher the clock speed, the faster the computer runs. A 486/66 MHz chip is probably the minimum speed for running Web browsers and other applications. I get along fine with my 90 MHz PowerMac and 486/120 MHz PC. But if you can afford a faster computer, by all means buy it.

What kind of computer do you need?

In order to connect to the Net, you need a computer that speaks the language of the Net. In other words, you need at least one computer that has Internet access software installed in it. This software enables the machine to communicate in the language of the Internet, TCP/IP (Transport Control Protocol/Internet Protocol). Most recent Macintosh and Windows operating systems come with TCP/IP built in. If your machine supports TCP/IP, you can install the great software programs (see Chapter 4 for some examples) that are among the big benefits of connecting to the Net.

As far as the Internet is concerned, computers that run Apple Macintosh or Microsoft Windows software work equally well. You can pick the system with which you're more comfortable. If you work in a university or other educational environment, where Macs are especially popular, you may prefer a Macintosh.

The Windows operating systems dominate the Internet just as they do the rest of the world. As much as I like the Apple Macintosh, it makes more sense to buy a PC that's running Windows 95, unless there's a compelling reason for you to buy a Mac. Windows gives you several advantages: cheaper prices; much more available software; and more widespread distribution.

If you intend to run your own Web, e-mail, or FTP server, a computer that's connected to the Internet or an intranet all the time and that provides Web pages and other files, you need a computer that has a very fast processor and that handles many requests for information simultaneously. If your site is popular, you can conceivably get dozens or even hundreds of computers connecting to your server, each requesting to see some of the files that you have published there.

Modems

A *modem* is a hardware device that converts the digital lingo that computers speak into signals that can be transmitted along a cable that leads to the Internet. There are many different kinds of modems, but you're most likely to encounter analog modems or ISDN terminal adapters.

Analog

The most common type of modem used by individuals and small businesses is an analog modem, which converts digital information to analog electrical signals that can be carried along a normal telephone line. These modems often come with a computer. Otherwise, you need an external modem (a little box that connects your computer and a telephone jack) or a card that plugs into your computer.

Plan to get a modem that transfers at least 28.8 kilobits (28.8Kbps) of data. 33.6Kbps modems are common, and 56Kbps modems are gaining in popularity.

Digital (ISDN) terminal adapters

In the case of an ISDN (Integrated Services Digital Network) connection, an ISDN modem is more correctly called a terminal adapter. ISDN is a good solution for small businesses that are in search of an affordable connection to the Internet that's faster than a dial-up modem. Terminal adapters can be purchased either as stand-alone units or as cards that plug in to PCs, Macs, or Workstations. See Chapter 3 for more about ISDN.

Other modems

Two attractive options for small businesses — cable modem services and DSL — use modem-like connections to move data to and from your computer. See Chapter 4 for more about these high-speed, low-cost options.

Using routers to direct traffic

If you have a local area network that uses networking software such as AppleTalk, Novell NetWare, or Microsoft Windows NT, you have the option of joining every computer on the network to the Internet. You can, of course, provide individual modems to the computers that you want to connect. A more elegant solution is to use a piece of hardware called a *router*.

Routers are designed to direct traffic between computers that are part of networks. The vehicles that they direct are called *packets* of information. Routers make sure that you're an approved user by checking the *IP address,* a series of four numbers separated by dots that identifies your computer on the Internet or on an intranet. If your IP address is on a preapproved guest list set up by a network administrator, you're allowed access through the router and are directed toward the computer that you want to connect to, which is also identified by its IP address. This IP filtering enables routers to serve as a security tool called a firewall. Figure 2-1 shows how one of the popular Cisco Systems, Inc. routers can act as a firewall between two computer networks within an organization and between the organization and the Internet as well.

If the prospect of choosing and setting up one or more routers has you bewildered, consider outsourcing your router service and maintenance to a telecommunications company. Sprint, AT&T, and Ameritech have staff people who can do the setup and troubleshooting for you.

Routers allow multiple workstations on one network to selectively communicate to individual stations on another network, passing all data information simultaneously through a common data port. Routers can either lead you from a computer on an internal office network out to the external Internet, or from a machine on a subnetwork to another subnetwork within the same organization.

Routers can connect to an internal office network through serial or Ethernet ports such as a 10BaseT port, which can transfer up to 10Mbps of data. However, some routers are customizable by the user so that they can accept even faster connections such as Fast Ethernet, which can move 100Mbps of information.

On the other side, the connection leading from the router out to the wider Internet can vary depending on how fast a connection the company needs and how much money is available. Routers can connect to the Net at 33.6Kbps or ISDN speeds, or at faster Frame Relay or T-1 speeds (see Chapter 3).

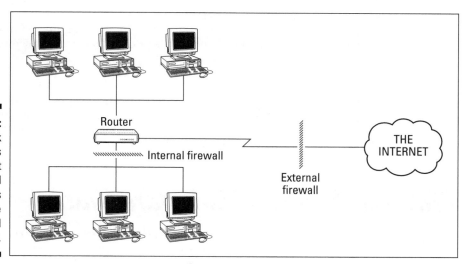

Figure 2-1: Routers link computers in different internal networks as well as the external Internet.

Some of the more frequently used routers are made by Cisco Systems, Inc. Cisco offers many different types of routers; some models that are targeted at small businesses are described at www.cisco.com/cpropub/univercd/data/ciscopro/catalog/cpa2500r.htm.

Cisco Systems, Inc.'s routers are among the more popular in the corporate world, but they're not alone in the field. Also check out the routers made by Bay Networks, Inc. (www.baynetworks.com/Products), Cabletron Systems (www.cabletron.com/products), and Ascend Communications, Inc. (www.ascend.com).

Security systems

You can find a lot of things on the Internet, but a very small number of unfriendly things may try to find *you* in turn. Viruses and Trojan Horses are computer programs that try to slip into your computer when you download a program or file. Unless you've installed antivirus software that destroys these programs, you run the risk of losing data.

If you open your office network to the Internet, it's advisable to restrict access so that only individuals with approved usernames or passwords can view or work on your files. A *firewall* is computer hardware or software that performs these kinds of security functions; firewalls and other Internet security measures are described in Chapter 10.

Internet software

Internet software has two big advantages over *proprietary* software, which is designed to operate on a specific type of computer and which usually has to be purchased from a computer retail outlet. In contrast, many Internet programs can be used on different kinds of computers and downloaded from the Net itself for free or for a small fee.

Specialized software enables you to conduct chat and real-time conferencing, transfer files, enter into discussions with newsgroups, compress files so that they take up less disk space when transmitted from one machine to another, and so on. Chapter 4 examines some of the common Internet software you may need when your office gets on the Net.

Finding the Right Software Wares

Setting yourself up as an Internet host by running your own server is no small matter. Hosting involves lots of money, equipment, and expertise. For instance, you probably need to dedicate a computer to run your server software. Most servers either run on the UNIX or Windows NT operating system, so you have to get a computer equipped with one of those systems if you don't already have one.

A less-elaborate alternative is to purchase your own server software and hardware but install and run the Web server at your ISP's office. Then you can get technical help, although you have to pay an extra co-location fee. Either way, you can easily add $3,000 to $9,000 to your Internet business costs if you decide to run your own server.

Server software

You need to implement simple server solutions if you want to set up an intranet and publish Web pages using Internet technology. The most common kinds of Internet server programs you're likely to install are

- **FTP Servers.** This software is used to make applications and other documents available to visitors who want to download them easily using FTP (File Transport Protocol) software.

- **E-mail Servers.** This software keeps track of e-mail addresses and passwords, stores incoming mail so that users can retrieve it, and routes outgoing mail so that it gets to the correct destination.

- **Web Servers.** This software enables you to make Web page text and graphics available so that users can view them with their Web browsers.

Some servers that perform many of these functions are readily available from the Web itself, such as

- **FastTrack Server.** A simple Web server provided by Netscape Communications Corp. that runs on Windows 95/NT computers. It costs $295. Read all about FastTrack at home.netscape.com/comprod/ server_central/product/fast_track/fast_track_data.html.

- **SuiteSpot Server.** Netscape's higher-level server provides e-mail, discussion group, and scheduling server software in addition to a Web server. You can try SuiteSpot out for 60 days by purchasing a trial CD for $10. The basic ten-user version of SuiteSpot costs $3,495. A Pro version and subscriptions to receive discounts on updates costs more. Go to home.netscape.com/comprod/server_central/product/ suite_spot/index.html to read about all of SuiteSpot's features.

- **Microsoft Internet Information Server.** This is a Web server designed to work with Windows NT server software. It's free and easy to use, and you can find out more about it at www.microsoft.com/iis. IIS is part of the Microsoft BackOffice Small Business Server package of business applications. Find out more at www.microsoft.com/directaccess.

✔ **WebSTAR.** This software from StarNine Technologies
(www.starnine.com) turns a Macintosh into a Web server. Check
StarNine's Web site for discounts if you purchase the program online.

ServerWatch is a Web site devoted to providing the latest information about
servers and server development tools such as proxies. Visit serverwatch.
internet.com to find out more.

All-in-one Internet gateways

Many businesses that need to provide Internet access to several employees
have to install separate devices including routers and server software
programs. They may also want firewall hardware or software.

An all-in-one device may include everything an office needs for the Internet:

✔ Internet access software

✔ A LAN-to-Internet connection

✔ Security features

✔ A file server that makes documents

✔ E-mail, Web, FTP, and discussion group servers

The following sections describe three of these convenient options you
should consider if you're interested in Internet one-stop shopping.

Whistle InterJet

Whistle Communications offers three all-in-one boxes that connect your
business to the Internet: the Whistle InterJet 100, 120, and 200.

Find out more at the Whistle Communications Web site (www.whistle.com).

FreeGate Multi-Services Internet Gateway

The FreeGate Multi-Services Internet Gateway is designed for businesses
employing between 20 and 200 users. To find out more, visit the FreeGate
Web site (www.freegate.com/home.html) or call 1-800-280-8816.

i-Planet solutions

i-Planet has three access units designed for businesses of various sizes. The
three units are compared at www.i-planet.com/P3family.html.

It's often a good idea to undertake your Internet project in stages. A step-by-
step approach helps ensure that you achieve your goals for getting yourself
or your office on the Internet. You can create a Web site, sell goods and
services online, and use e-mail and FTP, all while staying within your budget.

Chapter 3

Making the Right Connections

*W*hen it comes time to connect your business to the Internet, you face a dizzying array of options from which to choose. But they're the options with which you're already familiar. And because you have plenty of choices, you're sure to find the one that suits your company's needs.

Think of the ways in which you receive electronic communications every day. You dial up a friend on the phone, and in a minute, you're connected. You watch cable TV that either comes to you through a wire or a satellite dish. You make cellular phone calls or use a portable phone.

You can make your connection to the Internet in one of these ways:

- Your computer uses a modem to dial up a computer that's connected to the Net all the time. You're temporarily connected to the Net for the duration of the phone call.

- You have a cable run directly to your office or business.

- You get your Internet connection by satellite.

- You use the unused portion of your regular telephone line to exchange data with the Net. You're connected all the time and don't have to call up another computer using a modem.

  (This last option is called Asymmetric Digital Subscriber Line, or ADSL, and it's explained in this chapter along with the other types of connections that may be suitable for a small business.)

A small business manager who wants to connect to the Internet needs to be concerned with these kinds of questions:

- ✓ What type of Internet connection will best suit my needs and still be affordable?
- ✓ How much bandwidth do I need?
- ✓ How do I connect more than one computer, so that others in my office can also access the Net?
- ✓ How many e-mail accounts do I need to cover use by all my employees if I have only one Internet connection?
- ✓ How do I choose an Internet Service Provider, the company that gives me access to the Net?
- ✓ How many simultaneous visitors do I want my Web site to be able to accommodate?

These are important considerations because they affect the way you and your employees experience the Internet. The more people you expect to connect to the Net at any one time, the more you need a connection with high bandwidth. The capacity of your connection to the Internet also affects how quickly your customers reach you, and how much data you can transfer easily if you have to download (copy) files from the Net or send files from your site to someone else.

The best way to answer these questions is to determine your goals in getting connected to the Internet.

The type of connection and the Internet provider you choose depends on your goals in connecting to the Net in the first place. A small business may have these kinds of goals:

- ✓ **Post a billboard Web page.** You don't need *any* connection to achieve a rock-bottom presence for your business on the Internet. If you want only a simple Web page that lists your telephone number, products and services, and contact information, hire a consultant to create the Web site for you and put it on a Web server. Understand, though, that simply putting a Web page out there and leaving it isn't going to draw a lot of visitors.

- ✓ **Send and receive e-mail.** You may want to connect to the Internet not only to have a Web site, but also to exchange e-mail with clients and customers. In that case, a dial-up connection is adequate: You connect to the Net several times a day, send outgoing messages and download incoming messages, and then disconnect. If you want all your employees to be able to send and receive e-mail on the Internet without having to buy lots of modems and get individual accounts for each person, get a LAN ISDN connection, which is a low-cost way to give everyone in the office Internet e-mail.

✔ **Exchange files.** If you work in the graphics or printing industries, you may want to have a place on the Internet where customers and designers can send you files, and vice versa. In that case, you probably want a sizable amount of FTP space (10 to 20MB or more), and a fast ISDN, frame relay, or ADSL connection so that transfers of big files don't take hours at a time.

✔ **Do research.** You may need to be on the Web at all times to gather information, write reports, and communicate by e-mail. If you're looking for full-time access, a direct connection makes sense.

✔ **Handle lots of visitors.** The more visitors your Web site receives, the more bandwidth you need. If your customers start complaining that they can't connect to you or that your Web pages appear slowly, it's time to get a direct connection.

✔ **Send audio and video.** If you're in the film or entertainment industry, you may want to transmit audio or video clips to customers over the Net, or exchange files with partner companies. In that case, a really fast direct connection with a T1 or T3 cable, or an ATM networking solution, makes sense.

Making the right decision depends on knowing your options and knowing how to avoid a rip-off. The first part of this chapter runs through the most common Internet connection options; the second part discusses how to find a company that can provide you with the connection and actually give you a presence on the Net.

Making the Right Connection?

The following several sections run through the various ways that you can achieve your goals by connecting to the Net. First, simple dial-up modem connections are discussed. Then, you discover ways to have a dedicated Internet connection — that is, one or more of your computers connected all the time. Dedicated connections are generally much faster (and more expensive) than dial-up connections, too. The two types of connections are shown in Figure 3-1.

See Table 3-1, later in this chapter, for some estimates on how much each of the connection options may cost. Although they're only rough estimates, they'll help you prepare a budget for getting your small business connected to the Net.

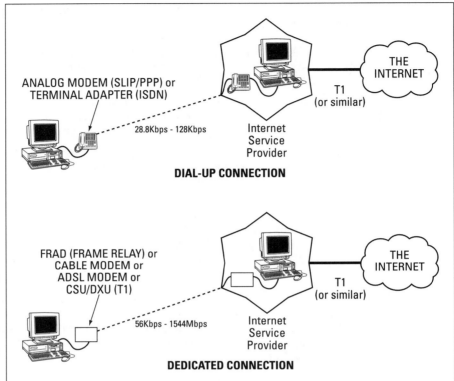

Figure 3-1:
Dial-up
versus
dedicated
Internet
connections.

Dial M for modem

A telephone line and a modem are as indispensable for most Internet businesses as a pair of sunglasses and a black fedora are for the Blues Brothers. The combination is the most popular and among the easier kinds of connections to set up. If you're just starting out with the Internet, all you do is get a computer, a modem, and a communications software package to facilitate the connection between your computer and another one, and you're in business.

Modems come in different shapes and sizes. Some modems can be installed inside your computer so that you never see them. The new PCMCIA modems are about the size of a playing card and fit into a handy slot that some computers have. The most common variety is an external modem, typically about the size of a paperback book.

Modems also transmit data in two different ways. *Analog* modems convert your computer's digital signals into analog data that can be sent along an ordinary copper phone line. *Digital* ISDN modems transmit digital data along an ISDN cable.

SLIP/PPP do dialups

Whether you use an internal, external, analog, or digital modem, or whether you have a PC or a Macintosh, your computer needs some software that enables it to make a phone call and connect to one of your Internet Service Provider's computers. This software uses one of two Internet protocols, PPP or SLIP, to make the connection between the two machines.

PPP stands for Point-to-Point Protocol, and SLIP stands for Serial Line Access Protocol. Both protocols enable your computer to connect to the Net. Don't go looking around your local computer store for a SLIP or PPP program, however. Usually, you don't buy such a program; you're issued a program by your Internet provider.

Over the years, I've used InterSLIP to connect to the University of Chicago from home, FreePPP (see Figure 3-2) to connect to my current provider with my Macintosh. On the PC side, I use either Dial-Up Networking or Microsoft Connection Manager, which comes with Microsoft Internet Explorer, to connect my PC to one of my provider's computers.

Figure 3-2: FreePPP, one of several programs used to connect computers to the Internet.

Be sure to invest in a modem that transmits information at a rate of 28.8Kbps. Anything slower and your Internet experience will be little more than a painful crawl. The common abbreviation *Kbps* stands for kilobits per second, so this kind of modem handles 28.8 kilobits or 28,800 bits per second of information per second — adequate for most casual Web surfing. However, prices are coming down on 33.6Kbps modems (I saw one advertised for $154.95). In fact, most computer stores sell 33.6Kbps rather than 28.8Kbps modems now. An even newer type of modem uses U.S. Robotics' x2 technology to reach speeds of up to 56Kbps, but the technology isn't yet supported by all Internet providers; check with your provider before you buy one.

If you are given a choice between SLIP and PPP, choose PPP. It's a newer protocol than SLIP and has better error-handling methods. Most providers use PPP because it runs into fewer transmission errors and runs slightly faster than SLIP.

ISDN: Another dial-up choice

ISDN service is a popular and practical alternative for many businesses that want a high-speed connection but don't need to operate their own e-mail, Web, FTP, or other servers in-house. ISDN (short for Integrated Services Digital Network) enables your computer to dial up to the Net and communicate at 64 or 128Kbps. ISDN achieves these speeds by means of special line-switching equipment that has to be provided by your phone company, and by combining standard copper wire telephone lines.

ISDN Basic Rate Interface, or BRI, is the most common type of ISDN. A BRI connection takes the two copper wires that are used for a standard telephone connection and divides them into three channels. Two of those channels (called B channels) can enable you to communicate at 64Kbps each. You can use either one of the channels to surf the Net at 64Kbps, or combine the two channels so that they serve as a single 128Kbps data pipe. A third channel, called the D channel, is also used in BRI ISDN.

Another advantage of ISDN is that it's digital rather than analog phone service. ISDN lines are clearer and more reliable than traditional phone lines.

There are lots of varieties of ISDN service, and they can be confusing. Setting up ISDN itself is not a terribly straightforward process, either. Home offices with only one computer have reason to check out personal ISDN service. I have ISDN service myself; here's how I set it up:

1. I checked with my provider and phone company to make sure that they could provide me with ISDN access.

2. I set up an appointment for a technician to run the ISDN line to my house, and found out what ISDN terminal adapters I could buy; my telephone company only supported two. I bought the BitSURFR Pro from U.S. Robotics.

3. The technician came and ran the line to a new junction box that he attached to the side of the house; he then extended the line to my office and put a new box on my wall.

4. I had to install a software program called MicroPhone in order to configure my modem to use the correct network switch type used by my phone company and to recognize some long numbers called SPIDs, which stand for Service Profile Identifiers (see Figure 3-3). This was the most confusing part of the process for me. I couldn't get the installation right the first time and had to have the phone company talk me through the steps.

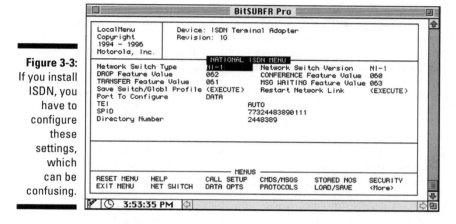

Figure 3-3:
If you install
ISDN, you
have to
configure
these
settings,
which
can be
confusing.

5. After I got the SPIDs right, I was able to dial up the network and surf at 56Kbps. (The advertised speed of 64Kbps is hard to achieve due to network traffic.) However, when my phone company switched area codes, my connection went down suddenly because the SPIDs were suddenly incorrect; I had to call the phone company and reconfigure the modem as in Step 4.

Although this process sounds laborious, I'm proud to report some big benefits. I not only enjoy a fast connection, but I also have an ISDN terminal adapter that comes with two POTS (Plain Old Telephone Service) lines ready and waiting for a fax machine and extra analog modem connection. Table 3-1 shows what everything cost me:

Table 3-1	Greg's ISDN BRI Costs
Item	*Cost*
ISDN terminal adapter	$353
Installation	About $100
Monthly phone charge for ISDN	$31
Monthly ISP charge	About $10

If you are a small business with 8 to 20 employees, you need LAN ISDN. This option connects your office LAN to the Internet with a router such as Farallon's Netopia or the Ascend Pipeline 50. You get e-mail accounts for all of your employees, a domain name, and access to e-mail and Usenet. You may also need one or more adapters to connect the ISDN line to your Ethernet network, and a 10BaseT hub. A good explanation of what's involved with LAN ISDN is provided on the Internet Express Network, Inc. Web site (www.ienet.com/access/lanisdn.html).

ISDN access is pretty widely supported by ISPs, but not all telephone companies provide ISDN service to all areas. Check with your Internet provider and telephone provider before you buy an ISDN terminal adapter (modem). Also make sure you buy a terminal adapter that's supported by your phone company.

PRI is a dedicated connection that can support up to 23 B channels. PRI ISDN is virtually the equivalent of a T1 line. (See the section "Full-time and part-time T1 and T3 lines" later in this chapter.)

With a PRI connection you can communicate at 1.544Mbps (that's megabits per second). You can handle a hundred or more visitors to your Web site at the same time.

The advantage of a PRI ISDN connection, compared with a T1 line, is that you can deal with your local phone company. If you want a T1 line, you usually have to deal with bigger Internet providers such as Sprint and MCI.

PRI ISDN is expensive, however. Ask your phone company if PRI ISDN is available, and how much it may set you back.

Going wireless with DirecPC

If some of your employees already think the Internet is something from outerspace, don't tell them about DirecPC. Just keep it your little secret. DirecPC grabs the Internet from a satellite circling 22,300 miles about the earth and beams information to a 21-inch satellite dish on your roof, which sends the data into your computer at a rate of 400Kbps.

Dedicated ISDN and Bandwidth on Demand

There are two variations on ISDN: dedicated ISDN and Bandwidth on Demand/Dial on Demand. Dedicated ISDN is a little misleading, because ISDN works with dial-up modems. In dedicated ISDN, you dial up a provider, and that provider enables you to remain connected constantly, for the length of a phone call. Depending on your telephone rate and whether the number you're calling is a local call or toll call, you can ring up quite a bill. It *can* work, however, if you have to make a number of calls per month (say, 100) for a fixed rate such as ten cents per call. (I have such an arrangement with my telco, Ameritech.) If your telco doesn't provide callpacks, look for a provider that offers you Centrex Flat Rate ISDN. You are charged a flat monthly rate for your phone calls instead of per-minute charges.

In connecting on demand, you are only connected when you need to be. Your ISDN modem is not connected to the Net until someone contacts your Web site. Your computer goes on, connects to your provider, and the provider sends data to the visitor. Then, your ISDN disconnects.

There's nothing wrong with dialing up

Direct connections to the Internet are great, there's no doubt about it. But the reality is that many businesses get along fine with dial-up modem connections. A small business doesn't need to be connected to the Internet 24 hours a day if its Web pages are stored on a server that's connected to the Net 24 hours a day.

If you ever want to experience what a T1 or T3 connection is like, go to a public or university library in your area that has computers for visitors' use. The connection's fast, all right, but you may notice that some Web sites still take a long time to appear. That's because the speed with which you access a Web site depends not only on the bandwidth of your connection, but also on the bandwidth with which the remote site's Web server is connected, as well as the processing speed of the computer that acts as a server. You can have cable modem or ATM speed on your end, but if you connect to a slow server, the result is still bound to be a less-than-hasty data download.

Most of the businesses I interviewed for this book have dial-up connections to the Net. StudioB, however, has a direct connection to the Internet.

Cost is not an advantage when it comes to DirecPC. The monthly charges you pay to DirecPC are in addition to your normal SLIP/PPP dial-up charges to your Internet provider and your telephone charges, too. To find out more, visit the DirecPC Web site at www.direcpc.com.

Make sure you have the right setup before you start signing up. DirecPC requires that you have a clear line of sight to the south from the roof of your building. The DirecPC access software is only available for Windows 95; Macintosh and Windows 3.1 are not supported. You also need a PC with a Pentium processor, 16MB of RAM, and 20MB of hard disk space. DirecPC does not support connections to online services such as America Online, either.

Direct connections to the Net on the cheap

Sooner or later, a direct connection makes sense for your operation. When is the time right to take the leap? You only need to consider a direct connection to the Net if

- ✔ You have money to burn. (It can happen!)
- ✔ Surfing the Web and using the rest of the Net is an integral part of your day-to-day business.
- ✔ You're lucky enough to live in an area where cable modem connections are available.
- ✔ Several employees use the Net all the time and you need to have constant e-mail communications available.

Two of the following alternatives to expensive T1 connections are exciting and relatively new: ADSL and cable modems. The problem with both of these options is that they aren't widely available.

Frame relay

Frame relay is a technology that provides high-speed access to the Internet at a reasonable price. In a frame relay system, data is sent in fixed-size batches called *generic packets*. Frame relay links several businesses to the Internet on one high-speed line, such as a T1 line, as shown in Figure 3-4. Because the line is shared, the participating businesses spend less than they would if paying separately. Frame relay is available in two speeds: 56K and 384K.

Your telephone company charges a flat monthly fee for the service, and your Internet provider adds a monthly fee as well. But for less than $400 a month, you can have a high-speed dedicated connection.

A great resource for everything related to frame relay is at `www.mot.com/MIMS/ISG/tech/frame-relay/resources.html`.

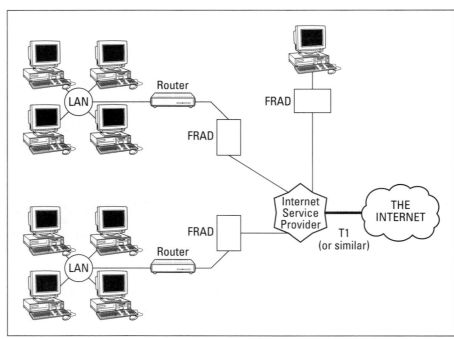

Figure 3-4:
In frame relay, like cable modem connections, several users share a fast data cable to keep costs down.

Case study: DayMen Photo Marketing

When is it time for a company to move from a dial-up to a direct Internet connection? Sooner or later, the moment arrives when it's wise to rid yourself of those analog modems and get a constant connection to the Net.

For DayMen Photo Marketing, a 30-person company located near Toronto, Canada that provides high-quality photographic equipment, the time came when the company moved into a new building. Prior to that, six of the DayMen staff were equipped with modems in order to connect their individual computer workstations to the Net. DayMen also has a Web site at www.daymen.com. Because the company did not have an internal e-mail server, the six individuals used their Internet connections to exchange e-mail not only with customers and suppliers, but also with each other as well.

The need to set up a convenient in-house e-mail system was just one impetus for getting a direct connection. Now, the company's Webmaster Doug Mummenhoff can set up an internal e-mail server that connects employees to each other and to the Net.

"As our Web presence grew we found that the constraints of having our Web site hosted by a third party Internet provider was too confining for our needs," Doug adds. "The slowdowns in service, the lack of content control, the lack of hard drive space, and inconvenient uploading of Web documents to the server were making it difficult to justify this setup."

The company opted for an ISDN connection because T1 was too expensive for their needs, and frame relay didn't allow them to integrate the digital telephone system they had already set up.

"For security, we have an integrated Cisco firewall hardware-software setup on the server which monitors users' actions while on the site. It prevents anyone from getting in and changing the site's contents."

"We get around a hundred-plus hits a day at our site — sometimes as many as eight to ten at the same time — so our lines are well-used. With global Internet usage growing by leaps and bounds, this may eventually not be enough but with the router service we purchased, we included the option to upgrade the line capacity to a T1, so we should be covered for a while to come."

ADSL is off to the races

Asymmetric Digital Subscriber Line, ADSL, is a technology that uses conventional copper phone lines to provide users with a direct connection to the Internet that, in theory at least, can reach speeds of 1Mbps to 8Mbps. Sound impossible? It turns out that the human voice only uses a part of a telephone line, the part that transmits signals of 3000 Hz (Hertz) in frequency or lower. ADSL borrows the part of your phone line that transmits signals that are higher than 3000 Hz.

ADSL requires hardware at your end of the telephone line; your telephone company also has to have the same piece of ADSL hardware. For that reason, your business must be located within a certain distance of a phone switch that supports ADSL technology. Because the data exchange is asymmetrical, the speed at which you receive data is different. Businesses with ADSL can upload (send) data to another location on the Net at 1.088Mbps, and download (receive) data at more than twice that rate: 2.560Mbps.

If ADSL is available in your area, find out if your provider will let you start at a relatively low speed, such as 640K/272Kbps (see the preceding example).

A similar technology that's just beginning to appear, Symmetric Digital Subscriber Line (SDSL) delivers data at the same speed in both directions. The speed is about the same as a T1 dedicated line.

ADSL and SDSL are seen as cost-effective "starter" types of direct connections to the Net. A business can start out with one of these connections and then move up to a faster option that uses fiber-optic cable, such as ATM.

For more general information on ADSL, see Dan Kegel's ADSL page at `www.cerf.net/dank/isdn/adsl.html`.

Cable me with cable modems

Cable modem connections are the most promising and exciting options around for personal and small business users. It's frustrating that they are only available in about 30 locations in the U.S. and Canada. (You can find a list of commercial cable modem services in North America at the Cable Datacom News Web site, `www.cabledatacomnews.com/cmic7.htm`.)

Cable modem services are shared by a number of users at once, so speeds can vary widely. MediaOne, which provides cable modem connections in the Chicago and Detroit areas, estimates that customers can send data at about 300Kbps and receive data at about 1.5Mbps. However, speeds for receiving data have been reported at up to 30Mbps.

To find out more about this promising technology, see the Cable Modem Resources web page at `rpcp.mit.edu/~gingold/cable`.

Megabits, gigabits, terabits, hike!

If you need a lot of bandwidth to do real-time communications or transfer audio or video, consider the direct connections that can transfer megabits, gigabits, or possibly even terabits of data per second.

One big benefit of really fast connections is the ability to deliver real-time video over an intranet or the Internet. London-based SohoNet (`www.sohonet.co.uk`) uses ATM to allow member businesses to quickly transmit film scenes, entire movies, and do videoconferencing over its network.

Another benefit of a direct connection is that you're able to operate your own servers in-house to provide you with e-mail, FTP, and Web pages on the Internet.

Full-time and part-time T1 and T3 lines

A T1 connection to the Internet is a copper cable run directly to your home or business. A full T1 connection delivers data at 1.544Mbps. T1 lines are widely used by Internet access providers who need to provide their customers with fast connections and keep Web servers connected to the Net all the time. If you get a T1 line, you pay not only the installation and sizable monthly fees, but you need to purchase a router and a box called a DSU/CSU (that's Data Service Unit/Channel Service Unit, for the technically-inclined). These can cost more than $4,000.

A good way for a small business to have the benefit of a direct connection to the Net while paying less than the cost of a full T1 line is a *fractional T1* line. Some providers advertise these as leased-lines with speeds that are a fraction of the full T1 speed. Most small business find that leased lines of 128Kbps or 256Kbps are adequate for their needs.

T3 connections are faster than T1 lines because they use fiber optic cables instead of copper wires. A T3 line can transmit data at up to 45Mbps. They're quite a bit more expensive than T1 lines, however, and most small businesses can satisfy their requirements with T1 connections.

Going into warp drive with ATM

ATM stands for Asynchronous Transfer Mode. ATM moves packets of data from one place to another incredibly fast along a computer network. ATM can replace existing local networks such as Ethernet, or Internet connections such as frame relay. ATM, like frame relay, works with packets of data that are a fixed size. The difference is that ATM works with packets that are bigger than frame relay can handle, and ATM is *really* fast: It can deliver data over conventional cables at up to 25 megabits per second, and over fiber optic lines at up to 622 megabits per second.

ATM is becoming available on the Internet, and prices for ATM hardware and software are going down. A good place to find more information about ATM is the ATM Forum (www.atmforum.com). There's also a good set of Frequently Asked Questions (FAQs) at www.fore.com/atm-edu/gd/atmgd1.html.

How to Choose an Internet Service Provider

You have an idea of what kind of Internet connection you need. Now, you need to find a company that can actually give you access to the Net. Here, too, you have lots of different options:

- ✔ **Commercial online services.** These are services that provide you with their own online content — discussion groups, publications, live chats, and so on — as well as give you access to the Internet. The best known are America Online and CompuServe.

- ✔ **Internet Service Providers (ISPs).** These are also sometimes called Internet Access Providers. Their primary purpose is to give individuals and businesses access to the Internet.

- ✔ **Web Hosting Services.** This is a term I came up with. I use it to describe companies whose purpose is to host business Web sites and give you a domain name, FTP space, and e-mail service. They don't give you access to the Internet, however; you still need an ISP or commercial online service for that.

How do you choose which service is best for you? Think *business.* Look for providers that have business resources, and especially accounts for small businesses and home offices. Find a service that your employees can enjoy working with, especially if they're inexperienced with computers in general or the Internet in particular.

Commercial providers versus ISPs

If you have only a handful of employees and they're all totally inexperienced (the Internet term is "newbies") with cyberspace, *and* if you don't expect to use the Web on a regular basis, the commercial online services may be right for you.

The online services came late to the Web and the rest of the Internet. Originally, they created their own online domains. If you subscribed to America Online, for example, you were limited to AOL's own content: its online magazines, reference materials, chat rooms, and all the rest.

Today, all of the online services provide their customers with Web access, and each enables you to use your Web browser of choice.

Surfing the Web through a commercial online service is like having training wheels on a bike, if you're used to sailing through the wide open spaces of the Web unencumbered. You can't always use the newest versions of the most popular browsers. And if you publish a Web site on the server space allocated to you by the online services, visitors may find that accessing your Web pages takes a little longer than it does on the Internet. For some reason, pages published on AOL just appear more slowly when accessed from the Web.

Pros and cons of online services

The online services have their own advantages and disadvantages for businesses. Here are some thumbs-up points:

✔ It's easier to get connected to the online services than to many ISPs. You install the software, supply some information, and you're ready to go.

✔ Online services are more secure than on the Internet. They are also more tolerant of blatant advertising.

✔ You can find lots of tutorials and online support on the online services. You can find tools that help you create your own Web pages quickly and easily and publish them online. It's also easy to find other business people to share ideas with through chat forums.

✔ The online services are nationwide, and they have access phone numbers all over the country. If you travel a lot, you can call up a local number to send and receive e-mail while you're on the road.

The online services are great if you're looking for a low-cost, no-fuss Internet connection. AOL, for instance, gives you the cheapest way to post a Web site that I know of. If you choose AOL's $9.95 monthly rate, you get five hours of access per month; each hour thereafter costs $2.95. You also get five screen names that you can create. Each of those screen names has a corresponding e-mail address so, in effect, you can have five separate e-mail addresses. Each screen name is allotted 2MB of space on a Web server, which is plenty of room to publish a simple Web site.

In order to get a complete picture, you should also keep in mind the following of using commercial online services to publish your business's Web site:

✔ You may not have as many options for connections as you would like.

✔ Online services do keep close watch over the content you publish. They sometimes monitor messages posted to discussion groups.

✔ Advertising or putting up a storefront on the online services can be really expensive. To promote your online store with a link to your Web page (if you have one) and a listing in its AOL Marketplace, America Online charges a flat fee of $100,000 to $125,000 plus 10 percent of sales.

If you have access to the Internet (for example, through a public library or through a friend), and are considering getting connected to one of the online services, check out one of the Usenet newsgroups that are set aside for individuals to discuss their experiences with AOL and other services. The newsgroups devoted to the online services have names like this:

    ✔ alt.online-service.america-online

    ✔ alt.online-service.compuserve

    ✔ alt.online-service.prodigy

Searching for an Internet Service Provider

If you're familiar with the types of Internet connections described in the first part of this chapter, you're way ahead of the game. No matter which ISP you choose, you should look for these features:

✔ **Flat rate access.** Most providers charge a flat monthly fee for unlimited access to the Net. The going rate is about $19.95 per month.

✔ **Telephone support.** Make sure you can call your provider for help; ask the provider and customers how long the typical wait is for phone support. Pick a company that won't keep you on hold, because lost time can mean lost business.

✔ **Web server space.** Expect your provider to give you space on a Web server where you can publish Web pages in order to advertise your business. By putting your site on their server, you benefit from your provider's fast connection to the Net (which is probably a T1 connection or faster). Another nice option is a virtual domain name. A domain name is an easy-to-remember word or phrase that you can use in your Internet address or URL. The shorter the name, the easier it is for customers to find you. A virtual domain name takes the form www.mybusiness.com, and gives an online business lots more credibility than a longer URL.

✔ **No business restrictions.** Make sure you can publish for-profit business Web pages on your provider's Web site, if that's what you want to do.

Where to find ISPs

There are thousands of ISPs around the country. Some ISPs are big and offer access anywhere in the country: They provide you with local phone numbers you can call so you can get a dial-up connection to the Net.

The best place to find a large selection of ISPs is the Web itself. However, you have to have a way to get on the Web in order to find them. Go to your local library and use a computer that's connected to the Net, if one's available, or ask a friend with Internet access if you can use his or her computer.

If you can't get on the Web, search the Yellow Pages for local access providers in your area. Call up a few and ask about their rates. If you can get on the Web, here are some good starting points for locating ISPs:

- Yahoo!'s index to Internet providers is at `www.yahoo.com/Business_and_Economy/Companies/Internet_Services/Access_Providers`.
- The List, which is among the old and well-established lists of ISPs is at `thelist.internet.com`. The nice thing about The List is that it's arranged by city, county, state, and other geographical areas.
- The Providers of Commercial Internet Access (POCIA) list has also been around a while. It's at `www.celestin.com/pocia`.

Perhaps the best way to find ISPs is to network with businesses in your area and ask about the providers they use. Call the chamber of commerce and local business groups for suggestions. Also check out the 476-page *Directory of Internet Service Providers*. You can order a copy by calling (800) 933-6038, or from the Boardwatch Web site (`www.boardwatch.com`).

Major Internet on-ramps

Several Internet access providers are large, nationwide telecommunications companies and other businesses that provide reliable connections, good rates, and support. Going with a big company can be comforting if you're new to the Net, simply because so many other individuals and businesses have already contracted to use the same firm, and it's likely the company will be around for a while because it's so big. Another advantage is that these companies typically offer toll-free numbers to use practically anywhere if you want to connect to the Net while you're traveling.

Local access providers

These days, your local area is covered by small Internet access companies. These companies may not offer the toll-free numbers or ready-made content that the commercial online services or big national ISPs provide. However, local access providers *may* provide you with better support than generally available from the bigger companies.

Web hosting services

Most Internet providers can give you a place to put your Web pages. Some may offer you the option of setting up a business Web site, which includes a virtual domain name (`www.business.com`), as well as lots of Web and FTP space.

Getting the "Internet backbone" straight

When you're shopping around for Internet providers, you sometimes find companies that advertise themselves as being connected to the "backbone" of the Internet. Why?

The backbone is a very fast part of the Internet that joins several main supercomputing centers. Smaller regional and local networks that make up the rest of the Internet spin off from those main centers. The resulting network of networks joins users around the country.

Does it make sense to connect with one of these providers in order to get a faster connection yourself? Probably not. These providers sell their fast connections to ISPs too. You don't get any speed advantage.

Deciding which setup is best for you

After you know about your Internet connection options, it's decision time. Keep in mind that virtually nothing is permanent when it comes to the Internet, including your choice of a provider and the software and hardware that you use to connect to the Net. Some providers do give you a special rate if you sign with them for a year. Others let you leave any time.

If you're dissatisfied with your present provider, go to Usenet to ask about providers. Ask questions and investigate newsgroups that are devoted to discussing issues related to the Internet access providers in your city, county, or state.

Word of mouth

References are the most reliable factor in choosing a provider. If you get good recommendations from two or three customers, you can be pretty sure that the ISP is an acceptable choice for you, too.

Co-location

Many small businesses that don't have a lot of space and need a fast connection to the Internet can consider co-locating your computer in your Internet provider's facility. If you want to co-locate, be sure to ask what hours you can have access to your computer, whether you can lock your location, and how much the provider charges for technical support.

Request that your provider gives you a report on how many hits your site is getting. If you're receiving a hundred visitors at the same time and some of your customers complain that it's hard to get in touch with you online, it's time to talk to your provider. Your connection may not be the problem: The computer on which your Web pages or other documents are stored and made available to the Net may be slow, too.

Chapter 4

Shake Hands with the Internet

- -

In This Chapter

▶ Understanding the inner workings of Web browsers

▶ Getting everyone in the loop with e-mail

▶ Collaborating with discussion groups

▶ Moving information with FTP programs

▶ Communicating with chat, Internet phone, and videoconferencing

- -

*W*hen one modem successfully connects to another one, the two share a "handshake." But, in the case of the Internet, simply making the connection isn't enough. You require the right software to help you and your employees navigate the nether reaches of cyberspace. You also need an idea of where you can go and what you can discover once you get online. With the right software, you and your business colleagues can communicate in new and exciting ways and discover sources of information you never imagined. This chapter is a rundown of the different software programs you need to download or purchase to fully use the Internet.

Web browsers *are* important, of course. In fact, the newer versions of Netscape Communicator and Microsoft Internet Explorer are all-in-one tools that enable you to access FTP sites and Gopher sites and participate in newsgroup discussions, as well as surf your favorite singer's new home page on the Web.

However, using the software that's specific to a particular part of the Net offers some additional advantages. Using an FTP program gives you the ability to delete or rename files on a remote FTP server, which is something you can't do with a Web browser. Some libraries can be accessed only by an old-fashioned terminal emulation program called Telnet. If you want to be able to fully research university databases and libraries, install Gopher software and start burrowing into "Gopherspace." This chapter, then, can help you understand the various services that make up the Internet and assist with the creation of an Internet software checklist to match your small business needs.

Sometimes, knowing what you *can* do helps you determine what you *want* to do. Understanding the kinds of services that are available on the Net may help you determine how you can use the Internet to your best advantage. If you want to give your customers a way to transfer graphics files to you, then setting up an FTP site may be the way to go. If you want to connect at-home workers with the rest of the office, check into real-time communications such as chat or videoconferencing. If you want to do market research, find some software that enables you to explore newsgroups. Keep your own needs in mind as you read this chapter (and this book); expect to run into the Internet services that can pull it all together for your small business.

Understanding Protocols

When you begin to learn about the many ways to access information on the Internet, some questions are bound to pop into your head. You may wonder: Why are there so many different parts of the Net? Why do they all look different? Why do you need special software programs to access them? The answers are easy to grasp if you consider how the Internet developed and what it was originally intended to accomplish.

For one thing, the Internet's evolution follows anything but a systematic plan. Different methods of communication develop as people look for more ways to share information. In order to transfer information between different computers that use different software and that are connected by a network, protocols came into existence.

A *protocol* is a set of standards that provides a universal method for locating computers and transferring data between them. You're probably already familiar with protocols from the first part of an Internet address called a Uniform Resource Locator (URL). The prefix that comes at the beginning of a URL tells you what protocol your Web browser or other software needs to use in order to access information on a particular site. Here are the most common examples:

- ✔ ftp:// is used for File Transfer Protocol (FTP)
- ✔ http:// is used for HyperText Transfer Protocol (HTTP), which is the protocol used to transfer information on the Web

The glue that holds everything together is TCP/IP, which stands for Transport Control Protocol/Internet Protocol. This is a combination of two protocols:

> ✓ Transport Control Protocol (TCP) is used to send the information from one location to another on a network.
>
> ✓ Internet Protocol (IP) provides a way for interconnected networks to transfer "packets" of information from one computer to another. Each computer has a standard IP address, a series of four numbers separated by dots, like this: 207.135.67.8.

In order to interact with the Internet, your computer needs to use software that supports TCP/IP. Then, depending on what part of the Internet you want to use, you install specific software like Fetch for FTP, Microsoft Internet Explorer for the Web, and all the other programs mentioned in this chapter.

Each Internet service has its own protocol for retrieving information from a host computer and transferring to a client computer (that's yours). Client software is the software that enables you to see and use the information. Table 4-1 lists the services that are available on the Internet.

Table 4-1	Internet Services
Service	*What It Does*
Anonymous FTP	Users can connect anonymously to an archive and download software and other data using File Transfer Protocol (FTP). Some of the more popular programs are Fetch (Macintosh), and WS_FTP or IFTP (Windows).
E-mail	Users send messages and attachments from one computer to another using Simple Mail Transfer Protocol (SMTP) and retrieve those messages using Post Office Protocol, Version 3 (POP3). They can manage their e-mail remotely using Internet Message Access Protocol, Version 4 (IMAP4). Eudora is one of the more popular programs for both the Mac and Windows computers; others are Quick Mail, Pegasus Mail, Netscape Messenger, and Microsoft Outlook.
FTP	Users are assigned a username and password so that they can gain access to a directory on an FTP server and transfer data back and forth.
Gopher	A way of locating information stored on Gopher servers and accessed through a series of hierarchical folders. TurboGopher (Mac) and WSGopher (Windows) are popular client programs.

(continued)

Table 4-1 *(continued)*

Service	What It Does
Internet Relay Chat	A method of conducting real-time communications on the Internet by enabling users to connect to a channel on a chat server and type messages to one another. MacChat and Global Chat (Mac) and Netscape Chat and NetMeeting (Windows) are clients.
Telnet	A way of using terminal emulation to connect to another computer on the Internet. NCSA Telnet and TN 3270 are examples of programs you can use.
Usenet	A global computer network that consists of online discussion groups (newsgroups) on lots of different topics. NewsWatcher (Mac) and NEWT News (Windows) are newsgroup programs.
WAIS	Wide Area Information Server, a way of searching for information on computers connected to the Internet. MacWAIS is a Mac program, and WAIS Toolkit is available for Windows NT.
World Wide Web	The graphical, colorful, multimedia-rich part of the Internet that uses hypertext to view information online. Netscape Navigator and Microsoft Internet Explorer are the "big two" browser programs.

Each of these services of the Internet has its own specialized software that you can install. But locating and downloading all that software takes valuable time. Luckily, you can access virtually all parts of the Net with one bit of software, a Web browser.

How Web Browsers Work

A Web browser is a must-have program for anyone who wants to use the Internet these days. A browser is a computer program that visually displays data and helps users locate information from remote sites on either a corporate intranet or the wider Internet.

The term "browser" is somewhat misleading because, although browsers do enable people to casually flip through "pages" of information looking for something that they may be interested in, they also do much more. Browsers provide a way of graphically presenting information contained on networked computers. They also enable users to interact with remote Web sites by submitting data entered on forms or manipulating images presented in the specialized graphics formats like GIF and JPEG. To borrow the name of the first graphical Web client, you can say that browsers present a "mosaic" of text and images that is not platform- or monitor-specific.

When a Web browser connects to a Web server, it downloads graphics and text files to your computer and stores them in a section of your hard disk called a *cache* (pronounced *cash*). The next time the browser visits the same site, it checks first to see if any information has changed. If it has not, the browser loads the information from the cache on your hard disk, not from the remote location. This makes the page appear on the screen more quickly. You can force the browser to reload a page from the remote site rather than from the cache by pressing the Reload button.

Web browsers are not created equal. Most, but not all, execute Java programs and display the results. Some browsers work faster than others and some display things like frames and animation that others cannot process. Some browser manufacturers create their particular extensions to standard HTML that only their own software can display.

If you plan on creating a Web site for your business, you need a variety of other software programs, such as Web page creation tools and graphics programs. See Chapter 13 for suggestions on programs you can use to make your own Web pages.

All-in-one Internet navigators

The two Web browsers that are tops in popularity, Netscape Navigator and Microsoft Internet Explorer, are roughly comparable in speed, ease of use, and flexibility. Together these two packages are used by more than 90 percent of all Web users.

The newest versions of these companies' products do more than just present Web pages. Rather, each is a suite of applications that, together, enable you to access virtually all parts of the Internet, including Usenet, Gopher, FTP, and Telnet. That's because they recognize not only HTTP, but also other protocols such as FTP, NNTP, SMTP, and Gopher. They also come with applications that give you the tools to audioconference or video-conference or share whiteboards — computer drawing tools that enable connected users to view diagrams and even collaborate on their construction. Simply purchasing or downloading one of these programs can solve many of your Internet software needs, as shown in Figure 4-1.

Web browser facts and figures

Where do you find these one-stop Internet browsers? You can purchase Netscape Communicator at 1-415-937-3777 or, if you already have another Web browser and can get on the Net, download Communicator from Netscape's Web site (home.netscape. com/download/index.html). The Standard Edition of Communicator includes the Navigator Web browser, plus e-mail, newsgroup, and conference software. This version retails for $79, but costs $59 if you purchase it from Netscape's online store (merchant. netscape.com/netstore/index. html). The program requires 16MB of RAM and 16MB of hard disk space. The Professional Edition of Communicator adds a calendar, mainframe access, and centralized management of Communicator, costs $79, and requires 16MB of RAM and 40MB of disk space.

Microsoft Internet Explorer 4.0 can be downloaded in minimal, standard, or full versions from Microsoft's Web site (www. microsoft.com/ie/download). The full suite of applications includes browser, e-mail, newsgroup, netscasting, chat, and administration tools. The Windows 95 version of the program requires 8MB of RAM; the NT version requires 16MB. Disk space required ranges from 11 to 20MB depending on the number of components you install. If you don't have enough RAM, you may as well stick with an older and less demanding browser.

Figure 4-1: Netscape Communicator gives you (from top) a Web browser, e-mail, and Web page composer, and other software all in one package.

Although Internet Explorer and Communicator dominate the Web browser market, when you develop your business site on the Internet, you should keep in mind that a small proportion of your audience use Web clients other than the "Big Two." Visitors to your site may choose less popular, and less full-featured programs like NCSA Mosaic, MacWeb, IBrowse, AOL's Web browser, or Spry Mosaic. Some users may even use a non-graphical browser called Lynx, whose patrons prefer to receive only textual data instead of having to wait for graphics to appear. You may want to keep your content simple, or provide text-only versions of your Web pages, so visitors with simpler browsers can get your message quickly.

For a small business, any Web browser you use needs to have some essential features:

- ✔ **Support for Java.** Even if you don't plan to add Java applets to your own Web page, you need to see what others are doing. Some applets provide stock quotes, others present the latest airline fares.

- ✔ **Support for colors.** Browsers can not only display colors, but also enable you to configure backgrounds and typefaces to suit your own tastes.

- ✔ **Support for forms.** There are Web page features, such as text boxes and check boxes, that enable you to submit information to a Web site.

- ✔ **Animations.** Most newer Web browsers enable you to view an image that consists of several separate GIF animations, all arranged to play in sequence.

How do you know if your browser lacks a feature such as animations if you can't see the animations in the first place? A good place to compare the capabilities of your browser is the Browser Capabilities Test at `www.itsi.net/browser_captest.html`. A clearinghouse of browsers you can download is located at the BrowserWatch Web site (`browserwatch.internet.com`).

Easy E-Mail on the Internet

After you're connected to the Internet, you may be "champing at the byte" to get your e-mail address on all of your business cards, newspaper ads, and brochures. An e-mail program is another must-have for everyone in your company.

The ability to send and receive e-mail with people all over the world is, after all, one of the big benefits of being Internet-reachable. I would even make the argument that having the Internet e-mail capability is at least as important, if not more, than having a Web presence.

My reason for such a bold statement is that e-mail enables you to do much more than exchange messages with someone. E-mail is also your ticket to important business functions such as:

- ✔ **File exchanges.** By attaching documents or programs to an e-mail message, you can use e-mail as a way to transfer data with customers and collaborators.

- ✔ **Communications.** E-mail is a way to deliver news and views about your company to subscribers on a mailing list. After your mailing list is set up, you can provide documents that are sent automatically to users who request them.

- ✔ **Discussions.** E-mail enables you to get the word out to everyone in your company all at once. A group of users can set up *mailing lists* for their workgroups in order to discuss the progress of critical projects. (See Chapters 7 and 15 for more on mailing lists.)

A small business that wants to send and receive e-mail online has three basic options:

Using standard Internet software

Issue each staff person a copy of an e-mail package that uses, at the very least, the Internet e-mail protocols SMTP and POP3. The better e-mail packages also support Multipurpose Internet Mail Extensions (MIME), a protocol that enables you to attach multimedia files to e-mail messages, and Internet Message Access Protocol, Version 4 (IMAP4), which enables you to access and file your e-mail messages remotely without having to download all of them.

Some of the better Internet e-mail programs come bundled with the Web browsers Netscape Communicator and Microsoft Internet Explorer 4.0. Communicator's e-mail component is called Netscape Messenger; Microsoft's is called Microsoft Outlook. Both of these programs recognize IMAP4, and enable you to search your e-mail messages as well as set up filters so you can process messages automatically as soon as you receive them.

Two other popular programs are Eudora Pro by Qualcomm and Pegasus Mail by David Harris (www.pegasus.usa.com). One advantage of these programs is that they permit lots of automated message handling. Eudora costs $59, while Pegasus Mail is free. Pegasus Mail is specially designed to work with versions 2.15 or later of Novell NetWare, and comes in versions for Windows 95, NT, and 3.1, as well as the Macintosh and OS/2.

Trying out the online services

If one or more of your computers are connected to America Online, CompuServe, or Prodigy, you're pretty much limited to using the provider's software for Internet e-mail. The online service's e-mail is completely separate from any local e-mail you already set up. Using AOL or another online service's software for your daily business e-mail needs is a perfectly practical solution for a small office, as long as someone on staff checks the e-mail regularly.

You do have two alternatives if you belong to an online service. For one thing, there's a highly rated e-mail package called E-Mail Connection 3.1a (www.connectsoft.com) that enables you to retrieve your e-mail from AOL and CompuServe as well as Internet Service Providers. It costs $50 and is available for Windows 3.1/95 only.

The other alternative is to obtain a shareware e-mail program. CompuServe users can download a program from Ozarks West software called OzWin II 2.12.2, which is an offline mail reader designed specifically for retrieving e-mail from CompuServe. Users can Go OZWIN on CompuServe to find out more and to download the program. The program can be downloaded for free but users are asked to pay a $69 registration fee.

AOL users can obtain a $35 shareware program called PowerMail 1.3 to read their AOL e-mail. The advantage of using PowerMail is that it has a spell-checking capability, and it enables you to encrypt your e-mail messages so unwanted recipients can't read them. The disadvantage is that you have to use the program at the same time you use your normal AOL e-mail software.

Sticking with your existing e-mail software

If you already have an e-mail network set up in your office that uses a popular e-mail program such as Lotus cc:Mail, Lotus Notes, QuickMail, or Microsoft Mail, and you want to open your network to send and receive e-mail, you have to make a decision: You can either install Internet e-mail programs in addition to your local area network e-mail, or you can purchase a *gateway* that adapts your local e-mail program to work with the Internet. A gateway is a software program that allows your existing local network to use TCP/IP software so your employees can communicate with the Internet.

If you use Lotus's Domino mail server, you can upgrade to version 4.6, which has added support for the Internet protocols. That way you can use any POP3-compatible mail software on the Internet as well as for local communications. Lotus Notes 4.6 is being positioned as a competitor to Microsoft Outlook and Netscape Messenger, in fact.

Your decision is influenced by whether or not you already have an e-mail program that enables your staff to exchange messages. These programs, such as Lotus Notes, Microsoft Mail, Lotus cc:Mail, or OfficeVision, are local area network (LAN) mail programs that require special gateway software to connect to the Internet. Why? Internet e-mail supports protocols like SMTP, POP3, and IMAP. LAN e-mail programs use protocols such as MAPI (Microsoft Mail) and VIM (Lotus cc:Mail). These gateways can either be quite expensive or difficult to use. Chapter 7 discusses the kinds of gateways you may need.

Should you spend the money to get an adapter for your local system so you can send and receive e-mail on the Net? That depends on how much you plan to use the Net and how many people in your office need Internet access. If you only plan to check your e-mail once a day from one computer, just install the e-mail software on the tone computer. If everyone in the office occasionally needs to be on the Net, better get an adapter, or have everyone download an individual copy of Microsoft Internet Explorer 4.0 and use Microsoft Outlook.

ABCs of FTP

At least one person in your office needs FTP software in order to send and receive large files if the occasion ever arises. FTP has only one purpose: to move data from one computer to another on the Internet. When you download the latest version of a game, Web browser, or spell-checking utility from a site on the Internet, your computer usually obtains the data using FTP. The program, in turn, is made available to you from a computer that has FTP server software installed. Here is a brief overview of these two important kinds of FTP software that your office may need.

Serving up software with FTP

Any computer that's connected to the Internet can be set up to operate as an FTP server. The machine itself can either be located in your office or at your service provider's location. The setup you choose depends on how much control you want to have over the machine and the data that's on it, and how much maintenance you are prepared to do.

Let your ISP do the serving

An FTP server works best if you have a computer that is connected to the Net all the time. If you dial-up to connect to the Net, your computer is only available to communicate with other machines on the Net for the length of the phone call. If you want to send someone a file using FTP, you have to arrange to be connected at the same time your clients or colleagues are ready to receive the data. Setting up a time to move the files can be pretty inconvenient.

If your computer does have a dial-up connection, it's more practical to purchase space on a server operated by a Web hosting service. Along with space for your Web pages, these services usually provide you with the option of providing you with your own FTP site as well. Many of the Internet Service Providers that provide access to the Net give you FTP space along with your dial-up account. Either way, you don't have to worry about setting up your computer to function as a server. You just use FTP client software to send and receive files.

Do-it-yourself FTP server software

If you do want to set up your own FTP site, it's by no means impossible. Inexpensive software is available to help you provide software and other files from your own computer.

The easiest FTP server software for the Macintosh is called NetPresenz by Peter N. Lewis, which is available as shareware for $10 from `www.stairways. com` (see Figure 4-2).

On the Windows side, you can set up an FTP server with a very good shareware program called WFTPD by Alun Jones. You can download it from the Texas Imperial Software Products Web site (`www.wftpd.com/wftpd.htm`).

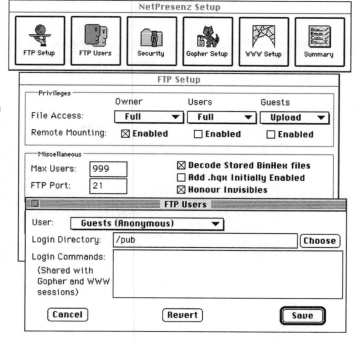

Figure 4-2:
Setting up NetPresenz is easy: Set access privileges for your visitors, create a folder that visitors can access, and you're ready to go.

FTP client software

FTP client programs enable you to download files from an FTP server (also called an FTP *site*) or send files from your computer to someone else's using FTP. The most common use of FTP software is downloading a file to your computer.

Many FTP sites on the Internet allow anyone to connect and download software freely: these are called *anonymous FTP* sites. Other sites require users to enter an approved username and password.

After you connect, FTP software enables you to navigate through the various directories on the site, and then either download files to your computer or *upload* them from your computer to the FTP site.

The preeminent FTP program for the Macintosh is called Fetch, which can be downloaded from any Macintosh shareware archive. A good program for Windows 95 is WS_FTP Pro by Ipswitch Software Inc. (www.ipswitch.com). WS_FTP, shown in Figure 4-3, can be downloaded for a free 30-day trial period and then registered for a $37.50 shareware fee.

Big FTP files can take a *really* long time to download. For instance, the 8.3MB files that make up the Standard Edition of Netscape Communicator take about 54 minutes to download over a 28.8Kbps modem.

Figure 4-3: It's not pretty, but WS_FTP gets the job done, transferring files from your hard disk, on the left, to a remote FTP site on the right.

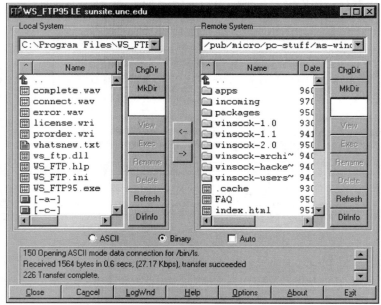

Joining in Usenet Discussions

Internet newsgroups are a huge and important resource on the Internet. Usenet (which stands for the original name of this part of the Internet, the User's Network) predates the Web by many years.

Newsgroups are group discussions on particular topics of interest. Anyone can participate in a newsgroup on the Internet by connecting to the group using a program called a news reader. On a corporate intranet, newsgroups are limited to employees or smaller groups within the company.

Users post messages, upload files, and read messages posted by others. Messages are sorted by topic, so you can read about subjects that interest you most.

One way to use newsgroups is to start your own discussion group, a process described in Chapter 8. Another is to "lurk" or listen in on group discussions in order to see what people are most interested in. The easiest way to access Usenet is to use the newsgroup tool that comes with a one-stop browser suite. Netscape's Collabra, for instance, has a particularly useful feature that enables you to search for discussion groups by entering part of their names. This is a handy feature because there are literally thousands of discussion groups, and subjects are often discussed by more than one group in the wide realm of Usenet. (For example, you can find two separate newsgroups, `alt.antiques` and `rec.antiques`.)

Chapter 8 goes into lots more detail about Usenet, but basically, you don't have to buy software to use Usenet unless you want to set up your own internal discussion groups. In that case, you have to purchase discussion group server software.

You can download NewsWatcher by John Norstad for free from `charlotte.acns.nwu.edu/jln/progs.html`. NewsMonger shareware for Windows 95 and NT costs $39.95. IWare InternetSuite, a mail and news reader, is offered by Quarterdeck Corporation as part of its suite of Internet applications for NetWare networks. Find out more at `ww.quarterdeck.com/qdeck/products/iware/iware-suite.html`.

Real-Time Communications Software

If distance prevents you from making face-to-face contact, and long-distance phone bills are piling up, consider using your Internet connection to facilitate real-time communications through your computer.

Real-time communications through discussion forms and chat rooms is an integral part of online services such as America Online, CompuServe, and Prodigy. If you already subscribe to one of these services, you probably know how to chat by typing messages through your computer.

The slower your connection, the worse your communications sound. Real-time conferencing and chatting works with a direct T1/T3 or cable modem connection to the Internet, or at the very least, a 33.6Kbps modem.

Getting together with Internet Relay Chat

Internet Relay Chat (IRC) also goes by the terms such as *Live Chat* or simply *Chat*. IRC works by giving computer users around the world a chance to gather in groups called *channels,* each one usually devoted to a topic of discussion. Private conversations are also possible.

IRC can provide a small business with a low-cost way to conduct real-time communications. IRC works well with slow dial-up modem connections, while videoconferencing and Internet telephony work best with direct connections or fast (128Kbps) ISDN modem connections.

The popular chat programs are all available on a shareware basis and can be downloaded for free or for a nominal fee from the Internet. Two IRC programs for the Mac are Global Chat by Quarterdeck (www.qdeck.com/chat), shown in Figure 4-4, and ircle (www.xs4all.nl/~ircle). On the Windows side, a popular program is PIRCH, which is available for $10 shareware by North-west Computer Services (www.bcpl.lib.md.us/~frappa/pirch.html). Microsoft Chat (www.microsoft.com/ie/chat), which is available for free either as a standalone application or a plug-in application for Internet Explorer, comes with a "comic book" interface.

Making Internet phone calls

If both you and your clients have a computer connected to the Net, and *if* you have Internet telephone software, you can save on long-distance calls.

Basically, you only pay for the local call to your Internet Service Provider (ISP). After you're connected, you launch a special software program that permits Internet telephony to help you connect to another computer on the Net that also has Internet telephony software. You speak into your computer microphone, which digitizes your voice and sends it across the Internet.

The cheapest tools for voice communications are the built-in conferencing tools that come with Netscape Navigator or Microsoft Internet Explorer. Internet Explorer is equipped with NetMeeting, which permits whiteboard and videoconferencing as well as telephony. Communicator comes with an application called Conference, which does the same thing.

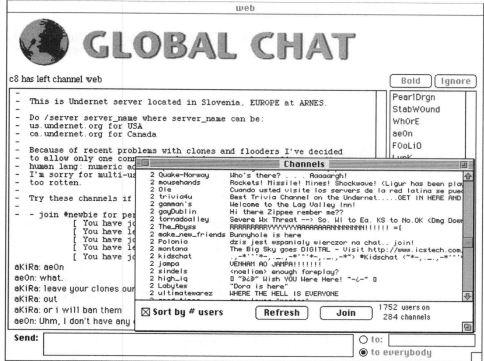

Figure 4-4:
Global Chat
enables you
to listen in
on chats
and type
your own
messages
to the
participants.

Videoconferencing

After you set up your computer for audioconferencing or chat, it's just another step or two to equip yourself for videoconferencing over the Internet. Videoconferencing requires the addition of a video camera to your computer and a video card.

Older Internet Technologies

Before the Web attracted everyone's attention, the Internet was already a happening place. In order to use the Internet to its fullest, you need a working knowledge of those once-popular parts of the online world that still hold lots of accessible information.

In many cases, you can use a Web browser to access these parts of the Net (though not every variety of browser enables you to connect via Telnet). Other times, your Internet Service Provider may provide you with special software that's tailored to each part of the Net you want to reach.

Burrowing with Gopher

Gopher is an information network that originated in higher education at the University of Minnesota, and if you need to find course catalogs or other college-related data, you may find it on a Gopher database.

If you use a Web browser, there's no reason why you have to install special Gopher software. Simply enter a Gopher URL in your browser's Open or Open Page text box and you'll go to a Gopher site:

```
gopher://boombox.micro.umn.edu/11/gopher
```

This URL takes you to a document on the University of Minnesota's Gopher server where you can download software for Windows and PCs.

A good place to start navigating Gopherspace is the Home Gopher Server at the University of Minnesota:

```
gopher://gopher.tc.umn.edu/1
```

This page includes lists of other Gopher servers around the world.

Searching with WAIS

A Wide Area Information Server (WAIS) is a server that enables you to search huge databases for free information. WAIS software is used by many of the popular Internet search services (see Chapter 16). When you send a query to a WAIS server, the matches that are most relevant to your query are listed first, and those that are less relevant follow. WAIS is no substitute for the search services like Excite, WebCrawler, and InfoSeek, however.

If your office network runs on Windows NT or UNIX, you can use WAIS to download two free programs of software that enable staff people to search your office intranet: WAIS Server and WAIS Toolkit are available from EMWAC (emwac.ed.ac.uk/html/toolchst.htm).

Getting down to basics: Telnet

Telnet is a terminal-emulation program that enables you to connect to another computer in much the same way a modem does.

You're most likely to use Telnet to access library databases on the Internet. Another big advantage of Telnet is that it enables you to connect to the information still stored in IBM mainframe computers. Although some corporations are developing Web interfaces to those databases, the organizations that are doing business the "old way" can still use Telnet.

Part II

Bringing the Internet to Your Employees

The 5th Wave   By Rich Tennant

"OH THOSE? THEY'RE THE SEAT-CUSHION-MOUSE. BOUNCE ONCE TO ACCESS A FILE, TWICE TO FILE AWAY—KEEPS THE HANDS FREE AND THE BUTTOCKS FIRM."

In this part . . .

The Internet isn't just for reaching out to computer users across the globe. It can help you reach your coworkers across the office, too. Part II is especially for small businesses that need to give all of their employees access to the Internet in order to exchange e-mail or improve access to company files.

Chapter 5

Helping Your Employees Use the Internet

In This Chapter

▶ Suggesting Internet business starting points for your employees

▶ Downloading free Internet training materials

▶ Providing books and magazines

▶ Setting guidelines for Internet use in the workplace

▶ Creating a new employee intranet

*A*ny new business venture needs to make sure all of its employees work together to achieve desired goals and be successful. Using the Internet to help your business grow is no exception.

When you have your connection to the Net and the right software installed, you can't just make a quick announcement and then let everyone fend for themselves. Give your employees a helping hand so they can get used to the new way to communicate and gather information.

Although everyone has heard of the Internet these days, lots of people don't have a clue about accessing its riches. Many others are unfamiliar — or even fearful — of computers. Luckily, Internet technologies themselves can give a business manager some easy ways to help employees learn to use the Internet without wasting their (or your) time. E-mail is a fundamental tool for communicating the information your staff needs to learn the Net. But internal documents published on a company intranet can help, too.

Most of this chapter assumes that you have one or more employees and computers, with the computers wired into a LAN (Local Area Network). If you are a one-person operation, then most of this doesn't apply to you, although the sections about getting up to speed on the Net and setting up a pilot project may help.

But even if you don't have your computers networked, you and your staff still need to learn about the Internet, and the suggestions in this chapter should come in handy. In any case you'll find that the Internet itself is one of the best sources of information for newcomers or "newbies."

The most obvious reasons to help a business's staff learn to use the Internet is to help them communicate with e-mail and to gather information from the Web or the online services. You may also want your staff to collaborate using mailing lists (see Chapter 7) or discussion groups (see Chapter 8). Training is a place where an internal version of the Internet, an intranet, can be particularly useful. It's a great way to convey personnel, financial, legal, or other company information to your employees.

If you do set up a computer in your office that has a connection to the Internet, make sure you train your employees on how to use it. Not doing so may hurt their morale. I know of one company that employs a very close relative of mine, and that has one computer equipped with a dial-up modem to make a connection to the Net. Only a handful of staff people know how to use the machine. When I wanted to send e-mail to this particular relative, she had no idea how to do it.

Learning the Net on the Net

If you want to learn about the Net, one of the best places to turn is the Net itself. That may sound strange coming from an author of computer books that show people the Web and the rest of the Internet. Books are great, and you should include a selection of good Internet starter guides — along with a copy of the book you're reading now, of course. But encourage your employees to visit some good Web and Internet resources for beginners, like these.

If you're in middle management, don't forget your bosses! You know, the folks who approve purchases of Internet hardware and software and who pay your salary, too. Start with management and get them used to the Internet before you start training everyone else.

Suggestions for beginners' Internet sites

If all of your employees do their wandering on company time, how can your regular work get done? You can save yourself and your employees a lot of productive time by giving them a set of URLs they can visit to get started on the Net.

You don't have to copy the contents of these sites to your computer. Instead, simply give your employees a set of URLs they can visit. Here are a few other sure-fire good sites.

- ✔ Free Online Dictionary of Computing (wombat.doc.ic.ac.uk).

- ✔ Try the Yahoo! Internet Life SurfSchool (www.zdnet.com/yil/filters/surfjump.html).

- ✔ There's a Web site devoted solely to "newbies," or newcomers to the Internet. It's graphically complex, but you may find it fun (www.newbie.net/CyberCourse).

- ✔ Although several years old, Brendan Kehoe's Zen and the Art of the Internet Web site still contains a lot of good information about the basic technical underpinnings of the Net (www.cs.indiana.edu/docproject/zen/zen-1.0_toc.html).

If the e-mail program you use recognizes MIME types (see Chapter 7), you can give your employees the URLs in the body of an e-mail message. The URLs appear as highlighted hyperlinks in the body of the e-mail message. Recipients can connect to the Internet, click on the link, and their Web browser accesses the site quickly. You can also save the links as a set of bookmarks (if you and your staff use Netscape's browser) or favorites (if you use Microsoft Internet Explorer). Your employees can use the bookmarks and favorites to open the URLs in their Web browsers (see Chapter 16).

Computer-Based Training (CBT) is growing in popularity. Plenty of companies will sell or create custom CBT training materials that you can issue to your staff people on a CD-ROM or floppy disk, or over your intranet.

Before you spend your money, however, check out the 15-Minute Series, a free collection of Internet training materials provided by InterNIC. InterNIC is an important resource on the Net. It's comprised of several organizations, including Network Solutions, Inc. The 15-Minute Series, created by Network Solutions and the Library and Information Technology Association (LITA), is a series of training sessions on the history and basic use of the Internet. Each subject in the series is available for you to copy without charge. They come in an HTML (Web page) version or a version for the presentation application Microsoft PowerPoint. They appear as a series of slides. They come in both HTML and PowerPoint versions. If you are enterprising, you can even add to the lessons and customize them for your company.

You or your staff can access these lessons on the InterNIC Web site (rs.internic.net/nic-support/15min) and view the materials with your Web browser while connected to the Net. However, if you only have one computer in your office connected to the Net, that isn't practical. Instead, InterNIC makes the lessons available to people who want to copy them to a computer on their local network. This not only makes the files appear faster, but lets people access the lessons without having to connect to the Internet. Employees only need to connect to the computer in your office where the files are.

Beginners' books you can buy

Before I ever thought about writing a book with *...For Dummies* in the title, I read other books in the series and learned quite a bit from them. Naturally, I suggest that you start with one or more of the *...For Dummies* books, too.

General Internet books

Provide your office staff with a few books about the Internet. Now in its fourth edition, *The Internet For Dummies,* by John R. Levine et al, published by IDG Books Worldwide, Inc., continues to provide a great introduction to the latest Internet technologies.

Internet business guides

If you want more specific guidebooks to doing business on the Internet after you read this one, here are some titles that I like:

- ✔ *How to Grow Your Business on the Internet,* by Vince Emery.
- ✔ *Marketing on the Internet,* by Jill H. Ellsworth and Matthew V. Ellsworth.
- ✔ *Grow Your Business Online: Small Business Strategies for Working the World Wide Web,* by Phaedra Hise.
- ✔ *Internet Business-to-Business Directory,* by Sandy Eddy Schnyder et al.

Magazines about the Internet

Every week or two, it seems, a new magazine about the Internet pops up on the newsstands. It's hard to keep track of them all. If you're going to sub-scribe to a magazine, you want one that is sure to provide useful content from issue to issue. In my office, the magazine area (a table in the hallway) was strategically located near the fax machine, water cooler, and bathroom. It was a great gathering place for people to browse and sometimes point out articles to one another. Here are a few suggestions:

✔ **Web Week.** This often-recommended magazine discusses the current state of Internet technology from a business perspective. You can check it out on the Web at `www.webweek.com`.

✔ **Internet World.** IW can be found at `www.internetworld.com`, and looks at the Internet from a wider perspective, reporting on trends and developments and providing advice on software, hardware, and content issues.

✔ **Wired.** This well-known glitzy magazine isn't so much a how-to guide as it is a chronicle of the culture of cyberspace. It has great articles about cutting-edge developments related to the Internet, and can get employees excited about exploring the online world.

✔ **Home Office Computing** and **Small Business Computing.** These are two really good magazines tailored just to the kinds of businesses they advertise. The Smalloffice.com Web site (`www.smalloffice.com`), which is produced by the editors of both magazines, is a good online resource, too (see Figure 5-1).

Figure 5-1:
Small-
office.com
is a great
small
business
resource.

Developing an Internet-Savvy Staff

The first step toward developing an Internet-savvy staff is to make sure your employees are okay with using Internet technology. Talk to them about your business's Internet connection at your staff meetings.

Be ready for some employee resistance. Some people just don't like computers, and some employees will never get used to the Internet. It may help to have them watch while someone else surfs the Web, or to assign someone to give them personal instructions. In my experience, virtually anyone can learn to send and receive e-mail. But some people do have a hard time getting around the Web on their own. You'll have to decide how much time you want to devote to hand-holding such employees.

Make sure your employees understand that being on the Net won't always save them work. The Net *does* help in some ways. You can look up facts and figures quickly, for instance. You don't have to print as many booklets; you can put them online. But on the other hand, someone has to report on your Internet research, and someone has to do the work of putting those publications online. Basic Internet business tasks like answering e-mail and maintaining your company Web site are new activities that you didn't have to do before. Tell your staff that being on the Net brings new responsibilities as well as new benefits.

Deciding who gets Internet access

Do you want to be the only person in your company who has access to the Internet? Do you want two people to have access, or everyone? If you are able to give everyone in your office access to the Net, great. However, your small business may not be able to afford it right now. Routers are expensive, as are LAN.ISDN and other direct connections. Maybe only one or two computers are Net-ready, and people have to dial up to the Net. How do you determine who gets access to the Net, to avoid conflicts and keep everyone happy?

It's helpful to familiarize everyone with the ABCs (or ISPs or FTPs or URLs) of the Internet so they know how to send and receive e-mail and discussion group messages. As for surfing the Web, using FTP or newsgroups, the ones who are really enthusiastic about those activities will select themselves. Here are some suggestions for giving everyone the introductory information they need.

Have a Webmaster conduct instructional sessions for your staff people explaining how to get on the Web or Net and how to use it. It's usually best to conduct these sessions for small groups of two or three people at a time rather than eight or ten at once. That way, people can take turns actually sitting at the computer and getting online and getting their feet wet.

Don't make yourself the arbiter of Net time. Instead, appoint an office Webmaster whose job is to maintain your Internet connection and monitor what software goes on the computer. Also consider creating a sign-in sheet so people can take turns getting on the Net at the times that are best for them, to avoid disagreements over who gets online when.

Sharing modems in an office network

Small businesses on a budget may not be able to afford a direct connection to the Internet. You may only have one dial-up modem connected to a single computer. If that's the case, for a nominal investment you can buy software or hardware that lets two or more networked computers share a single modem.

One such software package is WinGate by Deerfield Communications Co. (`www.deerfield.com/wingate/index.htm`). WinGate works with Macintosh or Windows computers. You install WinGate on one computer on your network, and all the other computers can share a single modem and Internet access account. WinGate comes in two versions, Professional and Lite. Both versions let a group of networked computers access the Net by FTP, the Web, newsgroups, and so on. The Professional version has added features such as advanced logging, accounting and auditing, and remote system alerts. You can download a 30-day trial version of the Professional version. The cost of the program varies from $60 to $700, depending on the version you want and the number of users you want to connect.

Identifying techies who can help you

Even if you don't hire a Webmaster (see Chapter 6), it's very important for every office that expects to use the Internet to have someone on staff who is really good with computers. This person should also be patient and pleasant and like dealing with people too. Often it's hard to find a computer type who really communicates well, too, but they are around.

Encouraging employees to help one another

Anything you can do to take the burden off you for computer instruction and support is desirable. You are busy enough managing the office and doing everything needed by your business.

Get your employees to help one another by answering questions. If you give people a start, in a few months you'll probably be able to check back and see who's into discussion groups, who has downloaded the latest beta versions of software, and so on. You can then ask those people if they would be willing to teach others what they know about their favorite parts of the Net. At the office where I worked for more than a dozen years, one person was especially good with e-mail, one person liked the Web, another was a graphic designer, and so on. Use peoples' built-in skills to help each other.

If you have the expertise to get high-tech about your training, Progressive Networks, Inc. lets you download training materials for free from their Web site (`www.real.com/products/server/intranet/demand.html`).

Streaming audio is audio data that has been compressed so it transfers quickly. The compressed data transmits from a Web server to a Web browser, where the data can be decompressed and played while the data is still downloading. An application called RealAudio Player allows the browser to decompress and process the audio signals.

Attachmate Corporation uses RealAudio technology to provide its employees with a guided tour of its extensive intranet. You can get an idea of how this internal site works by downloading the RealAudio Player plug-in and experiencing the company's sample pages at `www.realaudio.com/intranet/attach.html`.

Setting acceptable use policies

It's important for you to tell people in your office what constitutes acceptable use of your Internet connection. If you expect your staff to use the Net a lot, issue a memo — or better yet, publish a Web page on your intranet — that sets out your rules for acceptable use of the Net.

  ✔ Not to do unsolicited advertising.

  ✔ Not to send and receive personal e-mail messages during office hours.

  ✔ To always include a signature file on their e-mail and discussion group messages that includes the company name, e-mail address, and URL.

However, this isn't the only kind of acceptable use policy you and your employees need to know. Another important one is the Acceptable Use Policy issued by your Internet Service Provider. Not following your ISP's guidelines can get you kicked off the Net. The most common restriction is against spamming. So make sure all your employees know what it says by giving them the URL that leads to the guidelines as published on your ISP's Web site.

Copyright and legal issues

The last thing you want is for your business to get sued, flamed, mail-bombed (see Chapter 7), or otherwise catch heat for violating copyright on the Internet. It's true that this doesn't happen very often. It's true that copying graphics or other copyrighted material from a Web site is ridiculously easy and anyone can do it with a click or two of a mouse. It's also true that people put things on the Web that violate copyright all the time.

But just because it's easy doesn't mean that your workers should do it. Issue a warning about copying unauthorized material without permission, so you won't get your company in trouble.

Respecting privacy

Make clear what information employees should and should not give out about your business. Don't release information you don't want to share, such as contracts, future clients, and unreleased products. The Internet doesn't keep secrets!

When your employees get online, you can't keep track of every piece of software or every document they're going to download. Be sure you install virus protection software on every computer that's connected to the Net. If you have Macintoshes, one of the best programs is John Norstad's Disinfectant, which is available as freeware at `charlotte.acns.nwu.edu/jln/jln.html`. On the PC side, Virus Scan 95 by McAfee Associates, Inc. is a good program that's available for the Mac and Windows 3.1, 95, and NT. You can download a trial copy at `www.mcafee.com`.

Start with Your Internal Intranet

An intranet is like a miniature version of the Internet that can only be accessed by you and your staff. It's a great way for management to communicate with employees and for employees to collaborate with one another.

How intranets work

It's difficult to see real intranets because they only exist within an organization. However, here, too, the Internet can help. Lots of Web sites that sell intranet software or that design intranets provide online examples of what intranets *may* look like. You can use them to get ideas for what you may put on your own internal site. Here are some suggestions:

- Target Vision's Web site (`net-x.com/tvuecpresent/Emp.htm`)
- Epoch Internet (`www.epochworks.net/demotheater/intranet/handbk.html`)

How intranets differ from other LANs

An intranet, like other kinds of internal networks, uses central computers called servers that let networked computers access files. The difference is in the software you use. It's the same as the software you use to cruise the Net, much of which is cheap and readily available.

Using an intranet to collaborate

If your company has offices in more than one location, an intranet may be the best way for you to share information. Why? An intranet uses the same TCP/IP software you use to access the Internet, so you can reach the remote office easily through e-mail or other familiar Internet tools.

You don't *have* to install an intranet just because you have an Internet connection. If you are happy with your existing network, don't scrap it automatically. Some consultants believe that intranets have the biggest benefits to companies with 100 or more employees, or with offices scattered around the globe. You save on telephone, fax, package delivery, and more.

Building a Web team

Even if it only consists of two people, a team approach can be really helpful when it comes to creating your internal intranet (not to mention your external Web site). My colleague John Casler created an identity for the Web Team at one branch of Lucent Technologies near Chicago. The Web Team, which created the office intranet, had its own Web page and a tongue-in-cheek newsletter, both of which helped build morale and helped people work together.

Pilot Projects to Get You Started

If you're just starting with Internet technologies, it's best to tackle manageable pieces of your intranet rather than trying to create the whole internal Web site at once. It's no different than creating a business site for everyone on the World Wide Web to see (as explained in Chapter 13).

Pick a pilot project. Set a target date (perhaps a few weeks, or even a month to be safe) and assemble a team to put the information together using one of the Web page programs like Microsoft FrontPage or Netscape Composer.

The new employees' Web site

One universal topic that businesses large or small can put out on an intranet is a site where new employees can learn about your company. A new employees' site can be a good starting project for your Web team.

To create a site, you need to designate a computer to serve as an internal Web server. You also need some intranet server software. (These come with Microsoft FrontPage 97.) The computer can be one you don't use often; it can be a 486 PC, or an older Mac such as a Quadra.

Here are some things you can put on a Web site for new employees.

Welcome page

If your small business lacks people to do orientation sessions and give tours, a welcome page on your intranet can serve as a substitute. A "Welcome to New Employees" page should be friendly and provide the same kinds of hyperlinks you see on World Wide Web pages.

Company history/organization

A welcome page is an easy way to provide your employees with some background of how long you've been in business. You can also explain your company mission, and provide an organizational chart.

Human Resources information

Information about hiring and benefits is one of the most common types of content seen on internal networks. Bigger companies put out job openings in various departments. Smaller businesses don't need to do that, but can still put out lots of helpful information about group insurance.

Job records

If you already have a database of past job records, you can use a program called Cold Fusion to convert your database to Web pages (see Chapter 15). At the very least, include the job numbers and a list of past jobs so people can find them more easily.

Forms and other financial procedures

Properly filling out purchase requests, expense accounts, job records, and other business forms can be one of the most tedious and time-consuming office tasks (at least, it was for me). Scan a sample form that has been filled out the way you want, save it as a GIF or JPEG image, and publish it on your intranet along with any other special instructions you want to convey.

Care for your intranet

Be sure to designate someone to keep your intranet site up to date and looking good. When you've completed your projects, you can add CGI scripts, Java applets, and other high-tech goodies that work much faster over an internal network than they do on the wider Internet.

Also make sure you have a way to back up your files regularly. In the beginning, simply copying current files to floppy disks once a week is a start. As you accumulate more documents, use special software to update only the files that have changed since the last update. If you use Zip disks from Iomega, they come with software that lets you do this.

Adding e-mail addresses and URLs to business cards

Although this item comes last in this chapter, it's one of the first ways in which your business can and should take advantage of the Net. Adding e-mail addresses and URLs gives your Web site credibility. It impresses upon your employees that this new and exciting resource is real, and they should take advantage of it.

In some ways, you can measure the success of an intranet site the same as you would a Web site. Count the number of visits to your Web server; count the number of e-mail inquiries and newsgroup messages posted on any internal discussion groups you have. Saving hundreds of thousands of dollars because you don't have to print a booklet is one of the most tangible results.

Chapter 6

Working with Off-Site Employees

Connecting to the Internet enlarges your world. That applies to the world of work, too. When your office is online, you don't have to be on the premises to exchange messages, share files, and compare schedules with your coworkers. With a computer and modem at home or on the road, you can communicate with the office by e-mail and fax from your computer.

But being on the Internet gives you a new set of options that go beyond simple e-mail messages. For example, one trend in the American workforce is the increased use of "contingent workers" — temps, part-timers, and freelancers. Using Internet software, you can exchange schedules, transfer files, and work on projects collaboratively. It's faster and cheaper than long-distance phone calls or courier services.

This chapter includes what you need to know to include consultants, designers, or traveling staff people who can connect to you on the Internet.

Getting Connected, Internet Style

You probably have a general notion that the Internet can help you connect to your office when you're on the road or working at home, but how does that really work? You may also be wondering just what the Internet lets you do that other remote access systems do not allow.

One big advantage of the Internet is the *client-server system*. So much information is on servers connected to the Net, neither you nor your office must be connected all the time to exchange messages and files. (It's great if your office has a dedicated connection; it's just not mandatory.)

For example, if you are working outside the office, both you and the company can function as clients. You communicate by sending e-mail messages or files to a central server that is always available, such as the mail server or Web server operated by your Internet provider. You can dial up and send an e-mail message to someone in your office, and it's stored on the server until that individual dials up the Net from the office and retrieves the message later. You can also upload a file to your personal or business directory on your ISP's Web server. Someone in the office can connect to the server and download the file later.

If your office has a direct connection, a whole new set of possibilities arises. In that case you can use your office server to store messages and files rather than one of your ISP's machines. You can access your intranet by dialing in the URL in your Web browser. At that point, you enter the system through your intranet's security method.

When your internal company data is accessible from the Internet, the next step is to take precautions to avoid intruders. You may set up a firewall, a program that acts as a single gateway to your office network. See Chapter 10 for more on security measures.

You can accomplish many goals by giving your business access to off-site employees. You can

✔ Work at home yet still be available for meetings "virtually." The easy way is to send an e-mail message to the participants before the meeting, telling them what you want to contribute. After the meeting, send an e-mail message that summarizes the discussion.

✔ Access files stored on your office intranet server by connecting to the server from outside the office with your Web browser.

✔ Save time and money over long-distance calls or package delivery charges.

✔ Have designers send you Web pages or art files via e-mail or FTP.

Making All Employees Part of the Family

When you have an Internet connection, you can consider giving access to employees who are working in other locations, such as your client's office or their home offices. You can also connect workers who are at home because of injury or child care needs.

If you have one account with an ISP or an online service that you use for your office, do you need to get another account for your laptop or home computer? Not necessarily. You can use the disks that your access provider issued you when you signed up. In most cases, you can dial up the Net using the same username and password that the office machine(s) use. As long as you are not connected to the Net at the same time as the office computer, you can get your e-mail.

Even if the two computers *do* connect at the same time, it may not be a problem. Most ISPs allow multiple connections, although some may charge extra for this. It's generally simpler to avoid conflicts by getting separate accounts for your home and Internet connections, but it's not mandatory.

Setting up an office that's not too remote

Aside from the obvious equipment (computer, modem, phone, chair, desk), you need to consider the following:

- **Electricity.** Make sure your electrical circuits are not overloaded. You should have grounded (three-prong) outlets.

- **Surge suppresser.** Buy an inexpensive surge suppresser to keep your equipment from getting zapped if your voltage should spike.

- **Ventilation.** If you work from home full-time, it's tempting to leave your computer on throughout the night. Make sure you have good ventilation such as fans or air conditioning in hot weather, so your expensive equipment doesn't get overheated.

- **Phone.** Obviously, you need access to a phone line so you can call the office from your phone or computer.

Scheduling software you can use

Scheduling software lets you set up meetings with people in other offices by Internet. You can talk to people on the phone or (if you want to use the Internet to save on long-distance charges) use real-time communications techniques (see Chapter 9).

A calendaring and scheduling program lets you enter your upcoming tasks and meetings on your computer. You can then share your schedule with the other approved users in your company. You can check coworkers' schedules to arrange meetings or to review progress. You can even enter a meeting on someone else's calendar (if you have write access to that person's calendar, of course).

The big downside is cost, which ranges from $795 to thousands of dollars, depending on how many users you want to share calendars.

Netscape Calendar

If you already use Netscape Communicator to browse the Web, check e-mail, and perform other tasks, one way to keep your office informed of your day-to-day activities is to use Netscape Calendar. Calendar, shown in Figure 6-1, comes with the Professional version of Netscape Communicator. (It doesn't come with the Standard version.)

The big issue with Calendar is that your office needs the Calendar Server software on its intranet, which costs $995 for 100 users. Each Calendar server manages a group of individual calendars. The calendars may also exist on a user's local system so changes can be made. Then you can connect to the calendar server and synchronize your calendar with the other ones on the server.

Users can assign agenda items a level of Importance, Access level, and Start/End times. A message Inbox tells you about proposed events and lets you reply with your availability.

Synchronize and CyberScheduler

Another set of slick scheduling packages, Synchronize and CyberScheduler by CrossWind Technologies (www.xwind.com), lets all of the employees in an organization view and revise each other's schedules. Synchronize is the server program that holds the calendars; CyberScheduler provides a Web interface for the calendars.

Enter agenda items here   Completed and Uncompleted tasks are listed here

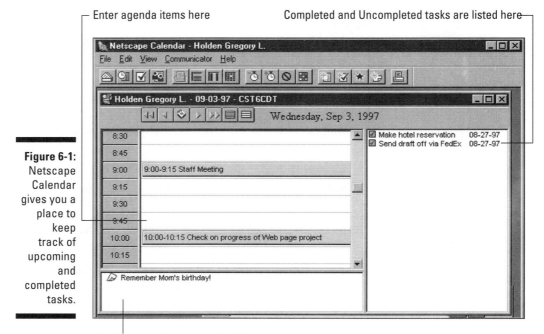

Figure 6-1:
Netscape
Calendar
gives you a
place to
keep
track of
upcoming
and
completed
tasks.

Reminders and notes are listed here

To get an idea of how Web-based scheduling works, you can try an online demo on CrossWind's Web site. The CyberScheduler Web page interface shown in Figure 6-2 lets you do such things as

✓ Set your tasks for the day.

✓ Check off the tasks you have done.

✓ Send yourself reminders.

Synchronize and CyberScheduler, like Calendar, require that you run server software on one of your office network servers. When this was written, the programs each retailed for $100 per user. However, if you purchase Sychronize, you can get CyberScheduler for free. Synchronize's server platform is only available for UNIX or NT systems. The client program that lets you access and edit your Synchronize calendar is available for Macintosh, Windows NT, and UNIX. CyberScheduler, at this writing, was only available for UNIX.

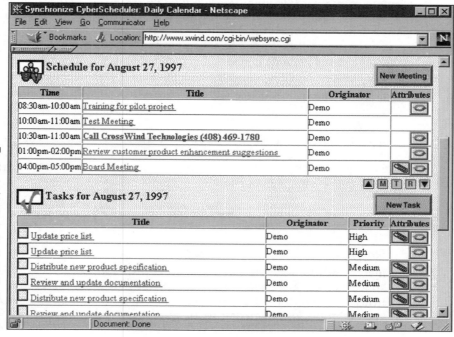

Figure 6-2: Cyber-Scheduler provides a Web interface so remote users can check office schedules easily.

Office Tracker Pro

For Macintosh users, a good alternative is Office Tracker Pro 3.0 by Milum Corporation (www.milum.com). Office Tracker Pro is available for Macintosh office servers. The Mac server version is PowerMac native; it requires a 68020 or greater processor, System 7.5 or greater, 4MB RAM, and OpenTransport 1.1.1 or greater. A 10-user pack, including one server program and ten Macintosh and Windows client programs, costs $795; a 20-user pack costs $1,395.

MeetingMaker XP

Another popular program, MeetingMaker XP by ON Technology, is available for Windows 95, NT, Power Macintosh, UNIX, and other platforms. You can download a free 30-day trial version from the company's Web site. Reach ON Technology on the Web at www.on.com or by calling (800) 767-6683.

A calendar service on your staff

Milum Corporation also offers a less-costly alternative to buying and running your own scheduling server and client software. For small businesses that don't have the in-house technical expertise or the money to run their own calendaring server, Milum also rents space on its servers.

Web-based schedulers for free

Server-based scheduling tools such as the ones described above are great, but they can be expensive and complicated. Whenever you run into a situation like this, just remember that the Internet is the Land of Free Software. This is especially true since the rise of Java, the powerful programming language that is cross-platform: it works the same on many different operating systems. Instead of buying server software, you mark up your Java or JavaScript calendar in your Web browser. You can then e-mail it to your coworkers or publish it on your office server so everyone can see it.

Here are some free programs you can use to publish schedules so your coworkers can see them:

Strong Software's Interactive Calendar

If your Web browser supports Java (and it should, because Java is becoming so widespread), you can easily try out a free calendar on the Web. It's not nearly as powerful as the previous schedulers, but it lets users know what you are doing in a given day, week, or month.

How do you know for sure if your Web browser supports Java? Here's what to do: One way is to connect to the Strong Software URL. If you see the FreeCalEditor, you're okay. If you only see a horizontal line across the Web page, upgrade your browser. There's another way to see what kinds of files your browser can display (or *play,* in the case of audio or video content). If you use Netscape Navigator 3.0 or an earlier version as your browser, select Help⇨About Netscape... (if you use Netscape Communicator, select Help⇨About Communicator). A Web page appears that tells you what version of Navigator you are using. Scroll down the page.

If you see a note that says *Java Compatible, contains software developed by Sun Microsystems Inc.,* you are Java-ready. If you use Internet Explorer, select View⇨Options.... When the Options dialog box appears, click on the Advanced tab. An option called Enable JIT Compiler should be available; select it. (JIT stands for *Just In Time* and is a way of *compiling,* or executing, Java code.)

You can test the FreeCalEditor applet on the Web, but it works faster if the applet is sitting in a directory on your computer. To get your copy of FreeCalEditor, just follow these steps:

1. **Open your Web browser, connect to the Net, and go to the Strong Software site (**www.strongsoft.com/FreeCalEditor**).**

   The Web version of FreeCalEditor appears in your browser window.

2. **Scroll down the page and click on the highlighted hyperlink Click Here.**

   A dialog box appears that lets you download the applet to your computer. This shouldn't take long, because it's only 57K in size. You need to have a copy of WinZip or StuffIt Expander available on your computer to open this compressed file archive, as explained in Chapter 5.

3. **Double-click on the archive** FreeCalEditor.zip**.**

   If you have WinZip already installed, WinZip will launch. You'll see the files that comprise the archive listed in the main WinZip window.

4. **Click on the Extract toolbar button.**

   A dialog box appears that lets you save the archive on your hard disk.

5. **Make sure the button next to the option All Files is selected. Then click on Save.**

   The files are stored in a folder named FreeCalEditor.

Because Java is a cross-platform programming language, you can open the applet on either a Windows or Mac computer. You only need a browser that supports Java.

Be sure to extract all the files to a single folder so you can keep track of them. Don't move the individual files, because the folder contains some important Java files with the filename extension .class that your browser needs in order to make the calendar work.

After you extract the files, open the page `default.html` in your Web browser. For example, if you are using Netscape Navigator:

1. **With Navigator open and running, choose File⇨Open Page...**

   The Open Page dialog box appears.

2. **Click on the Choose File button.**

   The Open dialog box appears.

3. **Locate the `default.html` document and double-click on it.**

   The Open dialog box closes and the Open Page dialog box reappears with the pathname for `default.html` in the text-entry field.

4. **Click on the Open button.**

   The FreeCalEditor page appears (see Figure 6-3).

The FreeCalEditor lets you easily select the month and year you want to schedule. You can then set the scheduling information for each day in the month. You can even add URL links to your scheduled event text.

Figure 6-3:
FreeCal-
Editor, an
interactive
calendar
you can
share with
coworkers.

Some other free scheduling options:

> ✔ **NetCal!** By iTRIBE (`www.itribe.net/netcal/about.html`), lets you publish a calendar for the Web from iTRIBE's server. The service is free, and both in-house and off-site workers can connect to the server by the Web and see the events for any particular day. The disadvantage is that there's no privacy; you can only add events using a username and password, but anyone can see them.

Consultants and Web Site Developers for Hire

Consultants can be an important resource when it comes to helping businesses use Internet technologies. Plenty of small businesses simply hire someone to do it all:

✔ Find a service provider.

✔ Purchase modems.

✔ Provide software.

✔ Set up an intranet or Web site.

✔ Train employees to use the Net.

Plenty of consultants are available, so it pays to shop around for the right person. Finding a consultant is like hiring a home remodeler: Get bids from at least three applicants, check references, and interview the candidates.

Want to take a peek behind the scenes at what consultants talk about among themselves? They sometimes discuss such issues as rates and payment schedules. Check out the Web consultants' BBS (`just4u.com/webconsultants/webbbs1//webbbs1.htm`).

It's often a good idea to break a big project into stages — Phase 1, Phase 2, Phase 3, and so on — and then tie payments to the completion of each stage. That way, if you or the consultant are dissatisfied, you can terminate the agreement.

Rates vary widely depending on experience and geographic location. A single page may take four to six hours to design and a couple of hours to put together and revise.

The field of Web page design and Internet consulting is new and unregulated. As yet, practitioners don't have to be licensed or certified by an "official" group. Word of mouth recommendations are important, so be extra-careful when you check out prospective consultants.

Evaluate your needs. You need someone to do the technical work, certainly. You may want your consultant to provide some very different talents, however, such as

- ✔ **Train your staff.** In this case he or she should be personable and communicate well.

- ✔ **Design Web pages.** In this case, the consultant should have experience with computer graphics programs, such as Adobe Photoshop and Adobe Illustrator.

- ✔ **Write and edit Web page content.** In this case, the consultant should have writing and editing experience, or work with someone who can provide content.

- ✔ **Market your business online.** In this case, business experience would help.

Wanted: A Webmaster

A Webmaster is a full-time employee who sets up and maintains both your internal and external Web sites. Besides being able to design Web pages and answer coworkers' questions with patience and clarity, a staff Webmaster needs to know some sort of computer programming language to make your company's Web pages more functional.

JavaScript is a language that adds functionality to Web page forms and other objects. Java is a high-level programming language that can do many things. Perl is a common and (relatively) simple language to create CGI scripts that accept form data and process it in a readable form.

Chris Faure, a Web consultant based in Chicago, says his most successful clients ask lots of questions and stay involved through the project.

Always sign a contract or simple agreement with any consultant you hire. It's important to have a written record not only of how much you're going to pay someone, but exactly what that person will do and when the work will be completed. It's always advisable to have an attorney review any complex agreements before you sign them. Sample contracts are at www.smalloffice.com/maven/bmresrce.htm.

You may not have to look very far to find inexpensive consulting. Your ISP's tech support staff can provide you with advice on relatively simple problems or questions, for instance. For an hourly fee, they may even do some setup and training on-site.

Transfers Are Smooth with FTP and E-Mail

When your business connects to the Net, you can use File Transfer Protocol (FTP) to transfer data to and from remote employees. FTP, which is described in detail in Chapter 4, is a down-and-dirty way to move files from one computer to another on the Internet.

It's not always practical to attach large files to e-mail messages. Files that are more than 500K in size should be sent by FTP or split into two or more e-mail messages. Large attachments can take a long time to transfer by e-mail.

Some available e-mail services, such as AOL, won't transmit very large attachments.

Intruders, Keep Out!

When you open your office's local area network to the Internet, you need to implement some sort of protection to keep intruders from getting a look at your files or copying them without your permission.

A *firewall* is a single computer that acts as a gate to the wider Internet; instead of equipping two or more employees with separate Internet connections, thus providing many different entry points to your system. Another is to use your network server software to assign each approved user an official username and password in order to gain access to any files stored on a server. The method for assigning passwords varies depending on the server program being used. See Chapter 10 for more on security practices you should undertake.

Working with contractors and others who can communicate and exchange files with the home office using the Internet helps a small business in many ways. You are able to get someone whose abilities are a precise fit for your company's needs. Outsiders also bring new ideas and a fresh perspective to your organization. They tend not to get into interoffice politics or personality clashes because they are focused on the project at hand. If the contractor doesn't work out or your needs change, you can end your agreement and find someone else to communicate with the new person via your Internet connection.

Case study: Dymaxeon Engineering

A good friend of mine, Nicholas Raftis, came to me with a problem. His small company in Bloomfield Hills, Michigan, Dymaxeon Engineering Ltd., creates training manuals for some of the biggest automotive manufacturers in the country. Nick had an e-mail account, but no Web page or FTP space. Yet, it's essential for Dymaxeon to transfer complex graphics files to and from its clients. The computer graphics programs require that the files be many megabytes in size, and sending them by e-mail can take hours. Not only that, but e-mail attachments of more than a megabyte can easily crash your computer before they download in their entirety. For only a small increase in his monthly Internet access fee, I set Nick up with a Web site and FTP space from his existing provider. He now uses FTP to send and receive files much more quickly and reliably than e-mail.

Part III

Improving Communication

The 5th Wave — By Rich Tennant

"IT'S JUST UNTIL WE GET BACK UP ON THE INTERNET."

In this part . . .

The Internet brings people together, and in Part III, you'll learn about ways in which having access to the Internet can help you and your employees communicate. Not only can you type and send messages with someone else, but you can carry on group discussions, transfer files, and even hear and see other users.

Chapter 7

Reaching Out with E-Mail

In This Chapter

▶ Learning to speak the language of e-mail

▶ Shopping for the right e-mail software

▶ Providing information to your customers by e-mail

▶ Teaching your employees about e-mail etiquette

▶ Starting your own mailing list

*T*he Web may be the part of the Internet that attracts all the attention these days, but in many ways, it's electronic mail that gets the job done. Users e-mail important documents, discuss urgent issues, and make new contacts by using this simple, convenient, and efficient part of the Net.

E-mail, after all, is the most frequently used part of the Internet. According to Intelliquest Research Group, a market research firm (www.intelliquest.com), e-mail is the most popular online activity.

Seventy-five percent of those who visited the Internet used e-mail in the month in which the firm took one of its surveys. According to CommerceNet/Nielsen research (www.nielsen.com), 80 percent of all businesses use e-mail.

E-mail is also the part of the Net with the widest reach, when you consider that all the online services — America Online, CompuServe, Prodigy, and the Microsoft Network — give their members accounts that enable them to exchange e-mail not only within the service itself, but also with the rest of the Internet as well.

E-mail can be used not only to exchange messages with coworkers and customers, but also to provide information automatically. You can set up a system that receives your e-mail request and sends back a document any time, without your having to worry about it.

Replying automatically to e-mail is a great way to save time and money, but it's no substitute for the personal touch. Whenever possible, designate some time during your week to respond to e-mail inquiries.

E-mail also gives you a way to access one of the Internet's great resources: mailing lists, which are self-selected groups of individuals who are interested enough in a topic to want to discuss it with others on their computers. Participating in existing mailing lists can help you research your market; starting your own mailing list can help you become an Internet resource and boost your credibility and marketability.

Internet e-mail can help meet many of a small business's communications needs. Here are some goals to consider when you're getting ready to set up an Internet e-mail system:

✔ Save money and time by corresponding electronically rather than using snail mail.

✔ Give customers another way to contact you.

✔ Stay in touch with the office when you are on the road.

✔ Respond automatically to e-mail requests by sending specific documents.

✔ Meet colleagues and research prospects by participating in mailing lists.

Of course, e-mail can also provide a way for a small business to explore electronic communications among staff members. A four-person research company in Chicago, Sense and Nonsense, has one account with America Online. Each AOL account can make use of five different "screen names," each with its own corresponding e-mail address. Each staff person can have his or her own e-mail address and send mail to the others.

E-mail doesn't work unless you check it periodically. A business with a dial-up connection to the Internet needs to assign someone to check the mail on a regular basis. Ask your provider about a special kind of connection, called a UUCP connection, that automatically dials your ISP, uploads outgoing messages, and downloads incoming ones.

This chapter provides examples of activities that a small business can conduct on the Internet using four popular e-mail programs: Eudora Pro, Pegasus Mail, Netscape Messenger, and Microsoft Outlook Express. Any of these programs can serve your small business well. If you want to automatically send files in response to e-mail inquiries, Pegasus, Eudora, and Outlook Express have an edge; Messenger can't respond by sending a file at the time of this writings. Personally, I recommend Netscape or Microsoft's products because they also come with other programs you can use for conferencing, accessing newsgroups, and surfing the Web. Of the two, Internet Explorer has the big advantage of costing absolutely *nada.* It also costs *nada* to try the programs out and decide which one you want to use for your own business.

Learning to Speak E-Mail Like a Native

In order to use e-mail successfully on the Internet to help your small business, you have to figure out how to speak the language. If you use e-mail long enough, it begins to seem like a world unto itself, where people you only know by their first names or e-mail addresses throw around strange terms like *flaming, spam,* or *mail bomb,* and where alphabet soup like SMTP and IMAP4 is mentioned casually.

Remember that many of the individuals with whom you correspond have been on the Net for many years. In order to create a good impression, take a few minutes to understand the language and workings of e-mail so you, too, can talk about *sig files* and *digests* and sound like an expert.

Following the e-mail trail

Imagine actually following the trail of an e-mail message from your computer to a friend's in, say, California — undoubtedly, an amazing journey. In order to reach its destination, your message may pass through several different computers, each one with its own operating system. You may use a program like Eudora to compose your message, but your friend can read it with a hot new program like Microsoft Outlook. Yet, your message comes through clearly, without any computer gibberish, and even with graphics and HTML formatting if you added them. (See the section entitled "Creating an Electronic Newsletter" in Chapter 15.)

Protocol alphabet soup

Two things allow alphabet soup to happen: the Internet protocols or standards as detailed in Chapter 4, and the *client-server* system that makes up the Internet. When you first compose a message and click on the Send button, it goes from your *client* computer to a computer at your Internet Service Provider's called a *mail server.* Usually, the mail server has a generic name like the one operated by my provider, InterAccess: smtp.interaccess.com. The purpose of a mail server is to receive messages and make sure that they reach either your mail Inbox or someone else's. The letters SMTP in this address stand for Simple Mail Transfer Protocol, which performs the task of delivering e-mail to the address you have specified.

After it goes through your SMTP mail server, your message is sent out through the twists and turns of the Internet. The message may pass through a number intermediate mail servers along the way. Each of these servers has to approve the transmission until the message reaches the mail server operated by your recipient's ISP. Once there, it goes into the individual's mail Inbox, where it can be retrieved using Post Office Protocol, Version 3 (POP3).

If one of the machines in the e-mail trail is unable to send the message along, it gets "bounced" back to you, usually with detailed information about where the problem occurred.

If you're not already overwhelmed with technical detail, it's good to know what all of the various protocols related to e-mail mean, since you can expect to see references to them pretty often. Table 7-1 lists the important ones.

Table 7-1	E-Mail Protocols
Protocol	*What It Does*
SMTP (Simple Mail Transfer Protocol)	Delivers outgoing mail to the correct address.
POP3 (Post Office Protocol, Version 3)	Enables you to access your unread e-mail and download it from the mail server to your computer.
IMAP4 (Internet Message Access Protocol, Version 4)	Allows you to manage your e-mail messages remotely. You can leave your messages on a mail server and organize them into folders without having to download the mail to your computer.
LDAP (Lightweight Directory Access Protocol)	Enables you to access individuals listed in a White Pages address book.

Flavors of e-mail

Much e-mail traffic consists of interpersonal one-to-one or one-to-several communications, but a number of other kinds of e-mail are common:

- E-mail can also be sent from one source to many readers (e-mail newsletters are an example, as are company-wide announcements).

- *Mailing lists* are e-mail messages circulated between subscribers who discuss topics of common interest.

- E-mail *mailbots* or *autoresponders* are used to send automatic replies to requests for information about a product or service, or to respond to people subscribing to an e-mail publication or service.

In terms of tone, e-mail messages fall somewhere between a brief note and a memo. E-mail correspondents have no way of knowing who is "important" and who is not, or who is rich and who is not, and most users react to this lack of context by treating everyone with the same level of polite, but informal, respect. People are usually on a first-name basis.

Case study: Travel Spirit

Travel Spirit, a three-person travel agency on the north side of Chicago, provides a typical example of how e-mail can act as a useful supplement to a business's existing customer service efforts. E-mail can't do it all, but it can help. "It's mostly good for getting back to people with information," says Elvira Kojro Eastman, president of Travel Spirit (spirit7@ix.netcom.com). We have some customers who don't like to talk on the phone too much. Others like to talk at odd hours. We can do both things with e-mail. "The company also uses a toll-free number and a fax number, plus the good old telephone to communicate with customers who aren't yet connected to the Net. Customer service is our biggest asset," says Eastman. E-mail is a useful supplement for many small businesses — a way to extend the personal touch.

Understanding message headers

Most e-mail messages consist of two parts and an optional third part. The *header* of the message is not always visible to the reader, depending on the software being used. The header contains a great deal of routing information that shows the path taken to get the message from the sender to the recipient.

The *body* of the message contains the actual message.

The *signature file* is the optional third part, and can be as simple as your name and address, but can also contain drawings made from alphanumeric characters.

If you're fascinated with the technical details of e-mail and want to know everything about the subject, just use your e-mail program's control for showing a message header. In Netscape Messenger, for instance, you choose View⇨Headers and then select All from the pop-up list of header options (Brief, Normal, All).

A more realistic reason to look at e-mail headers is to determine why a message bounced back to you. As shown in Figure 7-1, a typical header also contains the organization of the sender, the date and time the message was sent, the subject, names of people who received copies, and lots of scary-looking code that you can safely ignore.

Quoting

When you respond to an e-mail message, it's considered courteous to quote some of the original message you received. You don't *have* to do this every time you reply, but it can be a nice extra touch. This reminds the sender what he or she was talking about in the first place, and it can be helpful if some time has passed between the time the original message was sent and your reply. Quoting is particularly useful when you're responding to a mailing list or newsgroup message, because it enables the other participants to know what's being discussed.

The common convention for differentiating quoted material from the body of an e-mail message is to put a ">" character (right-angle bracket) in the left margin, next to each line of the quoted material.

Usually, when you tell your e-mail software to quote the original message before you type your reply, the program quotes the entire message. To save space, you can snip (delete) out the part that isn't relevant. In that case, it's also considered good e-mail etiquette to type the word <snip> to show that something has been cut. Then begin your message, like this:

```
pm wrote:
>Hey mate, wonder if I could get some info on <snip>
>those Hofner bass guitars you have for sale . . .
Hi pm,
I would be honored if you would purchase one of our
guitars. You can place an order online or call our
toll-free number, 1-800-GUITARS.
```

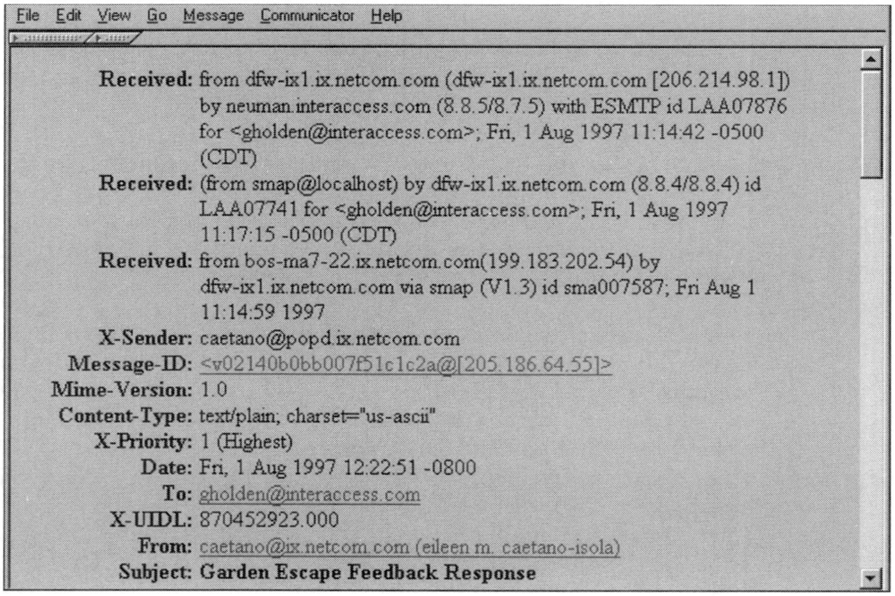

Figure 7-1:
An e-mail
message
header can
tell you the
path a
message
took to get
to you, the
format
of the
message,
and lots of
other
information.

File   Edit   View   Go   Message   Communicator   Help

Received: from dfw-ix1.ix.netcom.com (dfw-ix1.ix.netcom.com [206.214.98.1])
by neuman.interaccess.com (8.8.5/8.7.5) with ESMTP id LAA07876
for <gholden@interaccess.com>; Fri, 1 Aug 1997 11:14:42 -0500
(CDT)

Received: (from smap@localhost) by dfw-ix1.ix.netcom.com (8.8.4/8.8.4) id
LAA07741 for <gholden@interaccess.com>; Fri, 1 Aug 1997
11:17:15 -0500 (CDT)

Received: from bos-ma7-22.ix.netcom.com(199.183.202.54) by
dfw-ix1.ix.netcom.com via smap (V1.3) id sma007587; Fri Aug 1
11:14:59 1997

X-Sender: caetano@popd.ix.netcom.com
Message-ID: <v02140b0bb007f51c1c2a@[205.186.64.55]>
Mime-Version: 1.0
Content-Type: text/plain; charset="us-ascii"
X-Priority: 1 (Highest)
Date: Fri, 1 Aug 1997 12:22:51 -0800
To: gholden@interaccess.com
X-UIDL: 870452923.000
From: caetano@ix.netcom.com (eileen m. caetano-isola)
Subject: Garden Escape Feedback Response

Forwarding

Any e-mail program enables you to forward a message you receive so that someone else can read it. The only confusing thing is that, when you actually forward the message, the text of the message you're sending does not appear in the message composition window. Instead, the forwarded message is sent as an attachment, and you type a message in the composition window that enables the recipient to know what you're sending: "I'm forwarding this message I received from the Human Resources Dept.," and so on.

Adding emphasis

Although some e-mail programs permit you to send messages formatted with bold, italic, headings, and other kinds of emphasis, most people in cyberspace can only send and receive messages in plain text format, and in an old-fashioned typewriter typeface like Courier. Over the years, e-mail devotees have come up with some creative ways to convey emotion or tone of voice into an otherwise impersonal-looking e-mail message.

In order to add emphasis, they have to type some words in ALL CAPS, or add asterisks around others, like this:

```
I *really* want to tell you about this *amazing* business
            opportunity.
```

Before many e-mail messages cross your path, someone may send you one with a funny series of symbols that look like a sideways smiley face:

```
...You know what I mean :-)
```

This is the most common of a series of symbols called *emoticons* or *smileys*. They are made by typing a series of keyboard symbols. There are many of these, and if you really want to know all about them, visit the NetLingo Web site (www.netlingo.com/smiley.html). It's best not to overuse these though. The most common ones are :-), which means the author is smiling, and :-(, which conveys unhappiness.

Attaching files

Attaching a file to an e-mail message is a quick and convenient way to transmit information from place to place, and it's one of the more useful things you can do with e-mail. Attaching means that you send a document or file as part of an e-mail message. Attaching a document enables you to include material from any file on your hard disk. Attached files appear as separate documents that the recipient can download to his or her computer.

Many e-mail clients enable users to attach files with a simple button or other command. A lengthy series of attachments can be compressed using software such as StuffIt or WinZip in order to conserve bandwidth.

Another one of those "alphabet soup" protocols, called MIME (Multipurpose Internet Mail Extensions), enables you to attach graphic and other multimedia files to an e-mail message. They must be downloaded and read by an e-mail program that supports MIME. Virtually all the newer e-mail programs do support MIME, but in case your recipient has an e-mail client that does not support MIME attachments, or if you aren't sure whether they do or not, you must encode your attachment in a format such as BinHex (if you're sending files to a Macintosh) or UUCP (if you're sending files to a newsgroup).

A *signature file,* commonly called a *sig file,* is a useful tool for marketing with e-mail on the Internet. The sig file is a text file that's automatically appended to the bottom of your e-mail messages and newsgroup postings. It tells the recipient(s) who you are, where you work, and how to contact you. These files can be as simple as the one shown in Figure 7-2.

Sig files are easy to set up; you create a plain-text file and then have your e-mail software identify it as your signature file. The process is described in Chapter 12.

Figure 7-2:
Use your e-mail software's signature file options to add something about yourself to all of your Internet correspondence.

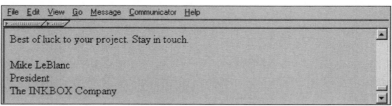

File Edit View Go Message Communicator Help

Best of luck to your project. Stay in touch.

Mike LeBlanc
President
The INKBOX Company

Choosing the Right E-Mail Software

After you set up an account with an Internet Service Provider (ISP), expect to receive (in the mail, or in person) a set of software programs that you can install on your computer and then use to navigate the Net. One of those programs is your key to sending and receiving e-mail messages.

With a little e-mail experience, though, you may want to shop around for something more powerful. Perhaps the program you're using doesn't support MIME and you get e-mail messages that are cluttered with HTML (HyperText Markup Commands) instead of seeing colors and images in a formatted message. Or maybe you want a program that enables you to sort and file your e-mail easily.

If you aren't issued e-mail software from an ISP, you can always use Microsoft Exchange, the e-mail program that comes with Windows 95 (see Figure 7-3).

Figure 7-3: Microsoft Exchange, part of Windows 95, files your messages and stores addresses in an address book.

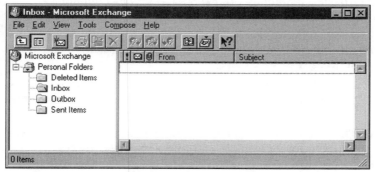

My agent, who depends heavily on e-mail for his business, has used Exchange for years. One of the good things about Exchange is that you can use it either on your local network or on the Internet. It enables you to sort your mail and do basic functions like forwarding, quoting, and accessing your mail from a remote computer such as your personal computer at home. Perhaps the best thing about Exchange is that it's free.

E-mail for free!

If you're really operating on a shoestring or if you just need more e-mail addresses than your Internet provider gives you, look into signing up with one of the many services that provide Internet users with free e-mail service. A recent article in CNET (www.cnet.com/Content/Reviews/Compare/Freemail) compared eight such services and recommended two: RocketMail (www.rocketmail.com) and Hotmail (www.hotmail.com).

With an address, you can access your electronic mailbox by pointing a Web browser to the e-mail provider's Web site. You enter your username and password, and voilà! You can get your e-mail messages from anywhere in the world. (You may have to endure seeing banner ads in your e-mail dialog boxes with some of these services, however.)

Features to look for

All e-mail programs enable you to display and scroll through an e-mail message easily. Most make use of functions such as copying and pasting, resizing a window, selecting all text with a single command, and so on. A good e-mail client enables you to easily move between messages, save messages in different mailboxes, and delete unwanted messages after you read them. Most e-mail programs display a list of the messages in an Inbox area, and some indicate which messages you already read, replied to, or saved to disk.

Other basic capabilities you need for everyday communications include:

- ✔ The ability to send and receive mail
- ✔ An address book where you can store frequently used names and addresses
- ✔ The ability to send and receive e-mail *offline* — that is, when you're not connected to the worldwide Internet, but to a local network such as an office intranet
- ✔ The capability to send an outgoing message while you surf the Web or your corporate intranet with the Netscape browser

The more advanced programs add features such as these:

- ✔ A search function that enables you to search your e-mail or news messages by keywords, sender names, and other elements
- ✔ A built-in spell checker that catches boo-boos in your outgoing messages
- ✔ The ability to set up filters and rules for automatically deleting, filing, or otherwise handling mail
- ✔ The ability to encrypt messages or attach a personal security certificate so that the recipient can be confident with your identity as the sender

Internet e-mail standbys

When you're shopping for software, it's often a good idea to use a tried-and-true program that's been around for several years. Such software has probably gone through a number of versions and is likely to have the bugs worked out of it. What follows are two suggestions.

Setting up a filter with Eudora Pro

For several years now, Eudora Pro has been one of the more popular Internet e-mail programs for both Mac and Windows users. That's because it's easy to use and powerful at the same time. One thing Eudora does well is automate mail handling. If you receive lots of e-mail, check out Eudora's ability to set up *filters*.

Filters are sets of rules that enable an e-mail program to recognize particular types of e-mail and automatically file, delete, or otherwise handle them. A *rule* is a directive that you give to your computer, as though you're giving instructions to an assistant. Basically, you're telling your e-mail program, "If you get mail from the president of the company, file it in the folder called Jones." Another kind of filter, called a "bozo filter," is a set of rules that automatically recognizes and deletes e-mail coming from someone you just don't want to hear from (such as, a "bozo").

Automated e-mail with Pegasus Mail

Pegasus Mail is another program that's enjoyed continued improvement during its long life on the Net. A powerful and full-featured e-mail program, Pegasus Mail is — best of all — absolutely free.

You can download Pegasus Mail for free, but the Web site (`www.pegasus.usa.com/ftp.htm`) doesn't make it clear which version of the program is appropriate for download. If you have a Windows 95 computer, try the file called `w32-254.exe`. If you have Windows 3.1, try `253up16.zip`. If you have a Mac, try `pmmac221.hqx`.

I use Pegasus Mail in this section to illustrate how to set up an automatic reply that you can send to visitors. You can tell your customers something like

> For more information about Acme Inc., our hours, and how to contact us, send an e-mail to us with the words **send info** in the body of the message. You can leave the subject line blank.

You can specify a set of response rules that tells Pegasus Mail: "When someone sends an e-mail message with the words 'send info' in the body of the message, you automatically send them our FAQ file, which has general information about the company."

After you download and install Pegasus Mail, which includes telling the program the name of your mail server, your username, and the password you use to retrieve your e-mail, start the program and then follow these steps:

1. **With Pegasus Mail's main window open on–screen, choose Tools⊅Mail Filtering Rules. Hold down your mouse for a moment and, when the pop-up menu appears, slide your mouse to the right and pass your mouse pointer over the option Edit New Mail Filtering Rules in order to select this option. Keep holding your mouse button down; another pop-up menu appears.**

   The third pop-up menu has two options: one that affects any new mail that arrives in the new mail folder while it's open, and another set of rules that are applied automatically when you close the new mail folder.

2. **Choose the option Rules Applied When Filter Is Opened . . . .**

   The dialog box called Rules for New Mail appears (as shown in Figure 7-4). This dialog box lists any existing rules or it's empty (if you have yet to add rules). In this dialog box, you can edit, ad, or delete rules.

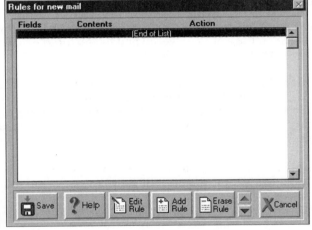

Figure 7-4:
This dialog box enables you to create filters in Pegasus Mail.

3. **To create a new rule, click on the Add Rule button.**

   The Edit Rule dialog box appears, enabling you to define or change rules. You can specify variables that tell Pegasus to look for text in either the header or body of the mail message.

4. **Click on the diamond next to one of the two options at the top of the dialog box that are called Always Trigger This Rule or This Rule Is Activated When the Trigger Text Occurs.**

   By clicking on Always Trigger This Rule, you activate your filter for every e-mail message you receive. By clicking on This Rule Is Activated When the Trigger Text Occurs, you tell Pegasus to operate the filter only when it encounters messages with the special "trigger phrase" in them.

5. Click on the diamond next to either In These Headers or As an Expression (as shown in Figure 7-5).

If you check the diamond next to In These Headers, you can tell Pegasus to look for key words in one or more of the areas shown. You have to click on one or more of the options: From, To, Subject, Reply-to, CC:, or Sender. Pegasus then looks for the text that you identify in any of the areas that you indicate.

If you check the diamond next to As an Expression, you tell Pegasus to look for information in a more global manner. Depending on what item you check, Pegasus looks for key words In Message Headers Only, In Message Body Only, or Anywhere in the Message.

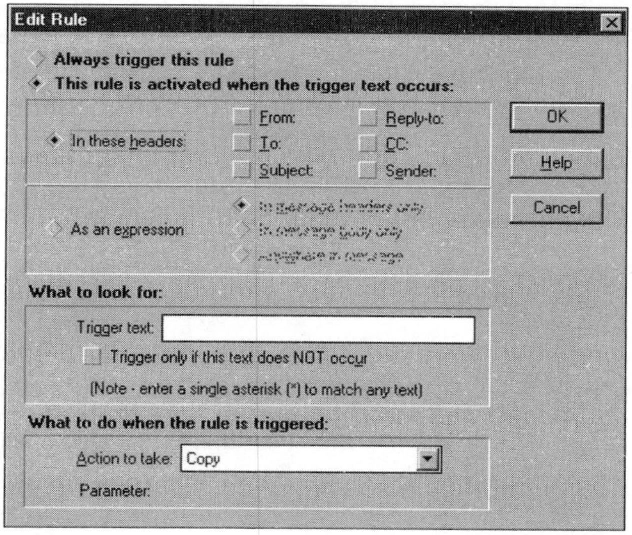

Figure 7-5: Specify the "trigger text" for your rule in this dialog box.

6. In the Trigger Text field, enter the words that you want Pegasus to recognize in order to trigger the rule.

This text may be someone's name, a product name, or some key word or words that are unique enough for your computer to answer appropriately. Try to choose words that you're sure are going to appear only in the messages in which you expect them to appear. Avoid words that are too generic or that have multiple meanings.

7. Now tell Pegasus what action it is expected to perform when it encounters the trigger text by selecting an option from the Action to Take drop-down list.

Pegasus, like Eudora, can perform a variety of actions when it encounters your trigger text. It can automatically print the file, forward the file to someone else, or move the file to another folder. To create an automatic-reply filter, select either Text File (to send a text document) or Send Binary File (to send a computer program).

When you select a send option from the Action to Take list, the Select a File dialog box appears, enabling you to select the file that you want to send automatically in response to the incoming e-mail message.

8. Choose a file in the Select a File dialog box, and then click on the OK button.

You return to the Edit Rule dialog box, and the full path of the file appears next to Parameter.

9. Click on the OK button to finish creating your new automatic-reply rule.

The Edit Rule dialog box closes and you return to the main Pegasus Mail window. Now the file you selected is sent to anyone who sends you a message containing the specified trigger text.

Of course, in order for the automatic reply to be sent, you need to create the text file that you want Pegasus Mail to send. You can create this file using any word-processing program. Type some general information about your company, or create a set of Frequently Asked Questions that can help answer the basic questions your customers may have. Be sure to save the file in plain-text format when you're done.

Pegasus provides small businesses with an easy, cost-effective way to provide automatic replies to e-mail inquires. The option's not as flexible as signing up with an Internet e-mail autoresponse service that can send a variety of files in response to messages sent to specific e-mail addresses such as jobs@mycompany.com.

For other ways to automatically reply to e-mail inquiries, see the section "Other Ways to E-Mail Information" later in this chapter.

Browser built-ins

As mentioned in Chapter 4, some of the more cost-effective Internet tools are suites of software packages provided by Netscape Communications and Microsoft Corporation. The e-mail programs that come with each of those packages are easy-to-use and full-featured. If you install one or the other, you don't need to go through the trouble of downloading and installing one of the programs mentioned in the preceding example (unless you want to set up your own automatic response mechanism, which isn't possible with either Netscape messenger or Microsoft Outlook). The following section presents an example of a program you can consider and a useful task you can perform with it.

Searching your e-mail with Netscape Messenger

One of the great features of Netscape Messenger, the e-mail component of Netscape Communicator, is its ability to search through the text of all your e-mail messages or newsgroup postings. You can search for all messages sent by a particular person, or for all the occurrences of a word in your messages.

The search component of Messenger actually enables you to not only search through e-mail messages but also newsgroup messages. The key to doing an effective search is determining what element is common to all the messages you want to find; you may want to locate all messages from a particular sender, or all messages with the word "Netscape" in the body of the message. Or, you may want to find all messages you received in a particular day or month. The search utility enables you to specify lots of different variables.

Unlike Internet search services like InfoSeek and AltaVista, the Netscape Messenger search utility only recognizes one keyword per set of variables. For instance, you can't enter: `the sender contains holden and greg`. If you need to search for two keywords, click on the More button and add a second keyword, like this:

```
the sender contains holden
and the sender contains greg
```

You can click on More and add a third keyword; and so on.

Other Ways to E-Mail Information

It's good business to reply quickly to all messages, whether they arrive by e-mail or via the good ol' telephone or postal box. An automatic reply signals receipt of their e-mail and suggests that they can expect you to get back to them soon. You can set up a system whereby you automatically reply to e-mail messages. You do this in one of four ways:

✔ Use a mail program that can recognize new mail messages and respond automatically (this is described in the previous section, "Automated e-mail with Pegasus Mail").

✔ Subscribe to an automatic reply e-mail service on the Net.

✔ Set up a UNIX shell account.

✔ Set up your own e-mail information server.

The next few sections examine the last three alternatives.

Use an Internet information service

If you don't want to go through the time and effort of installing software and setting up your own automatic-reply e-mail service, you can rent a software program called a *mailbot* from an Internet Information Service. A mailbot, also called an autoresponder, is an e-mail account that is set up to receive requests and deliver files automatically in response.

One such company, NetAssist (`www.nassist.com/revolutn.html`) can provide you with mailbots for $10 per month each plus a one-time $10 setup fee. You can find out more by sending e-mail to one of NetAssist's own mailbots: `faqmbot@nassist.com` for general information, or `pricemb@nassist.com` for a list of current prices.

Setting up an e-mail server

If your computer has a direct connection to the Internet, consider setting up your own e-mail server. An e-mail server is a program that receives e-mail from other computers and then routes the mail to the correct destination. The advantage of operating your own e-mail server is that you can set up nice features like automatic reply e-mail accounts and e-mail information servers without paying extra to an ISP.

An even bigger advantage is that, when you have your own in-house mail server, you can create as many e-mail addresses as you like — a great way to give Internet access to everyone in your business.

Don't confuse an e-mail server with an e-mail information server. An e-mail server acts like an electronic post office: It receives incoming mail and then delivers it to the recipient's electronic mailbox. An e-mail server that works on the Internet recognizes Simple Mail Transfer Protocol, enabling it to send and receive e-mail messages from your server and other servers across the Net. An e-mail server also provides e-mail accounts to individual users, which users then retrieve by means of a client program that recognizes Post Office Protocol (POP). An e-mail information server simply receives incoming e-mail messages and sends documents in response, based on commands within the received messages.

The following example shows how to set up your own e-mail server on one of your office computers using a shareware program called SLMail 2.5 by Seattle Labs. SLMail works best if you have a direct Internet connection, but it works with dial-up connections as well. The program operates with lots of different e-mail clients. In order to use your server to send and receive mail on the Internet, you need to obtain your own domain name (see Chapter 13) and your Internet access provider must provide domain name service for your domain. Be sure to talk to your ISP before you start so that your provider fully understands what you're planning. Your provider can then configure its computers to work correctly with SLMail, and your e-mail can make it to the right destination without getting lost.

Getting started with SLMail

SLMail is a versatile program that not only provides an e-mail server, but also mailing list administration and automatic replies to e-mail messages. A detailed examination of SLMail is beyond the scope of this book, but the following steps show you how to get started with the program.

SLMail 2.5 is available for Windows 95 and NT. A 14-day trial version can be downloaded from the Seattle Lab Web site (www.seattlelab.com), or by calling (425) 402-6003. To keep the program, you have to pay $199 for Windows 95 or $495 for the NT version. SLMail requires 32MB of RAM and 60MB of disk space. If you want to run an e-mail server on a Macintosh, download Eudora Internet Mail Server, which is available as freeware at www.eudora.com/freeware/servers.html.

Before you install the SLMail, make sure you know the IP (Internet Protocol; see Chapter 4) address of your ISP's mail server. An IP address consists of four numbers separated by dots, such as 207.245.86.5. Also, TCP/IP must be installed on your system. To check, click on the Network icon in the Control Panel. On Windows 95, you see TCP/IP listed on the Configuration tab. If you do not see TCP/IP in the list, click on the Add button to install TCP/IP.

After you download and install the program, start up SL Configuration from the Program Manager. When you start SLMail for the first time, it uses the settings in your existing Internet software to configure itself; the configuration window shows you some of the settings it chooses. It's a good idea to click around the tabs in the Internet Mail Server Properties dialog box (see Figure 7-6) to make sure the program is set up correctly, however.

The program automatically creates one user account called Root. To create a new user account, do the following:

1. **Either right-click on the Internet Mail Server Properties dialog box, or click on the Create New User button at the far left of the toolbar.**

    A pop-up list appears with five options that represent the five types of e-mail accounts you can set up with SLMail. These different accounts enable you to do much more than simply receive e-mail. The five account types are

    - **User.** These are the normal accounts that enable users to send and receive e-mail. Anyone who has an account on your SLMail server can use a POP e-mail client, such as Pegasus Mail or Microsoft Outlook Express, to access his or her mailbox.

    - **Alias.** This is the simplest type of account; it provides another name(s) by which an individual user can receive e-mail.

- **Responder.** A responder account enables you set up an automatic reply e-mail account such as info@company.com. You can identify files to be sent automatically in response to an e-mail message received at this address.

- **Forward.** A forward account automatically forwards e-mail to a new address, and can be useful if a staff person goes on the road and wants to receive mail through America Online or another service, or if a staff person moves to another company.

- **(Mailing) List.** As you may expect, this account enables you to create and manage your own mailing list.

Create new user button

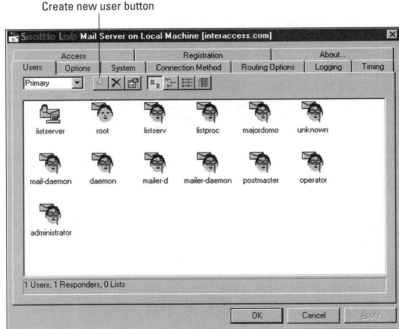

Figure 7-6:
The Internet Mail Server Properties dialog box enables you to add users and set up e-mail accounts.

2. **Select one of the account options.**

   An icon appears in the Internet Mail Server Properties dialog box. The name underneath the icon is preselected.

3. **Enter a name for your account and then click anywhere in the Internet Mail Server Properties dialog box.**

   A dialog box appears that enables you to enter more specific information about the type of account you want to create. If you select User, for instance, after you enter the user name, the Edit User dialog box appears so that you can enter the password and access privileges for that user. If you select Alias, after you enter the alias, the Add Alias dialog box appears so that you can enter the user ID of the existing user for whom you want to create an alias.

The SLMail online help file contains detailed instructions on how to proceed with any of these options. You can also refer to *Setting Up an Internet Site For Dummies,* 2nd Edition, by Jason Coombs and Ted Coombs (IDG Books Worldwide, Inc.),which describes an earlier version of SLMail called WinSMTP Daemon. The general procedures for setting up the two programs are pretty much the same.

Using the UNIX vacation program

If one of the many hats you wear has a propeller on it because you're a computer whiz as well as a businessperson, you have another option for setting up an automatic-reply e-mail account. Ask your Internet provider about getting a UNIX shell account. A UNIX shell account not only has its own e-mail address, but you can also make use of a special UNIX utility, called the *vacation program,* to reply automatically to incoming e-mail. Ask your provider if a vacation program is available and whether you can have access to it.

Publicizing your information service

After you set up an automatic-reply e-mail account or an e-mail information server, what do you do with it? You use the Internet to get the word out about where to reach you. You can find some suggestions for using the Internet for publicity in Chapter 12, but here are some ideas that are specific to Internet e-mail:

- Whether you set up mailing lists or automatic-reply accounts as described in this chapter, be sure to put your e-mail address on all of your company's printed materials, including all your business cards, letterheads, and any advertising you take out.

- Include a mailto: link on your Web pages. Put a link at the bottom of every Web page, like this:

  ```
  Webmaster@mycompany.com
  ```

- Prepare some documents that you can send out automatically to e-mail inquiries. One such document may be a note that immediately notifies people when you receive their messages and assures them that you plan to get back to them ASAP. That way, if you only go through your e-mail once a week, you won't keep potential clients waiting to hear from you. You can say something like this:

> Thank you for sending e-mail to Virtual Corporation. Due
> to the volume of mail we receive, it will take a few days
> to get back to you. If you need to get in touch with us
> immediately, you can call our customer service department
> at 1-800-999-9999.
> You can also visit our other information resources:
> WWW: http://www.ourcompany.com/
> FTP: ftp://ftp.ourcompany.com/

Another type of document you can provide is a set of Frequently Asked Questions (FAQ) that gives people the basics about your company and its products.

You can even send an entire World Wide Web document by e-mail. Many e-mail clients display the Web page immediately in the message window. Other users can save the file to their hard disks and view it offline using their Web browsers.

E-mail newsletters

Even if you never pictured yourself as a publisher, you can create an electronic newsletter that you present on your Web site and/or send to subscribers using e-mail. Newsletters do require some work to set up and produce on a periodic basis, but they can have great benefits for your business, such as

- ✔ **Customer tracking.** Giving your customers something to subscribe to builds a mailing list of names and e-mail addresses you can use for other marketing purposes.

- ✔ **Low-bandwidth.** An e-mail newsletter does not consume much memory and appears on the screen faster than many Web pages.

- ✔ **Timeliness.** You can put out information by e-mail faster than it appears in print. Your e-mail publication can provide updates to information in your brochures or ads.

For more on starting and distributing an electronic newsletter, see Chapter 15.

E-mail is as easy to *abuse* as it is to *use*. Don't send unsolicited e-mail, and don't send e-mail that begins with a generic "form letterish" type of address such as "Dear Valued Customer." Yuck! That's the opposite of one-to-one marketing, and it's likely to lose you far more visitors than you gain. Use the person's name whenever possible, and try to refer to his or her group or organization somewhere in your message. Even if the rest of the message is repeated to many recipients, it can still have a personal touch.

Employee Considerations

It's confession time. Ready? Before I became a full-time writer, I was a full-time employee in a "real" office in a very big organization. While I was there, I wasted a lot of time with e-mail — astoundingly easy to do. You send messages to your friends and to your coworkers. Then, you read the latest set of e-mail jokes and puns that are making the rounds. You set your computer so that a bell chimes when any new message comes in.

E-mail is a great way to get your staff to work together more productively, especially if they're in different locations. However, it's also a great time-waster. Don't be reluctant to establish and communicate your company's policy regarding the use of e-mail.

Minding your "cc's" and "to's": E-mail etiquette

Because it's so easy to reply hastily and less politely than usual via e-mail, users are advised to think reasonably before responding. E-mail does not convey inflection or body language, so clear communication is vital. Some emotion can be conveyed through the *emoticons* mentioned earlier. Express-siveness can also be shared through sharp and abusive language known as *flaming*.

Don't get burned by flames

Maybe it's the facelessness of e-mail communications that causes partici-pants to display more emotion than they would otherwise. The emotional potential of e-mail correspondence has its good and bad points. On the plus side, it's easy to develop good working relationships and close friendships solely by exchanging e-mail messages. On the downside, the distance of e-mail communication causes some people to get angrier online than they may in a face-to-face confrontation.

A *flame* is the opposite of what anyone trying to grow a small business on the Internet wants to receive. Flames are abusive, often profane e-mail messages sent from one person to another. If you do receive a flame, by all means try to avoid responding in kind, thus starting a *flame war* in which the participants exchange angry e-mail. Instead, wait a while for things to cool down and then respond as calmly as you can.

The danger with starting an e-mail fight is that you may trigger an even more destructive e-mail practice called mail bombing. A mail bomb isn't an explosive device that's sent through the mail. Rather, it's e-mail that's designed to overload the targeted person's computer system.

Stay away from spams

One reason you may receive a flame or mail bomb is that someone has judged you as guilty of *spamming* the Internet — sending unwanted e-mail messages advertising some service or product. Unfortunately, spams seem to be proliferating as more people get on the Internet. Typically, *spam artists* operate by sending advertisements for get-rich-quick schemes or to advertise their own Web sites.

Don't add to the flood of spam yourself, especially to mailing lists or newsgroups that have nothing to do with your business. The members of such groups feel that you're invading their privacy and violating the fundamental nature of the group. As a result, you may receive flames, mail bombs, have your phone lines jammed, lose customers, and get canceled by your ISP.

The way to promote yourself using mailing lists or newsgroups is *not* to advertise at all, but to participate constructively, providing advice and help when it is called for, so that people appreciate your knowledge and begin to consider sending some business your way.

Wait before you send

If I had a dollar for every time I clicked on the Send button and immediately wished I *hadn't* sent an e-mail message on its way so quickly, I could . . . well, I could buy a new e-mail program. I remember clearly how much trouble a coworker encountered when he bypassed our supervisor and sent an e-mail to all the top officers in the company, telling them exactly what *he* thought they should be doing with the company's Web site.

If your e-mail software enables you to save a draft of a message before you send it (Netscape Messenger lets you do this), make use of this feature if you're at all unsure whether you want to release a message. Always be sure that you're saying what you really want to say, and that it's going to the right people, and that everything is spelled correctly.

Respect privacy

Request that your employees not forward someone else's e-mail without the originator's permission. Also ask them to keep confidential anything about the office that you don't want to spread to the outside world. There's nothing secret about e-mail! The contents can be forwarded to newsgroups, Web sites, and sent to the competition.

Multimedia e-mail: Adding images and sounds

Your e-mail doesn't have to be a boring, text-only affair. You can send formatted e-mail with text and images to people who have a mail client that accepts MIME-compatible attachments. In the world of the Internet, MIME doesn't stand for a voiceless performer walking against the wind; rather, MIME can give color and voice to your e-mail.

MIME stands for Multipurpose Internet Mail Extensions. MIME is a set of standard designations that identify the *file type* of a mail file so that a computer can recognize what that mail file is and determine what to do with it. A MIME designation tells a computer that the mail file is something other than standard ASCII text. MIME types exist for graphics, sound, and other types of multimedia files.

If you attach a multimedia file to an e-mail message using a MIME-compliant mail client, a filename extension is added to the message header being sent to the receiving computer along with the message. For instance, if you attach a JPEG image to your e-mail message, the image file is designated with the MIME description `image/jpeg`. If the person who receives this e-mail message has Netscape Messenger or another e-mail package that recognizes MIME types, that recipient can set up the e-mail software to automatically recognize and process an attachment with the MIME type `image/jpeg`. A program such as Paint Shop Pro can be designated to open up and display the file when it's received.

If your recipients use a mail client that recognizes e-mail documents with the MIME type `text/html`, the software recognizes HTML documents and displays them in the mail window with formatting and images intact. You can send formatted HTML documents, such as newsletters, by attaching them to a message and simply e-mailing them. When the recipients open your message, they immediately see in the mail window, whatever headings, images, animated GIFs, Java applets, or other features you included in the document.

You also see the MIME type of the document when you view the "full" header of an e-mail message. See the section "Understanding message headers" earlier in this chapter.

E-mail communication for the computerless

If some of your clients or suppliers don't have e-mail, you can still send them e-mail messages from your computer. Just use one of the services that can convert your e-mail messages into faxes. Some of these services are free; most charge for their services. Kevin Savetz offers an extensive list of services in the U.S. and abroad at `www.northcoast.com/savetz/fax-faq.html`.

Using Mailing Lists

A mailing list is made up of a group of Internet users with similar interests. Members subscribe to a list in order to join it. Subscribers can then receive and read e-mail messages sent by other list members. Every e-mail message sent to the list is distributed to all of its members, any of whom can send e-mail replies that can develop into text-based discussions.

Mailing list discussions tend to be more focused than newsgroup postings because the number of subscribers is much smaller. The most common mailing lists on the Net are discussion lists, in which members exchange messages and develop threads, a series of replies and counter-replies on a subject. Another kind of mailing list is an announcement list, which provides only one-way communication: The list owner sends out news and updates about his or her organization.

You can find two types of discussion mailing lists on the Internet:

  ✔ **Moderated lists.** These lists are maintained by an individual who monitors discussions and adds and subtracts subscribers to and from the list.

  ✔ **Unmoderated lists.** These lists are maintained by an automated server, sometimes called a LISTSERV.

Mailing lists can be hard to locate, but there are a few sites on the Internet that present lists of the various lists. Do a search on one of the Internet search engines, or try the DTP Internet Jumplist: `www.cs.purdue.edu/homes/gwp/dtp/groups.html`.

After you find a list, subscribing is easy. You either find the e-mail address of the person who "owns" or runs the list, and send a polite message asking to be subscribed or, in the case of a LISTSERV, send a standard e-mail message such as

```
subscribe [your name] [your email address] [mailing list]
```

Expect to receive an automated reply along with instructions on how to use the list and how to unsubscribe (be sure to keep this initial message in case you ever do want to discontinue membership).

Traffic on mailing lists can be heavy, and it's not uncommon to receive dozens of messages a day. Mailing lists that reach a high level of traffic sometimes create digest versions that contain all the individual messages arranged in a specific way. Subscribers then receive one long message per day rather than many messages throughout the day.

Creating a mailing list with Outlook Express

If you're starting your first mailing list and only have a few dozen or even a hundred names on the list, you have two options:

- ✔ You can use a specialized program such as ListSTAR (described in Chapter 15) or Majordomo (hofdi.med.cornell.edu) to create an automated list for you. An automated list enables members to automatically perform common functions such as subscribing and unsubscribing.

- ✔ You can manage your mailing list yourself by typing in names and addresses in an e-mail program's address book. An address book saves e-mail addresses and other personal information so that you can send messages quickly without having to type in each address by hand. Most address books enable you to group together a number of individuals to form a mailing list. That way, you can send a message out to everyone in the list at once.

Mailing lists don't have to include hundreds of members, and they don't have to be open to everyone on the Internet, either. You can create a mailing list that only exists to members of your company on your business's intranet. A mailing list is a great way to keep everyone in a workgroup in the loop about a particularly critical project. A mailing list enables everyone in the group to communicate with everyone else all at once without the need to arrange conference calls or gathering everyone in the same place for face-to-face meetings. A small list that consists of only a handful of individuals is ideally suited to an e-mail program with an address book.

The following example shows how to compile a mailing list using the Address Book that comes with Microsoft Outlook Express. A mailing list in an address book is a group of individuals, each of whom receives a copy of any e-mail message addressed to the group's nickname. The list is represented as a folder in the Address Book window. To make your mailing list meaningful, you must have at least two individual users in your address book. The first step is to start up Outlook Express. Then follow these steps:

1. **When the program is open and running, click on the Address Book button in the toolbar (see Figure 7-7).**

   The Windows Address Book window appears.

2. **Choose File⇨New Group or click on the New Group toolbar button in the Address Book window to create a new mailing list.**

   The Workgroup Properties dialog box appears (see Figure 7-8).

3. **In the Group Name field, enter a name for your mailing list.**

   As you type the name, it appears in the Workgroup Properties title bar.

4. **In the Members area of the Workgroup Properties title bar, click on the New Contact button if you're entering the individual's name for the first time. If you're entering a name from your address book, click on the Select Members button.**

   If you click on New Contact, the Properties dialog box appears. The Personal tab appears in front by default.

5. **Enter the name of the person you want to add in the Name section of the Properties dialog box.**

   The individual's name appears in the Properties title bar.

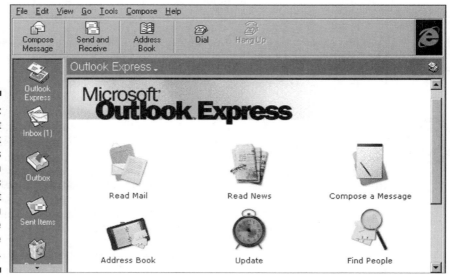

Figure 7-7:
Microsoft
Outlook
Express
comes with
an address
book that
enables you
to compile
a simple
mailing list.

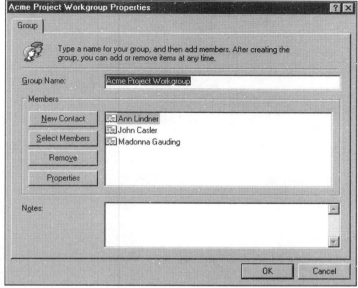

Figure 7-8:
Enter a
name for
your mailing
list in the
Workgroup
Properties
dialog box.

6. **In the Add New field, enter the individual's e-mail address, and then click on the Add button.**

   The address moves to the field at the bottom of the Properties dialog box (see Figure 7-9).

7. **For the purposes of compiling a mailing list, the only information you need to add is an individual's name and e-mail address. But you can also use an electronic address book to store someone's "real world" mailing address. You can record whether the person can receive secure e-mail as well. If you want to add this additional information, you can click on the other tabs in the Properties dialog box (Home Business, Other, Security, Certificates). When you're done, click on OK.**

   The Properties dialog box closes and you return to Workgroup Properties dialog box, where you can click on either New Contact or Select Address to add more names to the list.

8. **When you're done adding names, click on OK to close the Workgroup Properties dialog box.**

   You return to the Windows Address Book window, where your new mailing list or "Group" appears (see Figure 7-10).

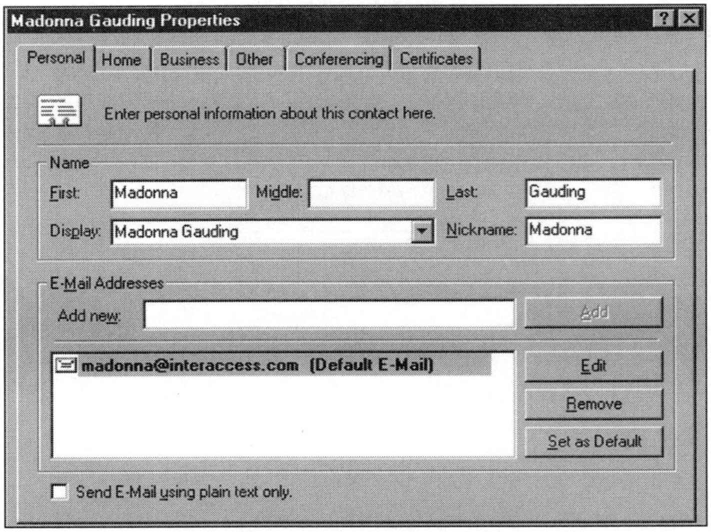

Figure 7-9:
Add a new
member to
your mailing
list in the
Properties
dialog box.

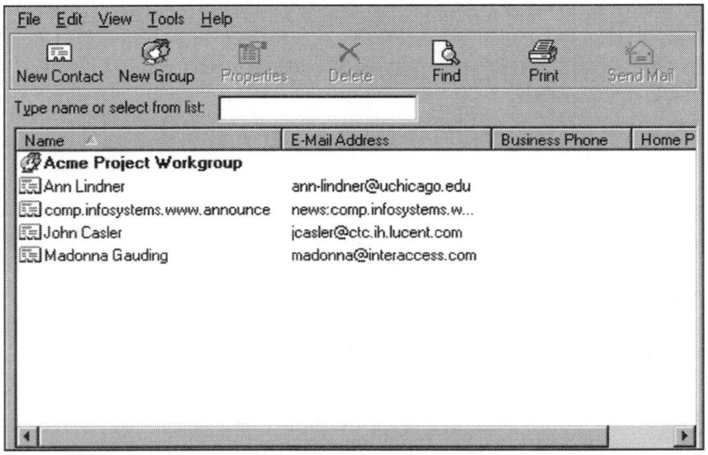

Figure 7-10:
Whenever
you want to
send a
message to
everyone in
your mailing
list, select
the group's
name in the
Address
Book
window.

When you're done, click on OK at the bottom of the Address Book window to return to the Outlook Express window. If you want to send an e-mail message to everyone in your mailing list, single-click on the group's name in the Address Book window, and then click on the Send Mail toolbar button. A New Message window appears so that you can compose your message.

If you want to start a mailing list using your ISP account, better check with the ISP first to see if the plan is okay. Mailing lists can generate a lot of e-mail in a short time, and not all ISPs permit you to do it. One ISP that lets you run a list is Web Communications (www.webcom.com), which provides its members with a cool Web interface to help them start a mailing list. You go to the Web page provided by Web Communications, fill in the name of your list, enter your e-mail address, and you're on your way.

Hiring an automatic mailing list service

As your business grows, your mailing list becomes bigger — sometimes too large to manage on your own. You may spend so much time adding and deleting names, sending and receiving e-mail messages, and making sure that your server doesn't crash, that you don't have time to actually participate in the list yourself. When administrative efforts become too time-consuming, you can do one of two things:

- ✔ Install software that automatically handles subscriptions and sends and receives e-mail for you. SLMail, described earlier, can do this for you. Another such program for the Macintosh, ListSTAR, is described in Chapter 15.
- ✔ Hire someone to run your mailing list for you.

Some Internet businesses do the grunt-work involved with managing a mailing list so that you can concentrate on important things like running your business, managing your staff, and finding time for your family. One such company is SkyWeyr Technologies, which is itself a small business that has found success on the Internet (see the case study that follows). SkyList, the mailing list division of SkyWeyr, handles the following services for its customers — the sorts of features to look for in any mailing list service:

- ✔ Handling of mail that "bounces" back, and deleting inaccurate e-mail addresses
- ✔ Managing requests from members to change their e-mail addresses
- ✔ Making sure all messages get delivered
- ✔ Handling all automated requests to subscribe, unsubscribe from the list, or to receive a digest version (a single message that contains a day's worth of correspondence)
- ✔ Maintaining searchable archives of past mailing list messages
- ✔ Providing reporting and statistics on use of the mailing list
- ✔ Offering support, personal attention, and a pager number in case of emergency

You only need a dial-up e-mail account in order to host a mailing list with a mailing list service. The list processing and heavy e-mail traffic takes place on the service's computers. The company operates "transparently" behind your company's Internet domain. For instance, if you obtain a domain name like `mycompany.com`, your list address could be `listname@mycompany.com`, even though the mail really comes to your mailing list service's computers for processing.

E-mail is a great business tool because it gives you plenty of ways to quantify results. You don't have to say, "It *feels* like this is working for us." Instead, you can count numbers and record data such as

- ✔ The number of e-mail inquiries your company receives in a given month.
- ✔ The number of people joining your mailing list.
- ✔ The e-mail addresses and names of people who make inquiries.

In addition, you can

- ✔ Add everyone who inquires to an address book and send them announcements in the future.
- ✔ Join mailing lists related to your own area of interest.

Case study: SkyWeyr Technologies

E-mail can help make your small business a success — just ask the folks at SkyWeyr Technologies. SkyWeyr Technologies was formed two years ago by Tom Biddulph, 10 years after he founded StarNine Technologies (which created ListSTAR, the Macintosh mailing list program described in Chapter 15). This rapidly expanding startup company performs Internet consulting services and develops cutting-edge Java application software.

Joshua Baer runs SkyList, the mailing list hosting division of SkyWeyr. SkyList currently hosts about 30 mailing lists. Discussion lists range from 25 to 1,500 members, and announcement lists can include tens of thousands of recipients. "I would consider a 600-member discussion list to be an active, healthy list for most topics," says Baer. "On the other hand, I have very active, healthy lists with only 250 or even 25 members, depending on the subject matter they're discussing."

As the founder and maintainer of the ListMom-Talk mailing list, an online discussion forum for mailing list managers on all platforms, Baer has this advice for small businesses thinking about starting their own mailing lists: "Keep in mind that most mailing lists are communities; as the list owner you want to facilitate the feeling of community. Make everything as simple as possible for the subscriber and your lists will thrive."

Chapter 8

Niche Marketing with Discussion Groups

. . . .

In This Chapter

▶ Finding the best discussion groups for your marketing niche

▶ Subscribing to groups and posting messages and replies

▶ Advertising your business on Usenet

▶ Starting your own Internet newsgroup

▶ Creating a discussion group on your intranet or Web site

. . . .

*I*t's my impression that many businesses, when they make the move to the Internet, think only about a Web page and an e-mail address. They don't consider making use of newsgroups, which is really a shame because in many ways Usenet is the *real* Internet. Usenet is a system of communication that enables individual computer users to participate in group discussions about topics of mutual interest. Someone organizes a group about a particular topic, such as parenting, antiques, or a particular brand of comic book. Anyone can take part by sending a message, which can be read by anyone in the group. The thing that distinguishes Usenet, however, is not the method of communication, but the character of the participants. The denizens of Usenet tend to be people who are passionately devoted to the topic at hand. Many are very knowledgeable, and generous with sharing their knowledge in order to help others.

The fact that Usenet is under-utilized by businesspeople is precisely the reason why those folks may be wise to look into using the system to help their businesses grow — and to help them assist others in the online community as they share knowledge and information.

Finding Your Niche

Online discussion groups are ideally suited to niche marketing: reaching out to narrow groups of people who are passionately interested in what you have to sell. People who consider an activity, a product, or a topic personally important love to participate in discussions with like-minded individuals, and they're also likely to make purchases related to that area of interest. These are the people who frequent newsgroups on the Internet.

For example, lots of people enjoy riding mountain bikes. An online 'zine (that's a term used to describe an electronic magazine that only exists on the Internet) called TREAD Online! is directed to this market.

TREAD Online! makes use of discussion groups in two ways. First, its own discussion area is called TREAD.Net on its Web site (www.tread.pair.com), where people who love mountain bikes can exchange questions, answers, and observations by typing messages to one another about safety, equipment options, and other topics. This isn't a Usenet newsgroup, rather, TREAD.net is a Web-based discussion area where participants can do things they can't do in Usenet, such as search for messages by keyword and view a table of contents. Later in this chapter, you find out how to create a discussion area like this for your own Web site or company intranet.

The newsgroup message displayed in Figure 8-1 by Netscape's Collabra discussion group software is a perfect one for a businessperson to provide helpful advice as a way of participating in the group and building credibility. (See the section "Searching Groups for Potential Customers" later in this chapter for more suggestions.)

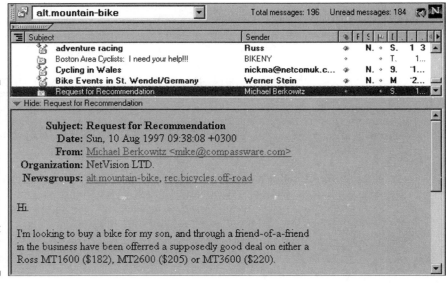

Figure 8-1:
Newsgroups
are text-
based
discussions
focused on
a individual
topics, like
this group
about
mountain
bikes.

Usenet newsgroups are only one kind of discussion group that you can use as a business resource. The online services provide plenty of discussion forums, too. And after you install Internet software, you can use it to set up internal discussion areas on your company's intranet as well. No matter where you find online discussion groups, the same principles of courtesy and generosity apply. This chapter takes all these groups into account by using, for the most part, the general term *discussion group* instead of *newsgroup* or *forum*.

Whether you're a *lurker* (someone who "listens in" on discussion group conversations) or a creator and moderator of your own group, discussion groups can benefit your business in many ways. Here are some goals you can keep in mind as you explore the world of online groups:

✔ Give your employees a place to exchange ideas online.

✔ Give your customers a place where they can post messages and discuss products related to your areas of interest.

✔ Become a resource on Usenet by contributing in newsgroups or even starting your own newsgroup.

✔ Do market research by listening in on newsgroup discussions as potential customers discuss topics that they're interested in.

Businesses don't exist in a vacuum. A fundamental goal of any enterprise is to contact potential and current customers and clients. Discussion groups are a great place to meet colleagues, to be part of a group, or to bring your staff people or your customers together.

In order to use discussion groups successfully, you have to figure out the ground rules. Many of the denizens of Usenet have been on the Net for many years, long before the Web. You're entering their territory, so plan to look into how discussion groups work before you start posting messages or creating groups yourself.

Understanding Discussion Group Communications

A discussion group is a forum on an intranet or the Internet that's organized around a specific topic or area of interest. Usenet (short for User's Network) is a popular part of the Internet that's older than the Web — although the Web was only created in 1990-91, of course. Using special discussion group software like the programs suggested in Chapter 4, you can read and post *articles* (also called *messages*) to those internal discussion groups and Usenet newsgroups that interest you.

A *news server* is a computer that provides groups to users on a network, using news server software that recognizes Network News Transfer Protocol (NNTP). Virtually all Internet providers have a news server that collects messages and posts them so that individual users like you can access groups and read messages using a newsgroup client. Not all news servers provide all available newsgroups. Some don't allow any of the `.alt` groups, for example.

To get started with a discussion group client program, the first step is to tell the program some basic information about your e-mail/news accounts.

✔ Your e-mail address

✔ The name of the news server that can route your newsgroup messages

Finding Internet discussion groups

Internet discussion groups have what's referred to as a *hierarchical structure*. Most individual groups belong to one of seven main categories.

✔ *comp* (computer issues)

✔ *misc* (miscellaneous issues)

✔ *news* (about Usenet itself)

✔ *rec* (recreational activities and popular culture)

✔ *sci* (science)

✔ *soc* (sociology and anthropology)

✔ *talk* (about many of the same subjects)

Most servers also subscribe to the `.alt` category, but may not subscribe to all the `.alt` subcategories therein.

Every category has subcategories, and many subcategories contain sub-subcategories. The components of discussion group names are separated by dots. Some examples include

```
alt.animals.felines.lions
rec.food.drink.coffee
soc.history.war.vietnam
```

Some groups are *moderated* by an administrator who judges the appropriateness of an article before allowing it into a discussion group. Most groups, though, are unmoderated: Anyone who wants to can post anything that comes to mind.

Online services' discussion groups

America Online, CompuServe, and Prodigy all have their own discussion groups, too, but you don't need a special program to access those groups. You use the same software interface that enables you to browse the other online service's resources or to send and receive e-mail.

Everything that's offered in this chapter about the do's and don'ts of dealing with Internet newsgroups applies to discussion forums on America Online and the other online services.

AOL also has its own set of newsgroups, which start with .aol, and which operate basically the same as the ones on Usenet. In truth, the division between Usenet and the online services is often fuzzy. You can access Usenet through the online services and you can get to some online services' discussion groups from Usenet. Both services provide gathering places for committed, passionately interested individuals.

There are tens of thousands of Internet discussion groups, and scrolling through them to find just the one you want can be a tedious process. The Usenet Info Center Launch Pad contains general information about Usenet, a browsable list of groups, and a way to search for a group of interest. You can see how many readers there are in each group and how frequently messages are sent by checking out sunsite.unc.edu/Usenet-b/home.html. You can also try DejaNews, a search service specifically designed for searching newsgroup messages (www.dejanews.com).

A new kind of software, an *intelligent agent,* also goes out to scour newsgroups based on your interests. See Chapter 16 for more about agents.

Don't go by the numbers. It's more valuable to your business to participate in groups that have a small and passionate number of users, rather than many thousands of individuals who are interested in an unrelated topic. You can get an idea of which groups are most popular by visiting the Web site www.tlsoft.com/arbitron, but the exact figures are far out of date.

Reading FAQs

It's a good idea to indulge in a little self-education before you start posting questions to a newsgroup. Most groups compile a list of Frequently Asked Questions, or *FAQs*. The FAQs for lots of groups are posted to news.newusers. questions. Become familiar with the goals and procedures of the groups that you plan to post to.

Although there's no such thing as a stupid question, it doesn't make much sense to ask in a posting when the answer is readily available elsewhere. The following groups also provide introductory messages to help you become acquainted with Usenet discussion groups:

✔ `news.announce.newusers` provides beginners with useful information on how to be a member of the Usenet community and how to start a newsgroup, plus hints on writing for newsgroups.

✔ `news.newusers.questions` is a place for absolute novices to shed any embarrassment and ask any basic questions about Usenet, FTP, e-mail, politics, friendship, life insurance — well, you get the idea.

✔ `news.answers` contains Frequently Asked Questions (FAQ) files.

You can also find the FAQs and figures about newsgroups via FTP or the Web. To find out all about Usenet newsgroups, get the FAQs. A good place to start, What Is Usenet, can be found at `ftp://rtfm.mit.edu/pub/Usenet/ news.answers/Usenet/what-is/part1`. A good place to find out more about the culture of the wild, wide world of Usenet is Yahoo's Net Legends FAQ at `www.yahoo.com/Society_and_Culture/Cyberculture/ Net_Legends`.

Subscribing to groups

Subscribing to a discussion group is a less complicated process than subscribing to a Web site or an online publication.

You're wise to subscribe to only a few discussion groups because a mind-boggling amount of groups exist. Having your software connect to all available groups in every session — and then scrolling through the list to find the one(s) that you want — can be very time-consuming.

It's a good idea to delete groups that you don't expect to visit often because it makes the other groups appear more quickly so that you can access them.

Anatomy of a discussion group article

Most Usenet articles, like e-mail messages (see Chapter 7) consist of several standard parts:

✔ **Header.** The header contains the subject of the article, the date it was posted, the person doing the posting, and the groups to which the article has been posted. The article can be posted to more than one group *(cross-posted)*.

✔ **Quoted material.** These are quotes from a previous posting. A common convention is to include the right-angle bracket (>) before each line.

✔ **The message.** The message portion of the article is the actual content, the new idea that someone just wrote. It appears as flush left, un-marked text.

✔ **Signature files.** These are text files that contain the sender's name and other information (see Chapter 7).

Searching Groups for Potential Customers

After *lurking* (staying in the background, reading discussion group exchanges, but not participating) for a while, you may decide to talk back to Usenet. Post an article in response to a question. Try to provide a helpful answer. Be sure to include, at the end of the message, a signature file that includes your e-mail address and the URL of your Web site.

If you're replying to a discussion group article, keep in mind that you can reply either to everyone in the group at the same time, or send a private reply only to the sender — or both. You can also cross-post — that is, send your message to more than one discussion group.

Netiquette

If you want to make money or find new clients by making contacts through discussion groups, you have to play the game right. Basically, the same rules that apply to e-mail work in the world of Usenet — only more so. The explosive growth of Internet communications has created an entire community with its own notions of what is and is not okay to broadcast on the Net. These notions are called *Netiquette*: the etiquette of Usenet and Internet communications in general.

Avoiding flames

The wrath of Usenet can be the kiss of death for a company that wants to do business on the Internet. There are all sorts of things that newsgroup users can do if they feel someone has broken their codes of conduct:

- ✔ **Kill files.** A kill file blocks any messages from an offending individual or domain from posting on a newsgroup.

- ✔ **Cancelbots.** These are software programs that delete offending messages and block future messages from a group.

- ✔ **Flames and mail bombs.** See Chapter 7 for descriptions of these not-too-pleasant communications that can hurt your business.

Don't post blatant press releases for your company, don't send attachments to a group unless that group's FAQ states that attachments are permitted, and don't post messages that are unrelated to the topic of the group.

Answering questions

The best reason to play by the rules is that the results are so good. Seeking questions and providing answers and advice, rather than presenting advertisements, are the best Internet marketing techniques that you can undertake.

Plenty of businesses publish Web pages that don't get many visits. But every business person who uses discussion groups the right way seems to have some success: more Web visits, more sales, more inquires, and more attention in general.

Placing ads and notices

Can't find a newsgroup to promote your business? Not to worry: Usenet has set aside some groups whose mission is to let people advertise products and services as well as items for sale. Check out the groups in the .biz hierarchy, such as biz.marketplace.

If you want to post a classified ad, check out any groups that show the words for sale, marketplace, classified, or swap in their names. Some of these groups are localized to a particular state or city, such as chi.jobs or chi.forsale.

Always read the FAQ for the group where you want to advertise. Make sure that your ads are actually related to the topic of the group. Look for the message Usenet Marketplace FAQ, which is regularly posted on the biz.marketplace group (or check out the FAQ posted on the Web at www.cis.ohio-state.edu/hypertext/faq/Usenet/biz-config-faq/faq.html). The popular group misc.forsale also has its own FAQ. Don't overuse CAPITAL LETTERS, the words *Free* and *Now*, the dollar sign *$,* and the exclamation mark *! ! !*

Starting a Usenet Discussion Group

Where do all these news groups come from? They're started by individuals just like you. Sometimes a new product comes out that grabs people's attention, so someone starts a discussion group about it. Some groups, like alt.parenting, are frequented by people genuinely seeking help and advice. But others, such as alt.clueless.newbie.whine.whine.whine obviously aren't going to provoke lots of intelligent give-and-take.

A small business may create its own discussion group on the Internet to offer a product. Another good reason for a new discussion group may be to prompt discussion about a provocative and controversial area of interest.

If you want to start a group that's open to everyone on the Internet, you can run it in one of two ways:

✔ **Read-only.** Only you can post messages; the group is basically a news outlet for your company.

✔ **Discussion group.** Everyone can initiate new topics, respond to postings, and make their own announcements.

After you decide on the kind of group that you want to create, you need to decide on the scope of the group. You have three alternatives:

✔ **Create a local discussion group which only exists on one server.** Only people who are connected to that server can see the group. Universities, for instance, have their own local groups that only students, faculty, and staff can access. ISPs have their own groups, too.

✔ **Create a global discussion group that's included on all news servers and that's voted on and approved by the Usenet administrators.** This process is almost universally described as laborious and time-consuming.

✔ **Create a global discussion group in the** .alt **or** .biz **categories.** You're allowed to create a group here without any formal voting process, although it's a good idea to seek approval by sending a proposal to the alt.config group beforehand.

You can read about new groups in news.announce.newgroups. Another resource, news.groups, is where new groups are hotly debated. Also look in news.answers for the message How to Start a New Usenet Newsgroup. If you don't see the posting in this or any other beginners' groups, send an e-mail to mail-server@rtfm.mit.edu. In the body of the message, type **send How_to_Create_a_New_Usenet_Newsgroup**. You'll receive an e-mail message that explains how to start your own group.

Creating an .alt discussion group

If you decide that you want to create a group in the .alt category, scroll through the long lists of postings in alt.answers and find the message So You Want to Create an Alt Newsgroup.

Don't try to propose an .alt newsgroup on a topic for which there are good groups in the other Big 7 categories already.

Interestingly, .alt was not originally named for alternative, although it has come to mean that. The term originally stood for Anarchists, Lunatics, and Terrorists. These days, .alt is a catch-all category where anyone can start a group if others show interest in the creator's proposal.

Creating a "Big Seven" group

If you're able to create a discussion group in one of the Big Seven main categories, you can earn the stamp of official Usenet approval. In order to do this, your group cannot duplicate the content of a group that already exists. You have to post a proposal, and your group is voted on in order to be accepted for distribution to the thousands of news servers around the world.

Here are a few tips to make sure that your proposal is accepted by the news administrators:

- ✔ Don't use a dot as a word separator, like alt.real.estate. Rather, use a dash: alt.real-estate.
- ✔ Don't use acronyms that people can't understand in a glance.
- ✔ Don't use numbers or special characters in a group name.
- ✔ Don't use joke names, such as alt.barney.die.die.die.

If the group you're proposing covers the entire United States, consider adding your group to the growing us.* hierarchy. To begin, you post your proposal to us.config. You find guidelines for the technicalities of starting a new group at www.cs.ubc.ca/spider/edmonds/Usenet/good-newgroup.html.

Setting up a discussion group server

Some programs do exist that can enable you to set up your own news server, but for most small businesses, self-made servers aren't necessary unless you're really good with computers and have a direct Internet connection. You can easily set up a group in the .alt or .biz categories on the Net, and because you can create your own discussion area quite simply with FrontPage, you don't really need to install news server software. For the server to work well, you need lots of available disk space and a fast Internet connection. Let your Internet provider bother with the technical work involved in serving up discussion groups, so that you can concentrate on the content you put online.

Creating a Discussion Area with FrontPage

An easy way exists to create your own discussion group, either on your internal intranet or on your Web page. Microsoft FrontPage 97 has one of the nicer systems for creating an internal discussion group. You can follow the program's easy-to-use wizards to create a Web-based discussion group that people can access from their web browsers without having to use discussion group software. Members can not only exchange messages and carry on a series of back-and-forth responses (called *threads*) on different topics, but newcomers to the group can also view articles arranged by a table of contents and accessible by a searchable index. Figure 8-2 shows the index page for a group created to discuss an office's new Web site.

You have to purchase FrontPage, because no demo or beta version of the software is available as this is written. I've seen the program advertised for $139 with a $40 mail-in rebate. At that price, FrontPage is a bargain considering all that it enables you to do. The program comes in versions for Mac and Windows platforms.

Creating pages

Follow these steps to set up your own discussion group with Microsoft FrontPage:

1. **After you install the program, start up FrontPage by choosing Start⇨Programs⇨Microsoft FrontPage.**

Figure 8-2:
FrontPage discussion groups are presented on the Web and include a searchable index.

Office Web Site Search Form - Netscape

File Edit View Go Communicator Help

Office Web Site

[Contents | Search | Post]

SEARCH FOR ARTICLE

Find articles posted to this discussion containing matching words or patterns.

Search for:

Start Search   Reset

FrontPage is a suite of different programs. The program that appears when you first start is called FrontPage Explorer. This application enables you to create or edit entire Web sites, which consist of groups of interconnected Web pages.

The Getting Started with Microsoft FrontPage dialog box appears first. This dialog box enables you to open a ready-to-fill-in collection of Web pages or use one of the built-in templates and Wizards that come with FrontPage. These are predesigned Web sites that save you the trouble of designing pages and, in some cases, writing computer scripts to process the data submitted by interactive Web page forms.

2. **To use FrontPage's discussion wizard, click on the button next to From a Wizard or Template in the section Create a New FrontPage Web. Then click on OK.**

The New FrontPage Wizard dialog box appears. This dialog box presents you, in the big field labeled Template or Wizard, with a list of preconfigured Web sites. All you have to do is fill in the content that's unique to you or your business. After you set up your discussion area, check out the items labeled Corporate Presence Wizard and Customer Support Web.

3. **Select Discussion Group Wizard from the Template or Wizard list. Then click on OK.**

The first of a series of Discussion Web Wizard dialog boxes appears. The first dialog box enables you to specify the location of your discussion Web. You can either set up a Web on your own computer, or publish (that is, transfer via FTP) the Web pages, graphics, and other files immediately to the directory on your Internet provider's web server that holds your Web pages.

By default, the server listed in the box under Web Server is the one that you specified when you set up Microsoft FrontPage. If you do not have authoring access on a web server, type in the full name and path of a folder on your local disk. If you enter a path to a folder that does not yet exist, FrontPage creates the folder for you. You can then set up your Web pages on your computer and test them out before you publish them on your remote Internet provider's web server.

4. **In the Name of New FrontPage Web field, enter a name for your discussion group, for example,** WaterCooler. **Then click on OK.**

The next Discussion Web Wizard dialog box appears. Go through this and the subsequent dialog boxes as they present you with questions that you answer to determine what kind of discussion group you're going to have. One of the dialog boxes enables you to select the features for your discussion group. You have five options:

• **Submission Form.** This is a form that users need to fill out in order to compose articles and send them to the group. This form is required, so the option is gray in this dialog box. You don't have the option to de-select it.

- **Table of Contents.** This is a page that presents visitors with links to all posted articles in the discussion group. It helps people find articles quickly.

- **Search Form.** This form presents users with a text box in which they can enter words or phrases to find articles that contain them.

- **Threaded Replies.** This is an arrangement that presents the articles in the group in the form of threads. A thread is a series of articles on the same topic. Presenting the articles in threads rather than in, say, chronological order enables you to select topics that you can easily reply to.

- **Confirmation Page.** This page enables people to know that their article is now posted to the group.

At any time as you go through the series of Discussion Group Wizard pages, you can click on Finish to finish the process. When you're done, the preset pages for your discussion Web appear in the FrontPage Explorer main window (as shown in Figure 8-3).

The FrontPage Explorer window shown in Figure 8-3 for the discussion group that I created shows the name of the group (WaterCooler) and its location (a folder on my hard disk C). The left side of the FrontPage Explorer window shows the arrangement of the documents that make up one discussion within the WaterCooler discussion group at the Office Web site.

The right side of the window is a visual map that shows how the discussion group is arranged and how the pages are linked to each other.

When you set up a discussion area with FrontPage, you have the option of designing your pages as a *frameset,* or a set of Web pages that are subdivided into separate frames.

Figure 8-3:
FrontPage's discussion group wizard helps you create a set of pages for your group.

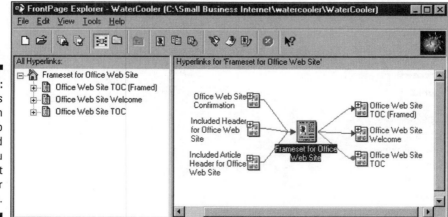

Editing pages

Once you have set up a discussion area, the next step is to edit your pages to reflect the content that you want visitors to read about and, hopefully, discuss when they visit your site. You edit by using another FrontPage component application: FrontPage Editor. Follow these steps to start the editing process:

1. **A quick way to access the editor is by double-clicking on the icon for the Welcome page in your discussion web.**

   The page you select opens in a new FrontPage Editor window, as shown in Figure 8-4.

2. **The toolbar buttons and menu items in FrontPage Editor enable you to alter the appearance of your Web pages. For example, it's a good idea to change the default grey background of your pages by choosing Format⇨Background.**

   The Page Properties dialog box appears.

3. **Click on the button next to Specify Background and Colors, and then click on the triangle next to Background, and select a color from the drop-down menu list. Click on OK.**

   The Page Properties dialog box closes and you return to FrontPage Editor, where your page appears with a new background color. Remember to pick a background color that contrasts with the type on your page and that won't make viewers' eyes bug out. There's nothing wrong with a plain white or cream-colored background.

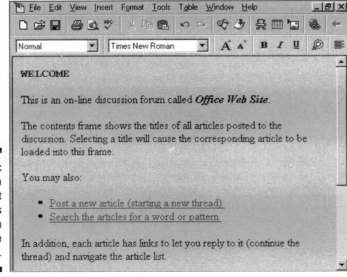

Figure 8-4:
You can easily edit Web pages with FrontPage Editor.

4. **Add a few sentences to the beginning of the Welcome page to tell participants more about the purpose and scope of the discussion group. You can add text by clicking anywhere in the text.**

   The vertical text bar appears in the text of the Web page so that you can insert new text.

5. **To edit more pages in your discussion group, choose File⇨Open.**

   The Open File dialog box appears. The files listed are the documents that make up your discussion group. You can double-click on a file's name to edit it.

6. **When you are done editing files, choose Tools⇨Show FrontPage Explorer.**

   You return to FrontPage Explorer.

Publishing your pages

Now your pages are ready to appear on the Internet or on your internal intranet. The next step is to publish your files — that is, send them to a server so that they appear to visitors. You can do that now by following these steps:

1. **Choose File⇨Publish FrontPage Web . . . from the Explorer's menu bar.**

   The Publish FrontPage Web dialog box appears.

2. **Enter the name of your directory on your ISP's web server (or your office intranet server) where your Web pages are published for everyone to see. For instance, the directory on my ISP's server is:**

   ```
   homepage.interaccess.com/~gholden
   ```

   You have to enter your password and username when you connect to the server. Click on OK.

   Your files are published on the server.

Testing your pages

After your discussion group goes online, test all the pages to make sure that they work. Open each page in your web browser and see how it looks. Enter the address for the home page of your discussion group in the Open Page dialog box of your browser. Remember that you have a new folder that contains your discussion group. The folder for my group is called watercooler, so my address looks like this:

```
http://homepage.interaccess.com/~gholden/watercooler/
```

When you connect, the Welcome page for your discussion group appears. If it doesn't, check to make sure that you entered the URL correctly.

Starting a discussion

Post a message to the group to suggest a topic for discussion by clicking on the link called `Post a new article (starting a new thread)`. **Fill out** the fields in your submission form and then click on the Post Article button. The article appears on your site.

Be sure to send an e-mail message to everyone on your staff to tell them about the site and encourage them to participate. Don't forget to tell them about the nice searchable index (see Figure 8-2).

Monitoring discussion

After you establish a group, your participation doesn't end. Be sure to regularly monitor the tone and content of the messages. If someone posts a distracting or annoying message, send a reminder notice to the group about the ground rules for discussion. After a while, you also need to suggest some new topics for discussion because previous ones become worn out.

Another way to start a discussion on the Net is to use Chat software. Announce a discussion either among your staff or on the Internet, or put up a notice on your Web site, and see who shows up. See Chapter 9 for more information on chat and other methods of real-time communications.

What you can do with an online discussion group

The preceding exercises showed how to set up an internal discussion group using FrontPage. However, the procedure for setting up a group on one of your business's Web pages and opening discussion to all of your visitors on the Internet is virtually the same.

What can you accomplish by enabling people to start topics, make responses, and engage in debate on your Web site? For one thing, people come back to your Web site. Having threads of discussions posted on the Web encourages visitors to return to keep track of responses.

Case study: How TREAD Online! connects with Usenet

When Chris Phillipo discovered many newsgroups about mountain biking and cycling in general, he embarked on a self-described "rampage of question-asking." Later, he studied the groups' FAQs and searched the Web. After he created his first Web pages, he decided to create a Web site devoted to cycling. "I did this for fun — the best way to start, in my opinion," he says.

After a year on his first-generation Web site, he says, "I worked about four hours a day for a couple of weeks to create the site that stands now. Others would likely have created a better site in less time, but I spent much of that time

learning how to use the graphics program, learning how to set up Perl and CGI scripts, and trying many scripts as well as making sure the page looked right in different screen resolutions whenever I made changes."

When he became serious about starting an online business, Chris made another important change: "I went from asking questions to answering any question I could and getting involved in most of the discussions. In essence, becoming a fixture. Add to that my new signature, and I started to get hits without resorting to bulk e-mail or other unscrupulous methods."

Encourage people to discuss issues related to your line of business. If you run an insurance company, have them discuss safety concerns. On your table of contents page, you can suggest a number of topics and even set up separate discussion groups for each subject.

If you run an online publication, a discussion page can provide a place for people to give their opinions about what they just read (something done by CNET [www.cnet.com], HotWired [www.hotwired.com], and many of the more successful online publications).

Connecting with discussion groups on the Internet by providing help and advice gives you tangible as well as intangible results. On the tangible side, hopefully you see more visits on your Web pages. You also get more e-mail inquiries, and make contacts with individuals from all walks of life, some of whom may return the favor by giving you feedback or providing advice. On the intangible side, you feel good because you're taking an active role in marketing your business on the Net, rather than simply waiting for visitors to find your Web site. An internal discussion area that you create on your intranet can also provide benefits in employee morale, feedback, and improved communication.

Chapter 9

Real-Time Communication

*T*hose television commercials make business conferencing look so easy. Someone pushes a button, and a roomful of executives in one office can see and converse with a roomful of colleagues in another office. In another commercial, a group of people in suits watch admiringly as the at-home worker, in her bathrobe, speaks with them and draws diagrams that they can all see instantly on a computer screen.

You may be thinking those solutions are just for big companies. Is real-time conferencing with clients or coworkers practical for a small business?

A connection to the Internet makes chatting or videoconferencing a viable possibility for businesses both small and large. If you and your fellow conferencers have a connection to the Internet, you can use the global network to talk to each other.

Applications such as Internet Phone and chat software can help your organization establish a presence on the Internet, too. These programs make communicating about as interactive as it can be without seeing or sitting in a room with others. You can use the Internet as a telephone, chat with others via interactive typed messages, exchange files, and collaborate using a *whiteboard* that you can draw on and that everyone can see. You can even use your computer as an answering machine to hold messages for you if you miss a call. For the most part, the software that enables you to do this is simple to use, doesn't require sophisticated hardware, and works with dial-up modem connections.

The Internet enables two or more connected users to communicate in real time through a central server. A *chat server* permits connected users to talk to each other if they're connected to a common chat area called a *channel*.

A *reflector* is another kind of server that enables users to videoconference. A *directory server* lets Internet phone users connect to each other. The users who connect to any of these servers need to have the same kind of conferencing software to be able to talk or type messages to one another.

Those all-in-one browser applications described in Chapter 4 can help, too. Microsoft Internet Explorer comes with a built-in application called NetMeeting that supports remote collaboration. Netscape Communicator comes with an application called Conference. Both of these programs enable users to chat, make Internet phone calls, share whiteboards, transfer files, and even engage in collaborative surfing — the ability for groups of users to surf around the Net together.

The range of uses for conferencing on the Internet is limited only by your imagination. Here are some goals to consider.

Using the Net for real-time communications can help small businesses in a number of ways:

- ✔ **Cost.** Being able to type messages or use your computer as a telephone can result in substantial savings in long-distance phone charges, especially if you communicate regularly with businesspeople in other countries.

- ✔ **Collaboration.** Some of your staff may have to stay at home because of illness or child-care responsibilities. Giving at-home workers the ability to chat or conference keeps them in the loop. It also enables you to collaborate with freelance designers or Web consultants.

- ✔ **Wider reach.** Chat is a hugely popular activity on the Net, as well as in the commercial online services. If your site is chat-, phone-, or confer-ence-ready, you can reach users who are more comfortable typing messages on a computer keyboard than calling you on the phone.

There's also an intangible result to consider — a novelty factor. Offering real-time communications with your business is cool and high-tech, which can attract the more techy Internet users to your site.

Checking Your Equipment List

Some varieties of audio- or videoconferencing require more memory and processing power than other Internet applications. Although you don't need anything exotic or expensive, you do require some hardware.

Shopping for hardware

Whether you want to hear audio or experience live video multicasts on the Web, you need to invest in some essential equipment for your computer — if the features aren't already installed. Basically, you need to make sure that your computer has a voice, so it can speak, and ears so that it can hear. Even if you don't expect to do a lot of videoconferencing, electronic ears and a mouth can make your own experience on the Web more fun.

For Internet phone or some other kind of audioconferencing, your shopping list may look like this:

- ✔ **Speakers.** Sure, every computer comes with its own speakers, but many of them are as feeble and tinny as an old AM radio. You can pick up a pair of speakers at any computer store for as little as $20 to $30. Look for powered speakers, which have amplifiers. If you prefer to keep your sound to yourself, you can buy a pair of headphones for even less.

- ✔ **Sound card.** A computer sound card is a thin, rectangular piece of plastic that's covered with chips and other electronic goodies. The card plugs into a special place inside your computer. Many computers come with a sound card already installed. If yours doesn't, buy one.

- ✔ **Microphone.** If your computer has one built in, not to worry. If not, you need to buy one, but they aren't expensive.

If you want to get visual and try videoconferencing, expect to purchase

- ✔ **Video capture card.** This is like a sound card, but it captures video images and turns them into digital information so that your computer can process and display them for you.

- ✔ **Video cameras.** Usually, these are little ball-shaped cameras that rest atop your computer. Black-and-white video cameras for the PC or Mac start at just $99, and color video cameras start at around $199.

Most PowerMacs and many PCs include video support. If you have a Mac, check your Control Panels to see what you have available. If you have a PC, do the following:

1. **Click Start⇨Settings⇨Control Panel.**

   The Control Panel window opens.

2. **In the Control Panel window, double-click on the System icon.**

   The System Properties dialog box opens.

3. Click on the Device Manager tab. Scroll down the list of installed hardware and click on the plus sign (+) next to Sound, Video, and Game Controllers.

A list of sound, video, and game devices appears. See if a video or sound card is installed.

Faster is better when it comes to any kind of conferencing, especially if you want to see your colleagues. A cable modem line or T1 connection is perfect. An ISDN line is good, too. However, if you have a high-bandwidth connection and your colleague uses a 14.4 Kbps modem to connect to the Net, you're still going to encounter camera image or audio signal delays. However, you *can* get by with a 28.8 Kbps connection if you stick to chat, and you can live with herky-jerky video images that lag behind the person's voice. Seeing someone on your computer outweighs the delay problem. Keep an open mind, and experiment!

Easy, No-Cost Solutions

If you hire a Webmaster to design a Web site for your small business, that person can set up some kind of real-time communications solution for you.

If you don't have the resources to hire a consultant, you can find some easy solutions in this chapter. I also describe your other options so that you can talk knowledgeably to your Webmaster or Internet provider if you want to set up one of the more advanced methods described later in the chapter, such as videoconferencing or whiteboards.

Chatting up your business

Chat is probably the most practical real-time communications you can set up for your business, either on the Net or using one of the online services.

The business uses of chat are limited only by your creativity. If you and your coworkers are able to connect to the same existing chat site on the Internet you can

✔ Set up a chat channel to have professional discussions with business associates around the world about the current state of your industry.

✔ Do market research by connecting to groups related to your areas of interest.

✔ Interview potential employees.

✔ Conduct classes or provide training using chat.

For instance, if you all have accounts or simply separate screen names on America Online, you can all connect at the same time to AOL and get into a private chat room that one of you sets up. You can then hold private discussions online. If you and your colleagues have accounts on CompuServe, you can do the same thing. If you're on the Web, you can set up free accounts at GeoCities (www.geocities.com) and set up a private chat room for yourselves, as explained in the section "Chatting on the Web with GeoCities."

While audio- or videoconferencing with NetMeeting or Netscape Conference is basically a one-to-one operation, you can conduct an online meeting with more people by using chat. Because chat doesn't use a lot of bandwidth, participants with slow Internet connections can still keep up with the conversation. If you *do* want to try group videoconferencing, try Enhanced CU-SeeMe by White Pine Software (www.whitepine.com).

How Internet Relay Chat works

Chat is sometimes called Internet Relay Chat (IRC), and has been likened to CB radio for computer users. It works like this: A chat server provides a place on the Net for users to connect using chat software. Users communicate by joining a chat room or channel and then typing messages to be sent to one another.

Usually, chat enables large groups of users to talk to each other. Each message can be read by everyone in the group. But a private chat room can be set up for smaller groups like office teams or departments.

You need some sort of chat program to connect to channels and communicate by typing messages. Some popular programs are PIRCH, mIRC, and Global Chat (see Chapter 4 for more information on these and other programs). A new kind of chat server uses the powerful programming language Java to set up a chat area on a web browser window. These sites enable you to chat by using a web browser rather than a separate chat program.

The culture of chat

No doubt about it, chat is used primarily for fun and recreation. Users often go by aliases rather than their real names. If you want to talk to someone you know, it's usually best to set up an appointment beforehand to make sure you're both online.

Remember to treat others as you want to be treated. Keep in mind that vulgarity and disruptive behavior are inappropriate online. If you're on America Online, you can read about our community guidelines at keyword **TOS**.

Looking for someone to call? A number of Internet telephone guides are available: Kevin Savetz maintains one at `www.northcoast.com/~savetz/voice-faq.html`; Cycor Marketing Services, a Canadian Internet Service Provider, maintains a list of public Internet phone servers on their Northern Lights server (`www.cycor.ca/iphone/serv.html`); and Yahoo! has People Search at `www.yahoo.com/search/people`.

Chatting on the Web with GeoCities

GeoCities, the Web site that provides Internet users with free home pages, e-mail, or other utilities, offers nine chat rooms for visitors to enter. For the most part, these chat rooms are intended to give GeoCities users a place to meet each other. However, anyone can join in on the chatting: You don't need to be a GeoCities member. Anyone can also set up his or her own private chat room, which makes it feasible for members of an organization who are connected to the Web to use GeoCities to chat.

To use the GeoCities chat areas you need a browser that recognizes the Java programming language. Most newer browsers support Java.

Because the GeoCities chat areas use Java, you don't need to access the chat rooms using a special chat program. You can just use your web browser, and the Java applet sets up the chat interface for you. Then, connect to the chat area at `www.geocities.com/BHI/newchat.html`.

Select one of the nine chat areas supplied. The nine rooms are assigned names that correspond to one of the neighborhoods in GeoCities. The chat page doesn't explain the theme of each group, but you can find out by consulting the list at `www.geocities.com/homestead/homedir.html`. Unfortunately, at this writing, there is no chat area set up for the Eureka neighborhood at GeoCities, which is oriented toward small businesses and home offices. By the time you read this, a Eureka chat area may be available. The available neighborhoods are described in Table 9-1:

Table 9-1	GeoCities Free Chat Areas
Chat Room	*Theme*
Heartland	Families, pets, hometown values
Colosseum	Sports and recreation
Fashion Avenue	Designers, beauty, and fashion
MotorCity	Cars, trucks, and motorcycles
Cape Canaveral	Science, math, aviation
Hollywood	Film and TV
Sunset Strip	Rock, punk, club scenes
Silicon Valley	Hardware, software, programming

These steps to set up a chat for you and your colleagues on GeoCities:

1. **Connect to the GeoCities Chat page (**www.geocities.com/BHI/ newchat.html**) and then click on the name of the group whose topic seems closest to your own interests.**

   Your web browser goes to the Expressions Login Page.

2. **In the User field, enter a name. This doesn't have to be your real name or your GeoCities username, if you have one. The name that you enter can be an alias. Then click on the triangle next to the Client field and choose the level of Java sophistication that you want to experience when you enter the chat room. Users with direct or very fast connections are wise to Java. Others can go for Java Light (the more powerful the Java, the slower everything appears on-screen). Then click on the Chat Now! button.**

   You go immediately to the chat area you selected. The Java applet may take a while to initialize and execute — your browser is actually interpreting and processing the Java program and functioning like a mini-computer. (On my 28.8 Kbps modem, it takes a full minute for the chat area to appear.) After the Java program does its stuff, you see a typical chat room screen like the one shown in Figure 9-1.

Current chat messages

Available chat rooms

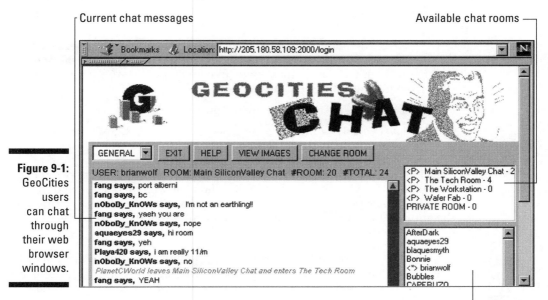

Figure 9-1: GeoCities users can chat through their web browser windows.

Currently connected users

Creating a private room

If you and your colleagues are all connected to the same GeoCities chat area, one of the participants can create a private room to carry on confidential business conversations. If you create a private chat room, you select your own name for that room. Then, you give the name to the other users so that they can join you there.

To create a private room, follow these steps:

1. **When you connect to a GeoCities chat room and there's an active chat session taking place, click on the words PRIVATE ROOM in the available chat rooms area on the right side of your web browser window.**

   The words PRIVATE ROOM are highlighted in black.

2. **Click on the Change Room button just above the chat message area.**

   The Enter Private Room dialog box appears.

3. **In the Room Name field, enter a name for the private room that you want to create. Then click on OK.**

   The Enter Private Room dialog box closes and you go to the new private room you just created. Since only you know the name of this room, you must invite other users into the room by sending them a private message.

4. **Re-enter the main chat area, click on the name(s) of the users that you want to join you, and type a message at the bottom of the screen. Send them a message like** Come join me in the WaterCooler chat area. **Then click on the Send button.**

   Your message is sent to the invited guests.

5. **Guests can follow the preceding Steps 1 through 3, and enter the name of your private room in order to join you there.**

The GeoCities chat area has lots of advantages — all free and easy. You can chat without leaving the comfort of your familiar web browser. You don't have to install special chat software, and you don't even have to go through the effort of becoming a GeoCities member, although that process is free and doesn't take that much time, either.

You don't have to provide information and run business discussions in order to get into chat. You can listen in on discussions and provide useful advice and help, just as with discussion groups. See Chapter 8 on how to market yourself through helpful participation in online talk groups.

Using America Online's discussions

If you have an account with America Online, it's quite easy to duplicate the process of setting up a private chat area on GeoCities, as described previously. Just connect to America Online, and then follow these steps:

1. **Click on People Connection in the America Online main window (or type Ctrl+K) and enter the keyword** Lobby.

   You go immediately to one of AOL's Town Square chat sessions, which is in progress. Your name appears in the box beneath People Here on the right side of the Town Square chat window, which contains a list of participants in the window.

2. **Click on the List Chats button.**

   The Public Rooms dialog box appears.

3. **Click on the Private Room button.**

   The Enter a Private Room dialog box appears (as shown in Figure 9-2).

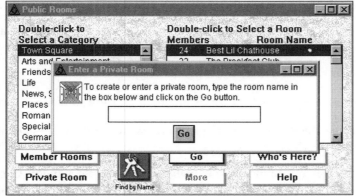

Figure 9-2: Setting up a private chat area is easy on AOL.

4. **Enter a name for the room that you want to create and click on Go.**

   A message appears in the main chat window notifying you that you have entered the chat room.

5. **Invite people into your private room by telling them the room's name. You send them what AOL calls an Instant Message. To send an Instant Message (or IM), simply select Send Instant Message from the Members menu, type each screen name in the To: field, type your message, and send it.**

   Your guests receive the message immediately and are able to reply directly to you.

Case study: The Motley Fool

The greatest success story to surface from an online business's use of chat and publication of good information comes from the Motley Fool, an investment discussion group started in 1994 by the brothers Tom and David Gardner. The Motley Fool started out as an online magazine on America Online (keyword **Fool**), and chats are still held regularly on AOL. Today, The Motley Fool employs more than 130 people, and earns revenue mostly through online advertising. Its Web site (www.fool.com) is tops among the popular investment sites on the Internet.

"I think the first move for the Web is not necessarily cool new applications in full-motion video, but rather, simple message boards that are very easy to use — as well as some sort of elegant chat applications." —Tom Gardner, from an interview in *EBusiness Magazine* (hpcc920.external.hp.com/Ebusiness/february/fool.html).

Setting up a private CompuServe forum

You and your colleagues connect to the same forum at a prearranged time. One person initiates a private discussion and invites the others to join in. Essentially, you're using your connection to CompuServe and the already-provided forum to hold a private business meeting. If you and your coworkers or clients are connected to CompuServe, the private forum can be a cost-effective alternative to long-distance phone calls.

CompuServe sets up these kinds of meetings. Here's how to get into one:

1. **From the main CompuServe window, select Services⇨Forums.**

   The Chat window appears.

2. **Click on one of the chat channels, such as the old standby, General Chat.**

   The chat window opens. The tracking dialog box contains a list of the current participants.

3. **Click on the Invite button in the Forum toolbox.**

   The Invite... dialog box appears.

4. **Check the box next to each of the participants you want to include. Then click on Invite.**

   The Conversation dialog box appears, and you can start typing messages to the invited guests.

Chatting with NetMeeting or Conference

The latest versions of Microsoft and Netscape's browsers enable you to chat as well as audio- and videoconference. You can connect to Internet Relay Chat or intranet chat sites using Net Meeting or Conference rather than relying on specialized software. Why? Convenience. You don't have to switch back and forth between your browser and another specialized chat program.

If you have Conference running, simply click on the Chat tool in the toolbar button to open up a chat window.

If you have NetMeeting running, With the Current Call tab active, click on the Chat toolbar button or select Tools⇨Chat to open up the Chat window.

One advantage of having a chat session with your Conference or NetMeeting participants is that you have a visual record of the chat messages that you exchange. Each program enables you to keep a log or record of the conversations you have. The messages are displayed in the text area in the upper half of the Conference Text Chat dialog box (the Chat Log). In NetMeeting, you review your conversations by clicking on the History tab.

Having a PowWow on the Web

Another interesting chat alternative on the Internet is PowWow. PowWow, by Tribal Voice, is a program that enables up to nine people to chat, transfer files, and cruise the World-Wide Web together. The program is available for Windows 3.1 and higher; check it out at www.tribal.com/powwow.

Setting up a Chat Server

The Chat Server, from Magma Communications Ltd., runs on Windows 95, NT, UNIX, and other platforms (chat.magmacom.com). Memory requirements are pretty heavy: Each chat room guest requires 8MB of RAM. The other thing that's heavy about the Chat Server is its price tag: The program costs $2,100 Canadian (approximately $1,550 U.S.).

Other Ways to Get Together

With a connection to the Internet, you can broadcast your voice or smiling face, share drawings and applications, exchange files, and collaborate in lots of ways that can save you money and time.

Internet Phone

VocalTec's product, Internet Phone, helps businesses communicate cost-efficiently across the country or around the world by using the Internet.

You can download a one-week (Windows) or two-week (Macintosh) demo version of Internet Phone from the VocalTec Communications Web site (www.vocaltec.com/download.htm). To use Internet Phone, you need a PC running Windows 3.1 or later or a Power Macintosh or compatible running System 7 or later. The Windows 95 version requires a 486 PC, 33 MHz (66 MHz for full duplex), and 8MB RAM (12MB recommended). The Mac version requires Power Macintosh or compatible 8MB RAM, System 7.5.1 or higher, Mac TCP 2.0.6 or Open Transport 1.1, QuickTime 2.1 or later, and Sound Manager 3.1 or later. Both platforms require a sound card, speakers, microphone, and TCP/IP connection to the Internet.

Creating a business presence with Internet Phone

Internet Phone gives potential customers another way to find and interact with you online. First, you enter your organization's name and contact window. Here's how:

1. **After you download and set up the software, connect to the Internet to check out Internet Phone's online global phone directory. Then double-click on the Internet Phone icon to start up the program.**

   The Audio Test dialog box appears. You can click on the Start Test button and speak into your computer microphone to test the quality of your sound output and make sure that your sound card and microphone are working correctly.

2. **When you're done, click on OK.**

   The main Internet Phone window appears (shown in Figure 9-3), followed by the Internet Phone Global OnLine Directory. This directory lists all the Internet Phone users around the world who are currently connected to the Internet and can receive phone calls. Just scrolling through the list of users may give you an idea of how using your computer as a telephone can help you connect with the entire world.

Figure 9-3:
Internet
Phone
enables you
to send and
receive
calls
worldwide.

3. **Before you start looking through the phone directory for someone to call, it's a good idea to enter your own personal information first, so that people can know something about you. Click on the Internet Phone window to bring it to the front, and select View⇨Options.**

   The Internet Phone Options dialog box appears.

4. **Click on the User icon.**

   The User Options tab comes to the front of the Internet Phone Options dialog box (shown in Figure 9-4). Enter information about your business. In the Comment field, enter a few words that describe what you do. Entering your user information is important because other Internet telephone users can learn something about you and how they may contact you.

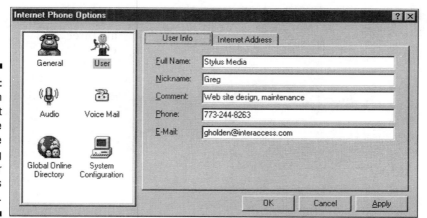

Figure 9-4:
Create an
Internet
phone
presence
by adding
your
organization's
data here.

5. **Click on OK to close Internet User Options and return to the main Internet Phone window. Now you can scroll through the list of users in the Global OnLine Directory (see Figure 9-5) and check your own listing. Click on the listing for TEST YOUR IPHONE HERE.**

A list of users who also want to test their Internet Phone appears.

Figure 9-5:
This
directory
contains
Internet
Phone
users you
can call.

6. **To make a call, click on a user's name in the directory and click on the Call button (or choose User➪Call).**

Internet Phone can make the call for you; turn up your speakers or put on your headphones, and say hello.

If you have a direct connection to the Net, consider leaving your Internet Phone software connected all the time, so that people can always see you in the list of users. Even if they can't reach you, people see your contact information (such as your Web URL and phone number), and they may think about contacting you again the next time they use Internet Phone.

You can use Internet Phone set up your own chat area.

1. **Choose Chat Room➪New/Private from the main Internet Phone window.**

The New Chat Room dialog box opens.

2. **Type in a name for a new Chat Room in the Name edit box, and then click on the OK button. If you wish to join a Private Chat Room, make sure that the Private Chat Room box is checked. (Remember that the other person you want to speak with must know the exact name of the Private Chat Room to meet you there.)**

   This creates the new Chat Room. If the Chat Room already exists because one of your colleagues has created it, you can simply join it.

Internet Phone, of course, is only one way to use your computer as a telephone. For more suggestions, see the helpful document by Kevin Savetz at www.northcoast.com/voice-faq.html.

Looking up phone numbers

If you're looking for someone in particular, or if you prefer to talk to a stranger, you can look for other conference users by checking a directory server. NetMeeting, Conference, and Internet Phone all connect you to their own directory servers, but you can connect to other servers if you know their names. Netscape's is dls.netscape.com and Microsoft's is ils.microsoft.com.

Using Conference and NetMeeting for phone calls

Both Netscape Conference and Microsoft NetMeeting enable you to conduct audio conversations on the Net through your computer. The same basic rules for using Internet Phone apply when you're using one of these programs: It's a good idea to enter information about your business in the user information area that appears on the directory server to which you're connected. Also consider being connected at all times so that people are aware that your company exists and can be reached by audioconferencing.

In either application, the first step is to find the person who you want to call. That person has to be connected to the Net and have either Conference or NetMeeting running. Then you can call that individual in one of three ways:

✔ Enter the IP address of the person's computer directly, if you know it.

✔ Look for someone in a Web Phonebook, otherwise known as a directory server (both Netscape and Microsoft connect you to their own servers when you run their conferencing programs). Usually, you can click on the name to select it and then click on the Call toolbar button.

✔ Use Speed Dialing to call an individual whose number you stored in the program's personal address book.

Just as you can get junk e-mail, you can get junk Internet phone calls. Most conferencing software includes a Do Not Disturb feature that enables you to block out calls from people you don't want to talk to. Whether you're using NetMeeting or Conference, the menu command is exactly the same: Select Call⇨Do Not Disturb. Be sure to select Do Not Disturb again to de-select it when you're ready to make yourself available to phone calls once again.

Having your computer take messages

Netscape Conference notifies you of any incoming calls you receive while you're away from your computer. You don't have to be up and running and connected to the Internet to receive voice mail. The message is stored in your e-mail Inbox or other folder until you retrieve it with other e-mail messages.

The person who was trying to reach you records a message. The recorded message is sent as an attachment to a regular e-mail message. When you open the e-mail message with Netscape Messenger, the attachment plays automatically.

Audio files can take up a good deal of room on your computer, and if you don't expect to listen to the message again, you can delete it. To delete a voice mail message, select the message by clicking on its subject line in the message folder in which it's contained. Then press the Delete key on your keyboard (or click on the Delete button in the toolbar of the Messenger window you're in). The message is transferred to the Trash folder. When you empty the Trash, you save space.

Advanced conferencing with browser tools

If you're interested in going beyond the basic, low-bandwidth varieties of online conferencing like chat and Internet phone, the conferencing applications that come with Netscape Communicator and Microsoft Internet Explorer are the most convenient tools you can use. If you're out surfing the Web or checking your e-mail and you want to talk to someone face to face (or voice to voice), all you need to do is click on a menu to switch from the Internet application you're in to the conferencing application.

Netscape's tool for conferencing is called Netscape Conference, while Microsoft offers conference connections with NetMeeting. Both programs operate in similar ways and provide roughly the same features:

- ✔ Chat
- ✔ Audioconferencing/Internet telephoning
- ✔ Videoconferencing
- ✔ File transfers between conference participants
- ✔ A whiteboard that enables participants in a conference to view files and send drawings to one another as illustration of what they're talking about

The programs' features differ. Conference offers collaborative surfing, which enables a group of users to surf around the Web together. NetMeeting enables users to share applications while they're connected.

Installing Conference and NetMeeting

The first step to enjoying the benefits of advanced conferencing is to make sure that you have Conference or NetMeeting installed. Conference does come with both the standard and professional editions of Netscape Communicator — if you downloaded the program from the Web or installed it from a CD, you probably have Conference. With any one of Communicator's programs running, click on the Communicator menu. Conference appears in the list of menu items.

NetMeeting only comes with the full version Microsoft Internet Explorer, which is available in minimal, standard, and full. If you didn't install the full version of Internet Explorer 4.0 because the program is simply too large (22MB) to download from the Web, you can download NetMeeting separately from `www.microsoft.com/netmeeting`.

You can run Conference or NetMeeting as a stand-alone application without starting up your web browser or other tools in order to conserve your computer's supply of RAM (Random Access Memory).

Using Netscape Conference

Netscape Conference gives you a pretty simple interface. The toolbar buttons provide you with the easiest way to get into the program's various functions, as shown in Figure 9-6.

Whiteboard button

Collaborative Browsing button

File Exchange button

Chat button

Figure 9-6: Netscape Conference's main window.

When you first install Conference, you see the window shown in Figure 9-6. In order to find someone to speak with, you can enter the person's e-mail address in the Email Address field and then click on the Call button. You can also click on the Address Book button if the person with whom you want to speak is included in your Netscape Communicator Address Book.

Using Microsoft NetMeeting

Microsoft operates a little differently than Conference. When you first start up NetMeeting, you're connected with Microsoft's Directory Server (ils.microsoft.com). All of the NetMeeting users around the world who are currently connected to the Internet and who are also connected to Microsoft's server are listed in the main NetMeeting window. You can access NetMeeting's chat, whiteboard, and file exchange functions from the Tools menu, as shown in Figure 9-7.

Microsoft NetMeeting's popularity can be measured in the length of time that it takes for a list of users to appear in its entirety. Many of the users have the X-rated or childish nicknames and comments that populate chat sites all over cyberspace.

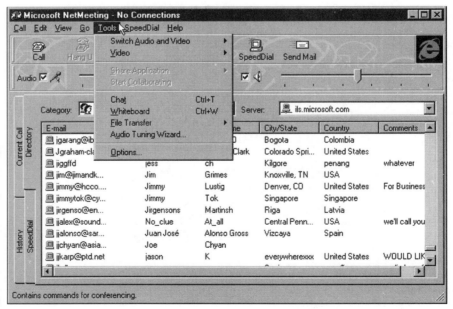

Figure 9-7:
A long
list of
NetMeeting
users
greets you
when you
start up the
program.

Other videoconferencing options

You don't have to use Microsoft's or Netscape's tools to conduct videoconferencing on the Internet. Here are some other options you can consider.

CU-SeeMe

One of the better and more popular programs for videoconferencing is called CU-SeeMe. This software, developed at Cornell University, has been available for the Mac for several years; a Windows version is now on the market as well. One nice thing about CU-SeeMe is that it's designed to work with low-bandwidth connections such as dial-up modems. See Chapter 4 for more information.

Kinko's

It's not an Internet solution to videoconferencing, but it may help in a pinch: Many branches of Kinko's can provide you with a videoconferencing site. Call 1-800-669-1235 for more information.

MBONE

When you start getting into the world of conferencing on the Net, you may hear the word MBONE being thrown around casually. MBONE stands for Multicast Backbone on the Internet — a virtual network that receives real-time video or other communications and distributes the signals to other points on the network. In order to receive MBONE broadcasts, you need to ask your Internet provider if it receives MBONE. A direct T1 or other fast Internet connection is recommended.

Whiteboards

Sometimes it's convenient to be able to see the things(s) you're speaking or chatting about, and sometimes you just have to draw a picture (which is, after all, worth a *lot* of words). Conference and NetMeeting both include a whiteboard that enables you and anyone with whom you're talking to share images and even interactively mark them up.

Both programs offer assistance for the artistically impaired by providing ways to capture images from your computer desktop, as well as loading images loaded from disk.

Conference and NetMeeting both include a basic set of drawing tools that resemble simple computer painting programs. NetMeeting's Whiteboard is shown in Figure 9-8.

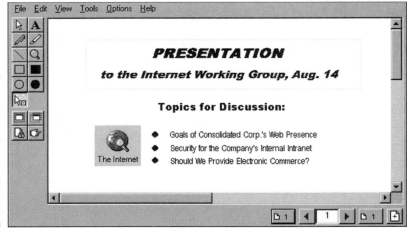

Figure 9-8:
Whiteboards
enable you
to illustrate
points and
create
drawings
while you
talk online.

Collaborative Web surfing

Conference not only gives you the ability to carry on voice conversations over the Internet, but also enables you to lead the person to whom you're speaking around the Net by controlling his or her copy of Netscape Navigator. The freedom to guide others can be a great way to teach someone how to use the Net or to direct someone to interesting Web sites. Conceivably, you can use the tour feature to conduct presentations over the Internet, leading remote viewers to sites around the Net by controlling their computers.

File transfers with NetMeeting or Conference

Usually, you can send files to other people across the Internet by transmitting the file to an FTP site or attaching the file to an e-mail message and sending it to the recipient of your choice.

Both NetMeeting and Conference give users another way to send text files, images, or entire applications back and forth, using The File Exchange Tool. This tool is especially convenient if you're talking to someone with Conference or Chat, and you mention a file that you want to send.

The results of making yourself available for real-time communications are similar to those of entering newsgroups or using e-mail: You make more contacts, and you get more visits to your Web pages. In addition, you and your staff are able to communicate in groups more easily. Your off-site employees are able to keep in touch with you, too. You can chat or conference with suppliers and partners in other countries. Expect your long-distance phone bill to decrease and your productivity to increase.

Part IV
Securing Your Business

"THIS SECURITY PROGRAM WILL RESPOND TO THREE THINGS:
AN INCORRECT ACCESS CODE, AN INAPPROPRIATE FILE REQUEST,
OR SOMETIMES A CRAZY HUNCH THAT MAYBE YOU'RE JUST
ANOTHER SLIME-BALL WITH MISAPPROPRIATION OF SECURED
DATA ON HIS MIND."

In this part . . .

Any business needs to protect its valuables, and information is what's really valuable on the Internet.

This part describes the security measures that are available to your small business and are rapidly making the Internet a secure place for sales transactions.

Chapter 10

Locking the Doors: Internet Security

In This Chapter

▶ Using certificates to verify your own and others' identities

▶ Protecting your computers from viruses, Trojan Horses, and other infectious diseases

▶ Encrypting your private e-mail and news messages

▶ Restricting access to your local network through firewalls and proxy servers

▶ Using IP filtering and authentication to keep out unwanted visitors

*W*hen you open a door that enables you and your employees to explore the Internet, you also put out the welcome mat to villains who may use your company's information for unscrupulous purposes. Even if your small business uses only one or two computers to connect to the Net, you need to be aware of some potential threats that can invade your computers.

Large businesses have large security concerns. Many use dedicated Internet connections to provide a gateway so that employees and colleagues can access their internal networks from the Net. Organizations don't want information to be available to their competitors or to unauthorized visitors. Businesses also want to keep personnel information confidential.

Concerns for Small Business Owners

For small businesses such as yours, security problems may be less severe but still need to be taken seriously.

Viruses can affect any computer that's used to download information from the online world. Credit card numbers, phone numbers, and other personal information can also be accessed by clever and unscrupulous criminals who send fraudulent e-mail messages.

Besides the potential for having your data stolen or damaged, as an Internet user you need to know something about how to keep your communications secure. A relatively new set of tools is available to ensure your identity and encrypt the messages that you send on the Net.

Even if your business only consists of one or two employees and the amount of information that you make accessible to the Internet is small, you can still use Internet security methods with the following goals in mind:

✔ Ensuring the correct identity of the Internet users with whom you correspond by using personal certificates

✔ Keeping private messages private by using encryption

✔ Protecting your computers and your data by installing virus scanning software

✔ Setting up a firewall and/or proxy server to help keep your internal network secure

✔ Making sure that only authorized users can access your office servers by requiring passwords

✔ Setting up your server so that it only provides access to computers with approved IP addresses

Problem? What problem?

Half the battle with protecting yourself is simply being aware of potential problems you may encounter, and what measures you can take to prevent them. Here are a few sample scenarios of what can happen when you connect to the Internet.

Viruses and macros

Whenever you connect to a Web site, you're downloading files to your computer. When you get your new e-mail messages, it's more than likely that you download them to your hard disk, as well as any files that are attached to them. Viruses can infect your computer during the download.

Not long ago, a virus infected the popular software program Microsoft Word. Microsoft issued software to eliminate the virus, but the contamination is still in circulation. While I was writing a previous book, my editor's computer was infected by a virus that caused her to lose files, and ultimately forced her to work in another office while her equipment was being repaired.

You also have to be concerned about the possibility that the Java applet or Active X control that you download and view in your web browser window may somehow invade your computer and destroy your data. Although security is being developed to keep these programs from being harmful, it's not impossible that a mean-spirited programmer may find a way to include, within the Java applet or Active X control, a program that harms your files in some way.

The solution: Every computer that's connected to the Net needs to have anti-virus software installed. Some good programs are listed in Chapter 4.

Keeping track of who's who

The Internet is a great place to meet people. But how do you know for sure who you're dealing with? Can you rely on the information people are putting forth? How do you know that people are who they say they are when all you have to go on is a URL or an e-mail address? Fraud can and does occur on the Net. People misrepresenting themselves as network administrators, for instance, ask customers for their usernames and passwords. They may easily pretend to be an authority and give out false information.

In the real world, someone checks out your identity and the government issues you a passport or a state ID. The solution in the online world: Obtain a personal certificate that you can send to Web site visitors or append to your e-mail messages.

Theft

Hackers, crackers, and phreaks are computer and telephone geeks who love to snoop on people. After they get access, they can raid passwords, addresses, phone numbers, job titles, and other personal information. They can also look through your files and copy information about your company.

Protect Yourself

Whether you're a one-person operation or a manager of employees who work in two or three different offices, to protect your computer and your identity when you go online. Here are some easy ways.

Picking good passwords

Passwords play an essential role in connecting to the Net, downloading software, subscribing to online publications, and other basic online activities. Here are some tips for picking passwords that thieves won't be able to crack.

A good method for choosing a password is to take an easy-to-remember phrase, and use the first letters of each word to form the basis of a password. Add punctuation and mix case letters to get a secure password. For example, take Special Report on High Technology, mix upper- and lowercase, and add punctuation to wind up with SRo]hT[.

- ✓ **Don't use the same password at more than one site.** If your password to one site on the Internet is compromised, your accounts at all other sites that use the same password can be affected, too. It's especially important not to use the password to an account to a commercial service like America Online or CompuServe as a password for an Internet site, unless you're willing to pay for someone else's ride on your service.

- ✓ **Don't use passwords that are in a dictionary.** Most passwords are stored on a host machine in encrypted form. If an intruder gains access to stored passwords, the simple encryption that protects the password is hard for a noncryptographer to break. It's (relatively) easy, however, to encrypt an online dictionary (like a spell checker) using common coding schemes and compare the words in the encrypted dictionary to the stolen encrypted passwords. If the hacker finds a match, your password is known. The point: Use a string of characters that's not in a dictionary.

- ✓ **Use at least six characters.** This makes code-crackers go through a lot more work.

- ✓ **Use capital and small letters.** This makes your password harder to crack, too.

One way to choose a good password is to make the letters of the password correspond to a phrase that you know well, such as The Charge of the Light Brigade. The password would be TCOTLB. Then add punctuation and mix case letters to get a secure password, such as TcOT]LB?.

Understanding Secure Sockets Layer

Secure Sockets Layer is probably the most widespread security method on the Internet. The term layer in Secure Sockets Layer is used because SSL is implemented at an intermediate stage between TCP/IP (the protocol for Internet communications) and application protocols such as HTTP (the protocol for the transmission on the Web).

Public and private keys

SSL uses a technology called *public key cryptography,* with software licensed from RSA Data Security, Inc. Public key cryptography uses a set of two keys, called the *public key* and the *private key,* and both must be used for the encoding/decoding process.

A message encoded with the private key can only be decoded with the public key, and a message encoded with the public key can only be decoded with the private key. Public keys are widely distributed, and private keys are never exchanged. If you want to send a coded message to your friend, you use *your friend's* public key (which your friend has distributed) to code the message. Only your friend has the private key to read the message.

When you read a secure Web page, the page is encrypted with the private key of the Web site that's serving that page. The public key is sent along with the page, and Netscape uses the public key to decode the page. Data transmitted to the server is encrypted with the public key from the server.

You can obtain a private key that's linked to the public key that you can send to other individuals or companies on the Net as part of your personal certificate, also called a Digital ID.

Certificates and digital signatures

Certificates are an important part of conducting secure transactions on the Internet. When you're communicating via a computer network and you can't ask someone for an ID card, you need to have confidence that customers or vendors are who they say they are. Certificates are supposed to do that.

A certificate, also commonly called a Digital ID, is an electronic document that's issued by a certifying agency. The agency states that the owner of the document matches the identification on the certificate. There is an electronic component to a certificate, too, in the form of your public key, which is included with the certificate. But certificates do require you to put a level of trust in the certificate issuer.

Technically, a certificate can be anything that documents the relationship between a person or organization and a public key. In practice, there's a widely used standard for the organization of certificate information into a file format that can be used by many programs on many different platforms: These files are called X.509 certificates. The X.509 standard is used by Netscape and many other encryption tools, such as Apple's developing PowerTalk technology and the public domain encryption programs PGP (Pretty Good Privacy) and MacPGP.

Obtaining a personal certificate

The VeriSign, Inc. Web site (www.verisign.com/) is the place to apply for a certificate called a Class 1 Digital ID. A personal certificate, which you can use to authenticate yourself in e-mail, news, and other interactions on the Net, costs $10, and you can try out a free certificate for six months. Follow these steps to obtain your Digital ID:

1. **Connect to the VeriSign, Inc. home page at the URL given above. Click on the triangle to the right of the box labeled Get Your Digital ID Now! and select an option from the drop-down menu. It's simplest to select the Digital ID Center button. Click on the Go! button.**

   The VeriSign Digital ID Center page appears. (The direct URL is digitalid.verisign.com/.)

2. **Click on the Request an ID button.**

   The Digital ID Enrollment page appears.

3. **Pick the type of ID you want: You can choose one that works with Netscape or Microsoft's web browsers, with e-mail programs, or with servers. Click on the link for the type of ID you want.**

   It's a good idea to pick browsers, since you can use a basic ID when you visit Web sites and when you want to send or receive secure e-mail. When you select either Netscape or Microsoft, you go to the Select Digital ID Class page. This page tells you that a regular Digital ID costs $9.95, while a Digital ID plus, which has a higher level of security, costs $19.95. However, you can get a free six-month trial version of the regular Digital ID.

4. **Click on Free Trial Class 1 Digital ID.**

   An application form for a Digital ID appears. The application process is pretty simple. First, you're asked for your personal information and a challenge phrase that you can use in case anyone is trying to imperson-ate you. You're required to accept a license agreement as well.

5. **When you're done filling out the application form, click on the Accept button at the bottom of the screen.**

   A dialog box appears asking you to submit a request for Netscape Navigator or Microsoft Internet Explorer to generate your private key. The private key is an essential ingredient in public/private key technol-ogy. Your browser generates the private key, you enter your password, and your Digital ID is generated and registered with VeriSign.

6. **Click OK to have your browser generate your private key.**

   You download the ID from VeriSign and to view it with Navigator.

After you have your Digital ID, what do you do with it? One thing that you can do is submit your certificate to a site instead of sending the usual username and password. After you obtain a certificate, you can try out one of the demos on the VeriSign Web site to see how this works. Figure 10-1 shows the dialog box that enables you to exchange certificates with a fictional human resources department on VeriSign's Web site.

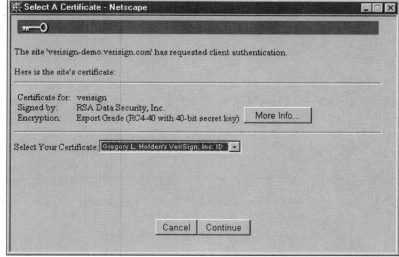

Figure 10-1:
You can exchange your Digital ID with sites that also use certificates.

Another thing that you can do with a certificate is send it along with e-mail messages, as explained in the following section.

You cannot encrypt nor digitally sign messages on any computer but the one to which your certificates are issued. If you're using a computer other than the one you used when you obtained your certificates, you must obtain a new certificate for the computer you're now using, or export your certificate to the new computer if your browser allows transfers.

Encrypting your e-mail messages

The method of Internet security being adopted by most information providers is *encryption:* coding transmissions to and from a remote server so that your sensitive information is rendered unreadable to thieves and snoopers.

After you obtain a personal certificate, you can send it along with e-mail messages to users whose e-mail software supports S/MIME (Secure Multipurpose Internet Mail Extensions).

Sending secure messages with Netscape Messenger

If you use Netscape Messenger, the e-mail application that comes with Netscape Communicator, you can use your Digital ID to

- ✔ **Send a digital signature.** You can digitally shrink-wrap your e-mail message using your certificate in order to assure the recipient that the message is really from you.

- ✔ **Encrypt your message.** You can digitally encode a message to ensure that only the intended party can read it.

To better understand how to keep your e-mail communications secure, read the online Secure E-Mail Reference Guide, which you can access at www.verisign.com/smime/nsemail.html.

If you use Netscape Messenger, follow these steps to encrypt or include your certificate with your e-mail messages:

1. **With Messenger running, click on the Security button in the toolbar of any of the Messenger windows.**

   A security information dialog box appears.

2. **Click on any of the highlighted word Messenger in the list on the left side of the security dialog box.**

   The following security options are displayed in the right half of the dialog box:

   - Encrypt your e-mail messages

   - Sign your e-mail messages with your Digital ID

   - Sign your discussion group messages with your Digital ID

3. **In order to activate Messenger's security features, check one or more of the check boxes. Then Click OK.**

   The security dialog box closes. You return to the Messenger window that you were in previously.

By checking one or more of the options in the Security dialog box, you activate Messenger's built-in security features for all your outgoing messages. In order to actually verify or undo those features (that is, if you want a message to be unencrypted or to be sent without a digital signature), you need to follow these additional steps:

Follow these steps to attach a digital signature to a message:

1. **With any Messenger window (Inbox, Message Center, or Message) open, click on the New Msg toolbar button.**

   The Message Composition window appears.

2. **In the Address area of the Message Composition window, click on the Message Sending Options button, which appears at the bottom of the three buttons on the left side of the Message area.**

   The Message Sending Options appear. If you clicked on the Encryption option in the Security dialog box earlier, the box next to Encrypted has a check box in it. If you clicked on the certificate option in the Security dialog box, the box next to Signed has a check box in it.

3. **If you want to undo either of these options, click on the check box.**

   The check box disappears.

4. **You can now address and write your message and then click on the Send button in the Message Composition toolbar.**

   Your encrypted or digitally signed message is sent on its way.

Sending secure messages with Outlook Express

Microsoft Outlook Express also enables you to send encrypted and digitally signed messages. The steps are similar to those for Messenger:

1. **After you obtain your own Digital ID, open Outlook Express and then click on the Address Book button in the Outlook Express toolbar.**

   The Address Book opens.

2. **Click on the name of the person that you want to receive your Digital ID. (If the person is not yet included in your Address Book, you need to create a new listing.) Then click on the Properties toolbar button.**

   The Properties dialog box for that user appears.

3. **Click on the Certificates tab to bring it to the front, and then click on the Import... button.**

   The Select Certificate File To Import dialog box appears.

4. **Locate your certificate file on your hard disk, click on its name, and then click the Open button.**

   The Select Certificate File To Import dialog box closes, and you return to the Properties dialog box, where your certificate appears in the box labeled Certificates Associated with the Selected E-Mail Address.

5. **Click OK.**

   The Properties dialog box closes and you return to the Address Book window.

6. **Select your recipient's name by clicking on it. Then click on the Send Mail toolbar button.**

   The New Message dialog box appears.

7. **Click on either, or both, of the security buttons at the extreme right of the toolbar. Digitally Sign Message enables you to add your Digital ID. Encrypt Message enables you to encrypt it.**

8. **Finish writing your message, and then click on the Send button.**

Your encrypted or digitally signed message is sent on its way.

Installing a personal firewall

If you're really serious about securing your own single computer, consider a product called eSafe Protect (www.eprotect.com/index.html). This product prevents any personal information from leaving your computer without your permission. You can also filter out any sites that you don't want to access, making this feature suitable for a childproofing filter if your kids also use the same computer you use.

The product is available for Windows 95 only. You can download a demo version. eSafe Technologies boasts that its product provides "a solution for every known or unknown threat coming from the Internet." The next few sections provide a brief overview of eSafe Protect's main features.

Resource Protection is a common way to protect your computer or network from unwanted visitors from the Internet. By clicking on the Resource Protection button at the top of the eSafe Protect main window (shown in Figure 10-2) you're presented with options that enable you to restrict access to files or directories on a computer.

As you see in Figure 10-2, you can specify that files or directories on your computer have any of five types of access:

- **Read.** Certain items can be read-only: The information can be reviewed, but no changes can be made.

- **Write.** The contents can be changed. This is particularly useful for a shared computer like a web server; you can allow visitors to only read files and not to change them.

- **Execute.** Programs can be run from the directory.

- **Create.** Someone with Create access can make new files and directories.

- **Delete.** Someone with Delete access can delete files and directories.

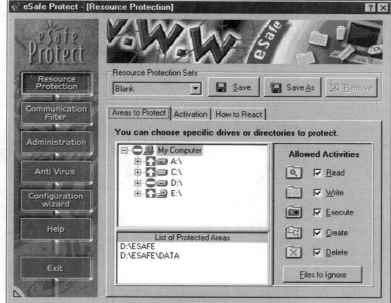

Figure 10-2:
eSafe
Protect
gives you
this set of
options and
lets you
protect files
on your
computer.

Communication filter

A common function of many firewall programs is to restrict access by identifying the IP address of computers that can either gain access or be shut out. An IP address is a set of four numbers that identifies your computer uniquely while it's connected to the Net.

eSafe Protect enables you to filter IP addresses by entering addresses in the Personal Firewall tab of the Communication Filter window (shown in Figure 10-3).

You can also prevent access to Web sites by specifying words in the URL or e-mail address, in the Forbidden Words tab. The Secret Info tab enables you to identify information on your computer that you don't want to transmit anywhere else.

eSafe Protect gives you plenty of virus-scanning options when you click on the Anti-Virus button. You can scan specific files or directories, or set up the program so that it checks your computer or a specific application every time it starts up — though this constant checking can be time-consuming, or course. See eSafe's Help file for the full range of virus-protection options.

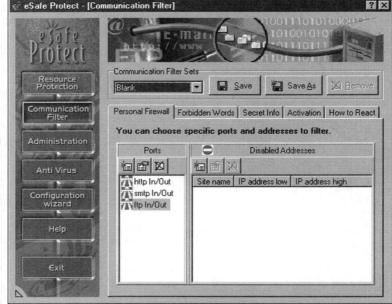

Figure 10-3:
You can
identify
computers
to access
or keep out
of your
computer in
this set of
options.

Protecting Your Office Network

After you protect your own computer, you may decide to take an additional
step and set up security measures to protect your internal office network
from being infiltrated by unwanted visitors from the Internet. The best
protection an organization has against the Internet hacker is a competent,
well-informed systems administrator. If you're the administrator, read on.

Keeping your Web site separate

For the ultimate Internet security experience, you can keep your local
network physically separate from the rest of cyberspace. Separation is
possible if you keep your Web site and other information on your ISP's web
server, without any connection to your office. That way, millions of people
can find out about your company, while your private corporate information
is kept off the Internet altogether.

Of course, this is no fun, either; you and your employees can't get to the
Internet to use it from your office. In that case, some alternative lines of
defense are needed. The simplest alternative is to only connect to the Net

through a dial-up modem, surf the Web or the rest of the Net for only as long as you need to, and then disconnect. For most small businesses with only a dial-up connection to the Internet, this amount of security is adequate.

If your company has a dedicated Internet connection, your network is available to the outside world 24 hours a day. This constant connection makes it wise to look into some simple security measures like firewalls and proxies.

Setting up a line of defense

Firewalls and proxies are computers and software programs that stand between your internal computer(s) and the wider Internet. Routers are hardware that enable a group of computers to access the Internet or another network. Each of these devices provides a single gateway into or out of your network, as shown in Figure 10-5.

The configuration shown in Figure 10-5 is only one possible setup for a perimeter network that stands between your internal network and the Internet. Some companies take the additional step of using two routers, one on either side of the bastion host. You can discuss which setup may be right for you by posing a question to the computer consultants who participate in the Firewalls mailing list. Send an e-mail message to majordomo@greatcircle.com. Put this single line in the mail message: **info firewalls**.

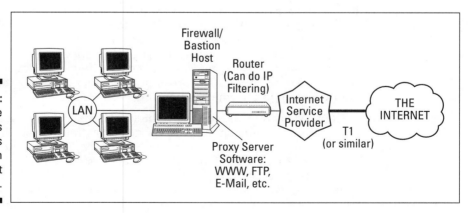

Figure 10-4: Where firewalls and proxies fit in an Internet connection.

Case study: Garden Escape, Inc.

Garden Escape is a company with 25 employees who work in its home office in Austin, Texas, and in two branch offices in other states. The company needs to maintain its security, especially because it has extensive information on customers who have made online purchases. Garden Escape also needs to provide its office staff in all locations, as well as the company's 35 suppliers, access to the organization's extensive intranet. Protection and accessibility are achieved through software that grants access privileges only to approved users or to computers with certain domain names. Suppliers can access the intranet and update their own inventories and manage orders themselves because they're granted a level of access that enables them to enter data in certain directories. This transfer of responsibility takes some of the burden of data entry off a staff that's relatively small.

Internet intermediaries

When you have a single entry/exit point, you can monitor who is or is not allowed into your network. You can also require that people enter by typing in approved usernames and passwords. Some of the security devices you're likely to set up (or have your systems administrator set up) include:

- **Firewalls.** Firewalls can be software programs or actual computers that are designated to serve as a company's gateway between the Internet and a local network. A computer that performs this function is sometimes called a *bastion host.*

- **Proxy servers (also called *proxy services*).** These are software programs that a firewall uses to transfer data between an internal network and the Internet. Your web browser, e-mail program, or FTP client requests a Web page, message, or program, respectively. But the proxy program that actually connects to a remote site on the Net and retrieves the data for you. The proxy program then transfers the data to your client program, which is how it gets to you.

- **Routers.** Many routers, such as WebRamp, have their own security methods for connecting to the Net. One common method is *IP Packet Filtering.* All communications on the Net use the TCP/IP protocols to transfer small batches of information, called *packets,* that are sent from one computer to another. Packet filters make sure only information from certain computers gets through the router. Many organizations use a combination of packet-filtering and proxy firewalls to achieve a higher level of security than packet-filtering alone can provide.

Counting heads and taking names

After one or more of these hardware/software options is set up, a company can also *audit* traffic to and from its server. The organization can keep track of who connects to a local network, what kinds of programs are downloaded from the Net, and act quickly if unauthorized users or programs are detected.

What's the password?

Authentication is another common security technique used in conjunction with firewalls and internal web server software. This measure involves assigning approved users an official username and password that they must enter before accessing to a protected network, computer, or directory.

Some organizations, like Speedware Corporation, Inc. (wwwdemo.speedware.com/Admin/coyote.html), enable employees to access their intranet from the external Internet, but require them to log on with an approved username and password, as shown in Figure 10-5.

The key to setting up some or all of the aforementioned security schemes is finding some user-friendly software that can help non-technical folks like you and me. Many programs are equipped to assist you. The software that enables you to set up a web server or provide information on the Internet is likely to come with its own system for setting up a user database and restricting access to its contents. Many security programs are only available for UNIX workstations or Windows NT systems. The following examples show how to set up and use one program that's available for Windows 95 as well as other systems, called WinGate Pro.

Figure 10-5:
A gateway from the Internet to a company's internal network.

Security with WinGate

WinGate, by Deerfield Communications Company, works with both Windows 95 and NT. WinGate's cheaper than firewall systems that are designed to work with UNIX workstations and networks of hundreds of machines.

The following steps show how to set up the program and some simple security features that can help your office without making your Internet experience slower and more difficult.

WinGate (www.wingate.net) comes in two versions: WinGate Pro and WinGate Lite. The Pro version has some nice additional security features that the Lite version doesn't have, such as authentication, auditing, and the ability to set up a database of approved users. WinGate Lite is appropriate for one- or two-person business users; WinGate Pro is only available for groups of five users or more. You can download a 30-day trial version of each product before purchasing it.

Setting up WinGate Pro

When you install WinGate, you first enter your user name and license key and then you come to the Basic Services screen. If you run a web server or FTP server on your office network, you need to click on the Advanced button next to each or both of the HTTP and FTP server options. You have to make sure that there is no port conflict between your server and WinGate. Enter the server's address and change the port number, if necessary.

This chapter doesn't examine every step involved in setting up WinGate, because clear instructions are included in the Help file that comes with the program. Double-click the Wingate2.hlp icon in the directory where you installed WinGate. Then follow the steps you find in the topic called Installing WinGate.

You need to assign an IP address for the machine that runs WinGate. Next, you have to set up private IP addresses for each computer on your network. Then, you specify the proxy applications that work with each of the programs that you use to access the Internet. You have to do this for every program you use, including your e-mail software, FTP program, and so on.

You have to configure each of the applications that you use to access the Internet to work with the proxy server of choice. After you perform the configuration, you won't even notice that you're using proxy applications. WinGate works transparently in the background.

Configuring WinGate Pro's security features

WinGate has a number of security features. One of them is a user database that enables WinGate to keep track of any computers that are connecting to WinGate from your internal network or from the Internet.

Restricting access to selected computers

Another way to protect your network is by selecting the machines that can gain access. You can select computers either as an alternative to authentication or in conjunction with it. You're actually using IP filtering, as mentioned earlier: You only allow access to machines from your own company or other approved users. You can also deny access to specific machines, such as a competitor's, based on that company's or individual's IP address or domain name.

An IP address is assigned to every computer that's connected to the Internet. Computers that are connected constantly, with a dedicated connection such as a T-1 line, have a static IP address — in other words, the address never changes. Computers that use a modem to dial up an ISP have an IP address that's assigned by the ISP's server — in other words, the address is different every time. An IP address consists of four single or groups of numbers separated by dots, such as 192.199.34.0. If you want to grant a supplier access to your internal network, you have to ask that supplier for the IP addresses of any machines that you want to add. WinGate enables you to use the question mark symbol as a wild card so that you can add a group of machines that are operated by the same company. For instance, a group of machines in a company may have the same first three numbers, and only the fourth number differs between each individual machine. In that case, you could use the ? symbol to grant access to all of the company's computers, like this: **192.199.34.?**.

Assigning rights

Suppose that you have an approved user who works in more than one location, such as a branch office, a client's office, or at home. In that case, you can give the user access if certain criteria are met. For instance, the user can gain access if he or she is working at machines with specific IP addresses.

WinGate's set of criteria is extensive: You can specify that the user has to enter a certain username, that the computer has to have a certain IP address, and so on. Look through the drop-down menu lists and read the Help file to get an idea of what you can do.

You can give off-site employees, as well as suppliers and contractors, access to your files. Authorized users can then work on the files remotely, taking the burden off your other staff people. You can also set up virtual workgroups that exist in separate locations: A group of writers and editors can prepare text in one location, designers can design publications in another, and so on. The point of Internet security is not to simply exclude people but make it possible to *include* select users without worrying about losing data or damaging files because of viruses.

Windows NT's built-in security features

If your company network, like many businesses, uses Windows NT to share files over a network, you have a lot of built-in security features that you can use if you open your network to the Internet. Those features include:

- **Directory permissions.** You can designate certain directories on a computer as being off-limits to anyone except those who enter user account names and passwords.

- **Auditing.** NT enables you to audit the traffic to and from your server so that you can keep track of who has accessed your files.

- **Encryption.** NT supports Secure Sockets Layer and enables you to secure sensitive data.

Windows NT also enables system administrators to designate permission levels for some directories, such as Read, Add, Change, or Full Control.

If you use Microsoft Internet Information Server to serve information on your intranet, you can also implement some of the firewall-type security schemes described in this chapter.

For instance, you can set up an IP filter by accessing the Advanced tab of the Service Manager window in Microsoft Internet Information Server. Once there, you can deny access to all users except those working on machines with approved IP addresses. You can also set Read-Only rights to some files or directories. Try out the security measures that you have on hand already before investing in firewall hardware or software.

Chapter 11

Conducting Secure Commerce on the Net

*G*etting paid is the bottom line, and having a convenient way for the customer to take care of the bill is good for everybody. Because the Internet encompasses so many different networks all over the globe, and because buyers and sellers can conduct transactions without actually seeing one another, online businesses need to take extra measures to avoid fraud or theft.

When information is sent from one computer to another on the Net, the intended recipient may not be the only recipient. The credit card number, for example, is vulnerable to being intercepted by criminals. Some hackers use software that does something called *packet sniffing*. Such software scans the packets of data for specific types of information, such as credit card numbers, that a growing number of consumers transmit over the Net when making a purchase.

The resulting security breach can spell disaster for small businesses that are just getting started in cyberspace. Enterprises not only risk lawsuits by irate customers, but also declining sales if word gets out that the business's site is insecure. If you have goods or services that you want to sell on the Internet, it's essential to take measures that help your customers feel safe because their personal data is protected.

The techniques used to ensure that commerce occurs in a secure environment on the Internet are extensions of the measures described in Chapter 10:

- ✔ **Identification.** By exchanging certificates, you can be sure of the identity of the person or business you're dealing with.

- ✔ **Authentication.** You can restrict access to a Web site that conducts purchasing transactions by requiring that each customer becomes a member and assigning individual usernames and passwords.

- ✔ **Encryption.** Credit card numbers and other personal information can be protected by scrambling as the confidential data is transmitted over the Internet. Hardware or software that acts as a firewall can provide additional security.

- ✔ **Verification.** After you receive a request for a purchase, the businessperson can verify the identity and the intentions of the customer. You can also check after delivery to make sure that the product was received and the customer is satisfied.

That first item, identification, helps protect you, the individual businessperson, as well as the prospective customer. You need to know that the people who are buying things from you are who they say they are. Certificates and digital signatures created by encryption help you do it.

White-collar computer crime is a problem that's growing dramatically. Agencies such as the Hi-Tech Crime Network and the National White Collar Crime Center (www.iir.com/nwccc/nwccc.htm) exist to combat the threat. For an idea of what to watch out for, visit the Home Business Scam Alert Network (www.world-wide.com/homebiz/scams.htm). If you've been the victim of fraud, report it to the National Fraud Information Center at 1-800-876-7060.

Advantages of online commerce

More and more people are becoming comfortable with shopping and purchasing on the Net. For example, *USA Today* reported that more than 6,000 tickets were sold to the 1996 Olympic Games in Atlanta in the first hour after the system went online, using credit card numbers submitted over the Internet. No cases of fraud were reported.

Shopping on the Internet is attractive to customers for a number of reasons:

- ✔ **Convenience.** Customers can browse catalogs and make purchases any time of the day or night.

- ✔ **Savings.** Prices are often better on the Net than in traditional retail outlets because of the low overhead associated with an online business (no building, no property taxes, no insurance, no rents, and so on).

- ✔ **Immediacy.** Purchasing on the Net gives immediate results, and gives the customer direct contact with merchants.

From a merchant's standpoint, setting up credit card purchases on your Web pages gives people another way to pay you. The ease of credit card use gives customers a way to make an immediate purchase on impulse; it doesn't require customers to go through the extra time and effort of calling you on the phone or sending a fax.

The fundamental goal of enabling commerce through your Internet site is to make it easy for clients and customers to purchase what you have to offer. Your goal is to provide buyers with the options that make it hassle-free for you and for them to do business.

"Currently, commerce over the Internet is gaining acceptance, but at a very slow pace," says David Shumate, President of Lakeville Engineering, Inc. Shumate uses Internet phone and videoconferencing to provide more personal contact with clients. "We feel that this is due to the fact that the ordering mechanisms are cold and impersonal, giving the user the feeling that he or she may never get what they are ordering or paying for. With video, you can talk directly to an individual, getting a warm collective feeling that the company selling the products cares about your satisfaction. You get a connection with the company through the individual and most likely increase the sales over traditional e-commerce applications."

Virtual storefronts

On the Internet, your Web page and your e-mail address serve as a virtual storefront. You don't have to set up a location that people can visit. Your overhead consists of your investment in computer equipment, the fees that you pay to Internet providers, and phone bills. By keeping expenses low, you can pass along savings to your customers and compete with larger suppliers. You may only be a one- or two-person operation, but visitors to your Web site don't know that. Your knowledge, professional presentation, competitive rates, and personal follow-up are what counts.

Case study: Charter Sailing Unlimited

Charter Sailing Unlimited is a one-person business that uses the Web to introduce customers to its services, but then follows up extensively with traditional communication: mainly, telephone calls.

Dennis Dori, the owner of Charter Sailing Unlimited, jumped aboard the Internet with a Web page in late 1995. In the beginning, the orders only trickled in. Dennis also had to fend off inquiries from youthful pranksters, as well as from tire-kickers who weren't seriously interested in chartering a yacht.

Dori and The Argus Company, his Web site consultants, got much better results by making the following improvements to the Web site:

✔ Providing a detailed interactive form that gives prospective customers a place to enter their information. A phone number is required, and visitors are told that they can expect to be contacted by phone for an initial consultation. The form asks people to suggest the area where they want to travel and to estimate the amount they want to spend.

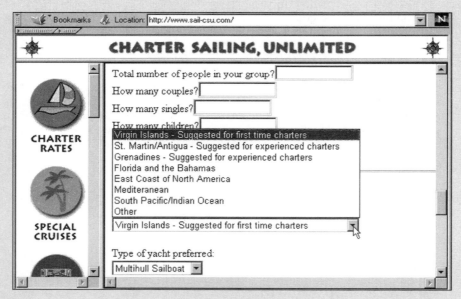

✔ Providing a definite call to action on the site, and encouraging serious inquiries only. Dori responds with an e-mail message that provides customers with options and asks how much they're willing to spend on a Caribbean vacation. Customers are able to qualify themselves as being serious about making a purchase.

✔ Following up with a monthly newsletter that Argus and Dori prepare. Information about everyone who makes an inquiry is saved in a database so that they can receive the mailings.

Potential customers may be turned off by a requirement to provide extensive information, but there's an advantage equal to the risk. Because he is honest and direct with visitors to his Web site, the owner of Charter Sailing receives fewer inquiries. However, a higher proportion of these inquiries are *serious* inquiries.

What Does Secure Commerce Mean?

Before you enable your customers to make credit card purchases online, establish some sort of secure ordering system for your online business.

The first shopping opportunities over the Web involved the danger of criminals intercepting personal data. Since the debut of online shopping, lots of big players in cyberspace have set up security procedures that make it impossible for criminals to get data they can misuse.

Providing a way for your customers to make purchases over the Net does not necessarily mean that you have to set up encryption and other security methods yourself. If you want to make it possible for visitors to your Web site to make online purchases, you need to strike a partnership with a business that already has a secure system in place. This can be an Internet Service Provider or a company like CyberCash or First Virtual, which can help you if you install its software and pay fees on a monthly basis or based on each transaction that you make.

For small businesses, the most practical and popular secure commerce options involve one of these alternatives:

✔ **Finding a secure server.** Your business pays an extra monthly fee to an Internet Service Provider to use the ISP's *secure commerce server*. Customers fill out a form on one of your Web pages and submit their credit card numbers and other information to you. The information is processed by the ISP's secure commerce server. The server software helps you with processing and customer authentication. But it's up to you to establish your business as an approved credit card merchant.

✔ **Using one of the CyberCash payment systems.** CyberCash is the most popular electronic commerce provider, according to a survey by Jupiter Communications, Inc. CyberCash has software that businesses can download for free. You register and pay a fee to CyberCash, and the software enables your business to process credit card transactions online, accept Internet checks, and receive micropayments.

✔ **Signing up with First Virtual.** First Virtual is another popular online payment service that acts as a transactions go-between.

✔ **Using ECash.** ECash is digital money provided by DigiCash. Customers have to open an account with Mark Twain Bank in St. Louis, and merchants have to install ECash software in order to use the service.

Setting Up a Secure Environment

No matter what electronic commerce system you decide to use, it's important to set up an environment through the Internet that makes visitors feel secure. This can be done by

- ✔ Creating interactive forms that ask customers for initial information without requiring that they make a purchase.
- ✔ Providing follow-up customer service contact over the phone or in person.
- ✔ Encouraging visitors with a call to action.
- ✔ Being clear about your services and rates.

Many of the goods and services that you can sell in the offline world can be sold in the online marketplace as well. The best products for Internet sales are simple, recognizable merchandise that doesn't require detailed instructions for users to understand: tickets, books, CDs, and computer programs are popular. Even cars can be purchased online.

Choosing the right items to sell online

A sales site on the Internet doesn't necessarily have to offer a gadget or group of items for sale. Sales can also be subscriptions and advertising.

Customer Service Review, an e-zine in South Africa, gets most of its subscriptions by credit card over the Internet rather than by fax or mail.

The next few sections describe the types of electronic commerce options that you can provide as part of your business site on the Internet.

Using the Web to make contact

The most common way to use the Internet to make sales is to rely on your Web page to get people to give you a call or come to your store. You don't have to finalize the sale on the Web. The Web makes a perfect front-end for transactions, which can be completed over the phone, by mailing a check, or with other traditional methods.

Be clear, be direct

Casting a wide Net (pun intended) has its advantages, but you also want a major portion of your inquiries to be from customers who are truly ready and able to purchase what you have to offer. You can weed out what Dennis Dori of Charter Sailing Unlimited calls tire-kickers by clearly describing what you do and including as much information as possible on your Web site about the process of selecting and purchasing.

Include a call to action

Web surfers are finicky. Visitors can easily click on a link and zoom from one Web page to another — keeping people on your site is practically an art in itself. Along with giving visitors useful content to read, be sure to put a call to action on your sales Web pages. Tell prospects what they need to do, lest they surf away to another Web site. Don't be bashful; feel free to employ obvious but effective phrases like "Buy Now!" and "Order Now!" Stay away from ho-hum statements like "For more information, contact us at. . . ."

The very successful HotHotHot hot sauce Web site contains a good example of a call to action. As shown in Figure 11-1, the very first paragraph on the company's welcome page (www.hothothot.com) ends with the highlighted phrase **come in and browse!** The greeting immediately encourages people to click their way into the site as soon as they discover it.

Figure 11-1:
This site provides a call to action that leads visitors toward making purchases or inquiries.

Advertising one-to-one

When it comes to getting prospective customers to travel to your Web site, you can take the high road or the low road. The low road is taking out a banner ad on a Web site or exchanging free banner ads through a brokerage firm like LinkExchange (www.linkexchange.com).

A middle road approach is listing your business on Yahoo!, either through its main Web site (www.yahoo.com) or one of the regional versions of Yahoo! that index Internet resources in specific metropolitan areas. Most business-people find that Yahoo! increases the amount of visitors who access their Web pages.

The high road requires more work on your part, but it can yield the best results. You reach customers one-on-one by providing personal information.

1. **Locate prospective customers.** Identify the market that's most likely to purchase your products or use your services. Hunt through discussion groups and mailing lists as well as Web sites.

2. **Listen to their concerns.** Get feedback about your prospective customers' concerns and what information they need by lurking in the background while chats or discussions take place online.

3. **Provide answers.** When someone in a discussion group, mailing list, chat room, or bulletin board asks a question that you can answer, provide a full and courteous response. Identify yourself and include the URL of your Web site. Become an active participant in a community and a resource that users can turn to when they need help.

4. **Offer information.** Create a newsletter or a mailing list of your own that customers can subscribe to. You can be sure that those who subscribe are truly interested in what you have to say, and by extension, may want to pay for your goods or services. See Chapter 15 for more information.

5. **Create a community.** Provide ways for prospective and current customers to exchange ideas and information. Set up a discussion group (see Chapter 8), a mailing list, or a bulletin board. The effort builds credibility for you and your organization, and makes people feel more at ease with making purchases from you. A perfect example is The Motley Fool, which puts out extensive information on both the Web and AOL, and conducts live chats and discussions about investing.

The Motley Fool is a great example of a virtual community of users that led to successful online commerce. When customers have a place to ask questions and discuss issues, they rely on the Web site as a source of advice, and feel at ease with making purchases on that site. See the article in *Wired* magazine (www.wired.com/wired/5.08/hagel.html).

Finding a Secure Server

The most practical way for a small business to enable secure Web commerce is an Internet Service Provider that has a secure server. This is a server that has secure commerce software and other security features like firewalls installed.

Working with an Internet provider

You pay an extra monthly fee to put your site on a secure server, but you can tell your customers that their information is protected if they submit it to you. My own provider, InterAccess, charges an extra $50 per month for setting up a secure business site. Others, like Traverse Communications Co., don't charge a monthly fee, but a fee based on the dollar amount of the transactions that you conduct. EarthLink Network, one of the bigger Internet providers, charges $95 per month for space on its SecurLink Server.

The advantage of this setup is independence: You operate your own secure system, and don't have to depend on companies like CyberCash or First Virtual to process orders for you. The secure commerce software is set up to work with companies that authenticate the customer's identity for you.

Interacting through Web page forms

In the secure server scenario, you create a Web page form on one of the Web pages on your site. A form is a Web page that can be used to enter personal information, including a credit card number. Forms also include a button that sends the data the user has entered either to an e-mail address (presumably yours) or to a file on a Web server that uses encryption and other security techniques to protect the information. Graphic Expectations, a small business whose Web page is shown in Figure 11-2, publishes its pages on a local ISP's secure server.

A computer script receives the data and converts it to a text file that you can read. (Chapter 14 includes instructions on how to create a simple form.)

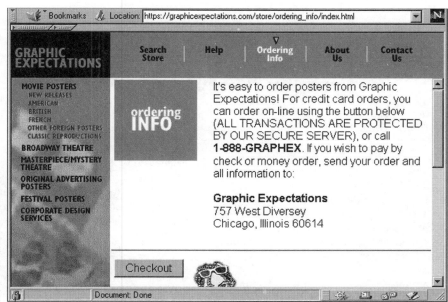

Figure 11-2: Graphic Expectations provides secure ordering on its site.

Closed lock icon indicates secure site

The customer, who must have a browser that recognizes secure servers, connects to your site and fills in the form. Your server sends the data to a processing service which processes the transaction while the cardholder is online.

In the background of this transaction, the computers send public keys back and forth to verify identity and data.

Installing your own server software

Server software is expensive to install yourself, but you can do it.

Here are a few popular commerce software packages that you can investigate:

- **Netscape's CommerceXpert** product family of electronic commerce solutions is being developed and sold by Actra, a joint venture funded by Netscape and GE Information Services (GEIS). Actra ECXpert, the foundation of Actra CrossCommerce application solutions family, is the electronic commerce software solution. Read about it at www.actracorp.com/public/pages/product/product1.htm.

- **Microsoft Site Server, Enterprise Edition** includes Microsoft Commerce Server. System requirements are extensive, including 64MB of RAM, Windows NT Server 4.0, and Internet Information Server 3.0. Find out more at backoffice.microsoft.com/products/SiteServerE/default.asp.

Case study: Graphic Expectations

Graphic Expectations is a small business with only two employees that has been in the same location on Diversey Avenue in Chicago for more than 20 years. In August 1997, Scott Bernberg created a Web site at www.graphicexpectations.com/main.html. A primary goal of going on the Web was to increase sales: Graphic Expectations deals in original movie and Broadway theater posters, artwork, and theater and festival promotion. "I think we have a product that lends itself to sales on the Internet," says Bernberg. "People on the Net tend to be fanatical about following their interests, and lots of people who are interested in particular movies are likely to order posters for that movie."

The company's ordering system is set up using Windows NT server using Quattro Pro and Java. Even though the site had only been online for a few weeks, Bernberg said he was already getting sales. "I'd say it's split down the middle: Half of the new customers use our toll-free number, and half purchase through the Web page. There is still a perceived feeling of risk with making a credit card purchase on the Web, though personally, I think the risk is more imagined than not."

✔ **Speedware OrderPoint** is electronic commerce software by Speedware. Examples of companies that use the product are provided. Learn more about OrderPoint at www.speedware.com/products/store.

✔ **Oracle Internet Commerce Server** enables you to set up and run a secure business on the Internet. It supports the SET protocol as well as CyberCash, and other secure commerce systems. Find out more at www.oracle.com/products/web/ics.

Shopping cart transactions

As an alternative to setting up a Web page form, you can also use shopping cart software, which enables customers to keep track of items that they choose while they continue to shop on your site. When the person is ready to check out, the program displays the selections, and gives the visitor the chance to make changes.

Setting up your business Web site on a secure server is only one half of a secure transaction. The other half is the browser program that your customers use. Their browsers have to recognize Secure Sockets Later encryption and must be able to access secure sites for the secure transaction to be secure. Most newer Web browsers, such as Netscape Navigator and Microsoft Internet Explorer do work with Secure Sockets Layer. It's a good idea to put a notice on your site that secure browsers are required.

Before you can start accepting credit card numbers over the Internet, you have to set your business up as an approved credit card vendor. It can be more difficult for a small business to establish a credit processing account with a bank for credit card purchases over the Net than it can be to actually set up the secure ordering forms and processing scripts. The process can take weeks, and some banks charge merchants a higher interest rate for purchases made online than for conventional credit card purchases. Ask your bank about its rates, and shop around for the best deal if you can.

An online business called Credit Card Network provides you with an online form that it can forward to one of its member financial institutions for a fee of $200 to $400. Credit Card Network can also provide you with ready-made online forms for your customers to fill out when they want to make purchases from you. The Network can also handle the processing of your customers' credit card information. A complete list of options is at www.creditnet.com/info/info-rates.html.

Working with CyberCash

CyberCash estimates that half a million customers are using one of the electronic commerce provider's payment options on the Internet today.

CyberCash has energetically developed several different commerce methods, and has pledged to support Microsoft's Wallet and Site Server commerce systems, as well as SET protocol for electronic transactions. Small businesses are smart to consider CyberCash as an option if they want to enable customers to make online purchases.

SETting the stage for commerce

CyberCash's software, CashRegister, recognizes a secure commerce protocol called SET (Secure Electronic Transactions). SET's development is attributed to big-time financial organizations and credit card companies like Visa and MasterCard. SET is intended to

- ✔ Keep payment information confidential.
- ✔ Provide proof to an Internet businessperson that the person is a valid user of a credit card.
- ✔ Prevent intrusion from outsiders.
- ✔ Work on all software and hardware platforms.
- ✔ Create a protocol that can be used beyond the Internet, on areas of commerce like America Online and smart cards.

SET basically provides a collection of encryption and security specifications used as an industry-wide, open standard for ensuring secure payment transactions over the Internet. One advantage of SET is that, if your Web server is equipped with SET-compliant software, the server contacts a financial institution to verify a credit card holder's name and address.

If you conduct business on the Internet, don't forget about sales tax requirements that may apply. If you own property, or have employees or an office in a particular state, you may have to collect pay taxes for that state in a timely fashion. If one of your customers is from another country, you may have to pay VAT tax to that country. Check with your state tax office or your accountant to find out.

CyberCash and credit card payments

All the steps that apply if your business accepts credit cards in the real world apply on the Internet, too. You have to be approved by a bank as a credit card merchant; you obtain a merchant ID and a terminal ID; when a customer makes a purchase, you need to verify his or her identity; and you have to pass the data about the transaction and the purchaser to a financial institution for processing.

If you own a store, the customer waits by the cash register while you do the work. If you own a virtual storefront on the Internet, the customer waits by his or her computer. But who does the work?

That's where CyberCash comes in. CyberCash provides online businesses with software called CashRegister that they can install to facilitate the processing of credit card transactions.

You need to select the correct operating system for the server that holds (or is going to hold) your online store. The CashRegister software only runs on Windows NT or UNIX servers and the files you download are quite large, ranging up to 18MB in size. After you download the software, you need to generate public and private keys and exchange them with CyberCash. Then you set up a secure purchasing area on your Web site. If you want help with the process, you can contact CyberCash through its Merchant Support site (www.cybercash.com/cybercash/merchants/support).

Internet checks

Although credit cards are the most popular way to make purchases on the Net, they require you to be a credit card merchant. As an alternative, you can also set up your company to accept electronic checks.

You install software that enables you to set up a Web page that, in effect, acts as an online blank check. A shopping mall called Mall Direct (www.mdb1.com) enables advertisers to submit electronic checks by filling out the form shown in Figure 11-3.

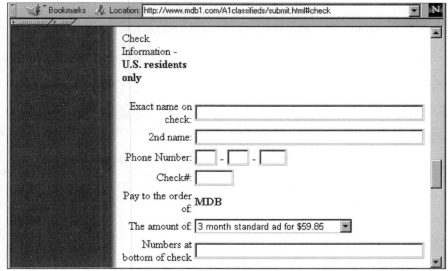

Figure 11-3: Electronic checks are one alternative to online credit cards.

The customer enters the information that's usually entered on a check: the date, dollar amount, name, bank, account number, and so on. The software enables your Web server to accept and verify information while the customer is still online. You can deposit the check in your bank as a *preauthorized draft,* a normal check that the customer has approved but that does not require a physical signature.

CyberCash offers this option, which it calls the PayNow Service. Payments come directly from a customer's checking account. Other services that provide online checking include

  ✔ **CheckFree Corporation.** CheckFree Corporation (www.checkfree.com) has a number of electronic payment solutions, including E-Bill, which enables businesses to send electronic bills to customers.

  ✔ **VersaNet (**www.versanet.com**).** The merchant buys software ($300) that works with a Web server to accept U.S. and Canadian checks on the Web. You pay a $1 to $1.50 processing fee to VersaNet for each transaction.

Electronic checks have some advantages over credit cards, but credit card systems like SET and CyberCash seem to be currently dominating electronic commerce. So, if you want to play the game with an established business, plan to make purchases via a credit card.

Micropayments

Small payments — in the range of 25 cents to $10 — are not sizable enough to process conveniently with a credit card. *Micropayments,* a way to pay without credit card charges, can be used to secure pay-per-view areas, pay-per-play computer games, and special reports and newsletters.

The CyberCoin service provides special tools to deliver information to the user, which can be either the content the user is paying for, or an electronic receipt that provides access for the user to get to the content elsewhere.

CyberCoin can also be used with an Internet Wallet, a software program that holds payment information and protects that information by encryption. A plug-in application in the user's browser transmits the encrypted data to the merchant's site, where wallet server software decodes the data.

You, the merchant, pay a transaction fee to a financial institution for each one of these micro-transactions, and CyberCash gets a percentage of that fee. You probably pay the bank about 8 percent for a $25 sale and up to 30 percent for a $10 transaction.

Alternatives to Using Credit Cards Online

Setting your business up to accept credit card purchases is hardly a straightforward matter for any business, let alone those who choose to market over the Internet. You have to apply to a bank and pay interest on each purchase.

Many small businesses prefer to use the Net as a front door for the initial contact. The sale is then finalized over the phone, through the fax machine, or by using the e-mail. Many customers feel more secure if you take their information by traditional rather than electronic means.

Some secure and simple ways to facilitate online transactions involve a two-step process. Credit card numbers never go directly from customer to seller.

Doing the e-commerce two-step

One simple alternative is to use a Web page form to take the order information over the Web, but to accept credit card information by fax or mail. One business that promotes this option transactions is Computer Literacy Bookshops (www.clbooks.com), shown in Figure 11-4.

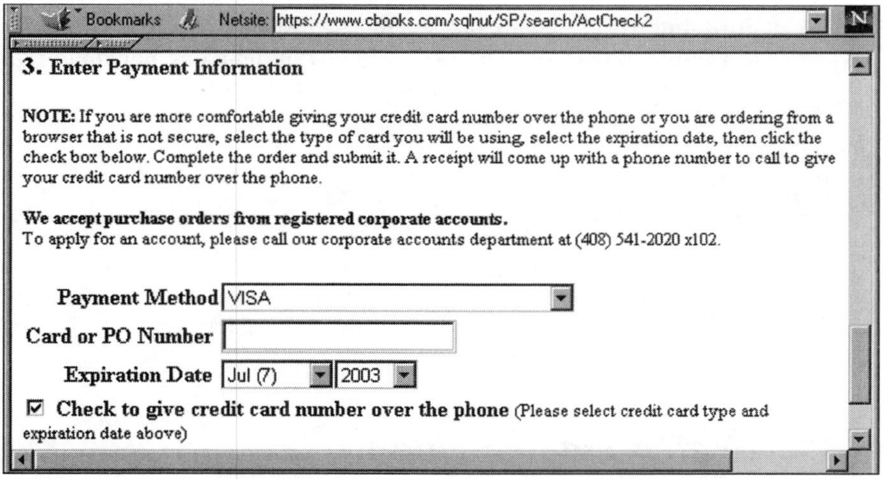

Figure 11-4:
Receive orders online, accept payments offline: a simple two-stage transaction used by this online bookstore.

> Bookmarks   Netsite: https://www.cbooks.com/sqlnut/SP/search/ActCheck2
>
> **3. Enter Payment Information**
>
> **NOTE:** If you are more comfortable giving your credit card number over the phone or you are ordering from a browser that is not secure, select the type of card you will be using, select the expiration date, then click the check box below. Complete the order and submit it. A receipt will come up with a phone number to call to give your credit card number over the phone.
>
> **We accept purchase orders from registered corporate accounts.**
> To apply for an account, please call our corporate accounts department at (408) 541-2020 x102.
>
> **Payment Method** VISA
> **Card or PO Number**
> **Expiration Date** Jul (7)   2003
> ☑ **Check to give credit card number over the phone** (Please select credit card type and expiration date above)

Using First Virtual as a go-between

FirstVirtual Holdings, Inc. (www.fv.com) gives businesses a different way to accept online transactions without resorting to credit card purchases. First Virtual acts as a go-between customer and merchant. When the customer makes a purchase, that customer sends his or her credit card information, followed by an e-mail message to confirm it. In return, First Virtual sends the customer a password. The customer uses the password to make purchases from the First Virtual seller.

When the purchase is made, First Virtual sends the customer an e-mail message to verify what was purchased and at what price. The customer confirms by e-mail. Then First Virtual bills the credit card and pays the seller.

Becoming a First Virtual seller requires you to fill out a registration form and pay a $10 annual fee. You also pay 29 percent per transaction, 2 percent of the charged amount, and $1 each time a deposit is made to your account.

Issuing ECash

ECash, which was developed by DigiCash (www.digicash.com), differs from credit cards and other electronic transactions in that it allows the customer to remain anonymous. The service uses electronic coupons for its transactions.

Although the ECash system seems secure and customer anonymity is an attractive option, ECash doesn't have the big-name backing of other electronic payment options, and isn't gaining in popularity.

Other Secure Commerce Schemes

Each of the secure commerce systems already mentioned requires that you, the small business owner, rely on another business for help in processing credit card data or making electronic payments. Here are some other alternatives that you can set up yourself.

Pretty Good Privacy

Pretty Good Privacy (PGP) is a *very* good encryption system that is effective and easy to use. PGP uses the private/public key encryption system described in Chapter 10.

When someone sends you a message that includes sensitive data, that person encrypts the message with your own public key. You then use your private key to decode it. PGP works the other way too: You can encrypt data with your private key, and the recipient unlocks the contents with your public key.

In order to distribute your public key to prospective customers, you can post it on your Web page, or on a special Internet site designed to store PGP public keys.

PGP can be used in the U.S. and in Canada but the U.S. government forbids its export. To find out more about PGP, visit the Web page quadralay.com/www.Crypt/PGP/pgp00.html. For commercial use, you have to purchase PGP from ViaCrypt Products, 602-944-0773, or by sending e-mail to viacrypt@acm.org. For personal use, read the README file at ww.eff.org/pub/Net_Info/Tools/Crypto.

Cybermalls

Another easy way to enable people to purchase your goods and services online is by joining a cybermall, the online world's equivalent of a shopping center, where you set up a Web page for your business and use the mall's own built-in purchasing systems.

Perhaps the biggest advantage of joining a cybermall is support. Some malls can help you set up good-looking Web pages. You also get to use the mall's own secure credit card processing and shopping cart systems.

Another advantage is traffic: A popular mall can bring in lots of visitors who may choose to visit your particular set of Web pages — your site — in the mall. iMALL reports that it receives more than 14 million hits per month.

The big disadvantage is cost. Malls have to make money, and many of them charge rent, such as Virtuocity (mall.virtuocity.com) which charges $187 per month for a virtual storefront. Mall Direct (www.mdb1.com) charges $19.95 per month for a 450-words-or-less classified ad.

Other malls levy a commission on sales. The Internet Shopping Network (www.internet.net), which concentrates on computer sales, does not require a rental fee, but does charge between 10 and 15 percent of sales.

To find a mall that offers goods and services in your area of interest, check out Yahoo!'s index at www.yahoo.com/Business_and_Economy/Companies/Shopping_Centers/Online_Shopping.

Microsoft Wallet

Electronic Wallet software is offered by companies such as Verifone and Microsoft, and has the advantage of enabling customers to pay for goods without having to enter personal information more than once.

Wallet software such as Verifone's vWallet (`www.verifone.com/products/software/icommerce/html/vwallet.html`) or Microsoft Wallet (`www.microsoft.com/commerce/wallet`) are programs that enable users to store password and address information on their computers and transmit the information to sites using a wallet application that works as a plug-in within a Web browser.

In transacting business with a Wallet, a shopper only has to enter a Wallet ID number to make a purchase from a Web site, rather than entering his or her name, address, credit card numbers, or other information. In order to receive a Wallet from a user, you need to use CyberCash, which supports Microsoft Wallet, or special merchant's software that you can download from Microsoft or Verifone for free.

Sealing the deal

Be sure to confirm all sales with the customers by a return e-mail message or telephone call before you ship the order.

Verification is especially important if you take orders from suppliers or other businesses over the Internet. If your business accepts purchase orders, you can bill your account with the company either monthly, weekly, or whenever the order is made. Before you ship anything out, however, make sure that your employees confirm by phone that the order is legitimate, and be certain that you get a written, signed document to verify that everything is on the up-and-up.

Be sure to ask your customers for feedback on your online ordering system. Ask them if they had to wait a long time before their order was verified. Make a purchase yourself to see how well the system works.

Measuring the success of online commerce is easy. You only need to count how many orders you get.

Part V
Selling Your Products

The 5th Wave   By Rich Tennant

In this part . . .

An important aspect of marketing in cyberspace is putting out information that builds credibility and gives value to your presence on the Internet. Part V also addresses ways to get your catalog or other information online, and gives you tips for creating Web pages that stand out from the crowd. You'll also learn how you can provide effective customer service through the Internet that will keep your clients satisfied.

Chapter 12

Getting the Word Out

● ●

In This Chapter

▶ Assembling an Internet publicity toolkit

▶ Broadcasting your message with e-mail

▶ Using Gopher, newsgroups, and FTP to widen your exposure

▶ Advertising for free with LinkExchange and Internet indexes

▶ Placing banner ads and hiring Internet marketing consultants

● ●

*E*very successful business needs to get the word out to potential customers. Yet, small businesses are often at a disadvantage compared with the Big Players in their given fields. The giants — like Mammoth Corp. and Gargantuan Inc. — can hire public relations and advertising specialists to create extensive ad campaigns, flood the media with press releases, and identify potential customers. How can a small business manager compete with a bigger company's publicity machine?

Internet to the rescue! The Net can provide you with impressive, cost-effective marketing. Through one well-placed online ad, you can reach thousands or even millions of people every week. As two well-known business authorities, Don Peppers and Martha Rogers, Ph.D., explain: "The World Wide Web represents an order-of-magnitude increase in the cost-efficiency of marketing — with customers or prospective customers, family members, associates, and strangers."

These days, when people consider using the Internet for publicity, they think two words: Web page. If they're Web surfers, they can place banner ads on someone else's Web page for a fee, like taking out an ad in a newspaper.

Effective advertising on the Net involves more than using the Web. You have many more options than paying to place a banner ad on a Web page. And those options are less expensive and more effective than the banner ad alternative. Many of the examples in this chapter use LinkExchange, an advertising network that spreads your ads around the Net for free.

To many people, the Web *is* the Internet. The most effective Internet advertising uses a Web site in conjunction with the rest of the Internet, including e-mail, newsgroups, and FTP (File Transfer Protocol).

Whether you simply have a Web page or e-mail address or decide to use all parts of the Net, the key to success lies in finding the right places to post your ads, to publicize yourself without breaking your budget, and to make your ads fit the style of the Internet. Self-promotion is intended to intrigue those users who find you inspiring them, to discover more about you. In order to do this, you only have to understand three things.

- ✔ **Target.** Identify members of your target market and reach them by placing ads on sites that your customers frequent or by contacting them through electronic mail. Locate sites that your customers visit, and publicize your business there.

- ✔ **Interact.** Internet ads don't just sit on a page — they're made to be clicked on. Customers can visit your Web site, find out more about your products, and send you an e-mail inquiry.

- ✔ **Inform.** On the Net, information sells. The more useful data you provide, either on the Web or on other parts of the Net such as FTP, the longer potential customers stay on your site. The longer their visits, the more likely they are to make a contact or a purchase.

Setting Your Internet Advertising Goals

Before you start blowing your horn, you need to have an idea whose ears you want to fill. Knowing which goals apply to you can help you decide what you want to say and where you want to say it.

Take a moment to stop and think about the goals of an Internet advertising campaign. Here are some goals:

- ✔ **As many hits as possible.** A *hit* is a term that describes a visit to a Web page. Many Internet businesses simply want to get as many visits as they can, regardless of who their visitors are. The more visits they get, the more advertisers are willing to pay to place an ad on their sites.

- ✔ **Supplement existing advertising.** An e-mail address, Web page, and URL can help increase responses to your existing ads by giving customers other options to contact you.

- ✔ **Hold your existing customer base.** Attracting customers is important; keeping them interested in you is just as important. The Net can be a great avenue for software updates, instructions, documentation, and other forms of customer service that keep your VIPs (Very Interactive

People) coming back for more. You may even receive the ultimate online compliment: Someone bookmarks your site, so that they can return to it easily at the click of a mouse button.

✔ **Give your business credibility.** A connection to the Internet carries a cachet. It shows customers that you're serious about your business.

After you determine your goal, you can settle on the advertising approach that's right for you, and select where you want to place yourself. If your goal is to get as many visits as possible, for instance, use mailing lists, Internet indexes, and banner ads to broadcast your company name to as many publicity sites as possible. If you want to target your message to just the right group, try responding to messages or placing links on newsgroups, mailing lists, and Web sites that your customers are most likely to frequent.

Before you start using your Internet connection to blow your horn, you need to have something to say. The first step is to assemble an essential set of Internet tools that you can use as an Internet publicity kit.

Online versus Traditional Marketing

Internet marketing is notably different from traditional marketing. To understand what's so special about marketing on the Internet, it can be helpful to compare online marketing with traditional marketing techniques.

Interactivity

One of the big differences between online and traditional ads is in the *ease* with which potential customers can interact with an ad. Only one mouse click takes a prospect to your Web site.

The goal is not just to get people to see your name and take note of your e-mail address or toll-free number. Ultimately, you want viewers to click through to your Web site to find out more about you.

Cost

On the Net, the price you pay for a conventional banner ad in a newspaper or magazine depends not so much on the physical size of the ad, but on how many visits the Web site typically receives. The more popular the ad, the higher the cost. For instance, an ad in the printed version of the *Chicago Tribune* can easily cost hundreds of dollars for only one day. A six-line ad in the online Tribune Sunday Business section's Internet Directory costs $50. A small business can find plenty of ways to get its e-mail address or Web site URL publicized without spending a penny, however. Many Internet sites include a link to your site for absolutely *nada*. They make money by getting visits, and they get visits by putting out lots of information from people like you and organizing that information in ways so that people can find it easily, thus saving them time and money.

Broadcasting versus narrowcasting

The traditional broadcast media delivers short bits of information to huge numbers of people — basically, everyone in their coverage areas who happens to be tuned to a particular radio or television station. The Net *can* enable you to do that, too, if you're lucky enough to get your company mentioned on one of the sites that draws millions of hits each day. But the Internet really excels in one-to-one communication that TV and radio can't touch. By targeting particular Web sites, you can reach small groups of people — or even one prospect at a time.

Direct mail

Many similarities are apparent between direct mail and e-mail on the Internet. You target a group of recipients, prepare a mailing, and send it off. One big difference is postage and printing: You don't have to pay a certain amount for each piece of e-mail.

Relationship building

Often, on the Net, advertising isn't an end in itself. Rather, it's a result. People find out about you because you provide information, you set up contests, you answer questions, and you provide a rich Web site.

Useful content sells

The best way to advertise is the opposite of what works in print: the more useful information you put on the Web, the more relationship-building you can achieve, the more hits you can get, and the longer people are inclined to stay on your Web site. The longer the stay, the more likely the contact about acquiring your goods or services. Provide information or services that people can use, and you're sure to gain attention.

Assembling Your Internet Publicity Toolkit

Remember those old-time press agents with white shoes and ears glued to their telephones. These veterans were great at cooking up publicity kits. A publicity kit is a good way to publicize any event or business. Someone puts together a press release, photos, and background information, packs it in a folder, and sends this bundle to media people.

You can do the same with media and publicity services that you want to reach on the Net. An Internet publicity kit consists of tools for creating communications that can be sent to indexes, announcement services, columnists, magazines, and other places on the Net — the objective: to draw attention in your direction. No matter what your business does or what your goal is, you can choose one or more of these tools to serve your purposes.

The following sections describe the kinds of tools you can work with.

Creating an Internet business card

Wherever you go, you carry a business card, don't you? In fact, most businesses start up operations with a fresh batch of business cards. On the Net, start by making your own electronic business card.

E-mail address

On the Net, your e-mail address is as important as a toll-free phone number or street address in the offline world. Keep it short, simple, and easy to remember. If possible, stay away from random addresses like these:

```
101334.9788@compuserve.com
QSNd78f44@prodigy.com
```

With most providers, such as America Online, Earthlink, or AT&T World Net, you're invited to create your own username, which becomes the first part of your e-mail address. There's nothing wrong with using your first initial and your last name as your e-mail address. An e-mail address isn't the place to apply creativity. Ideally, customers can *guess* your e-mail address.

URL

Uniform Resource Locators (URLs) are like e-mail addresses. Don't keep customers scratching their heads. Short, obvious URLs work best.

Usually, when you or a consultant create a Web site (that is, send it to a computer that makes files available on the Web) you're given space in a directory on a Web server. Your URL corresponds to that directory, such as

```
http://users.aol.com/username/
```

If you can, pay $150 to an organization called InterNIC that can assign a shorter alias to your URL — an abbreviated version that only uses the domain name part of the URL, like this:

```
www.business.com
```

The less time people take looking for you, the more time they can spend visiting your site and finding out about you. (If you're interested in getting one of those short domain names, see Chapter 15.)

Signature file

A *signature file,* also called a *sig file,* is a three- or four-line signature that you add to your messages. It can look like this:

```
Joe Blow
President, Blow Enterprises
Web site http://www.blow.com/
```

Creating a signature file takes only a little more time than putting your name on the dotted line. Just follow these steps to create your own sig file:

1. **Open up a text editing program. This example uses Notepad, which comes built in with Windows 95. If you're a Macintosh user, you can use SimpleText.**

   A new blank document opens on the screen.

2. **Press the hyphen or equals sign key (=) to create a dividing line that separates your signature from the body of your message.**

   You see a short series of dashes, hyphens, or equal signs (=). Pick the symbol that you want to use.

3. **Type your name, job title, company name, e-mail address, and Web site URL, if you have one. Press the Return or Enter key after each line.**

   Your signature now occupies three or four lines. If you're feeling ambitious at this point, you can press the spacebar to arrange your text in two columns, as shown in Figure 12-1.

Figure 12-1:
A signature
file often
uses a
divider line,
and can be
arranged to
occupy less
space on
the screen.

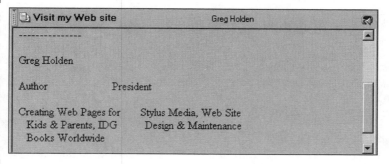

4. **Choose File⇨Save.**

   A dialog box appears, enabling you to name the file and save it in a folder on your hard disk.

5. **Enter a name for your file that ends in the filename extension .txt. This identifies your file as a plain text document so that you can locate it more easily. Then, click on the Save button.**

   Your text file is saved on your computer's hard disk.

After you create a plain-text version of your electronic signature, you need to identify that file to the computer programs that you use to send and receive e-mail and newsgroup messages. Identification enables the programs to automatically make the signature file appear at the bottom of any messages that you compose; you don't have to type your signature over and over again. The method for attaching a sig file varies from program to program; check your own e-mail software's Help file for details.

 Plan to make the first recipient of an e-mail message with your signature file none other than yourself — to verify correct spelling and proper spacing. Remember, the signature is going to appear on *all* of your e-mail and newsgroup messages, unless you tell your software *not* to attach the sig file you specified earlier. So make sure everything reads the way you want.

 Looking for Finger software for Windows 95? Look no further than WSFinger32, which is available as shareware for $10 from the Tidewater Systems Web site (www.empire.com/~jobrien).

A Netscape address book card

An *address book card* is a special feature that comes with the most recent version of Netscape's Web browser, which is called Netscape Communicator. Communicator enables you to create an address book card that you can attach to an e-mail message. (Attaching means that you join one or more files to an e-mail message, so the message and file(s) are sent together.)

Letting visitors finger you

Another kind of electronic signature is a *Plan file*. Plan files are short text documents that (like signature files) give your name, URL, and any information about you and your business that you want people to read. In order to see the plan file, visitors have to *Finger* you by using a terminal emulation program such as Telnet, or a more specialized software program called Finger (Mac) or WinSock Finger (Windows).

Finger is a throwback to the days before users were connected to the Internet with dial-up phone software like PPP or SLIP. According to one of the larger ISPs in Chicago, InterAccess, a small but significant number of customers still connect to the Net from remote terminals rather than via PPP or SLIP. Nonetheless, if you want to cover every Internet publicity base, or if your targeted customers include programmers and serious computer enthusiasts, try setting up a Plan file.

First, call your ISP. Not all ISPs let you post a Plan file. If you can, prepare a simple text-only document that says something about yourself and your company like this:

```
Stylus Media
Information Stylists, Publications Professionals and
        All-Around Nice Guys
We do Print * Text * Web Sites * Advertising *
        Networking * Programming
1826 West Cornelia, Chicago, IL 60657
Voice/Fax: 773-244-8263
E-mail: gholden@interaccess.com
WWW: http://homepage.interaccess.com/~gholden/stylus/
        / —— \  / |    |  |   /
        \   |  \ / |    |  |   \
        /   |    |  |__ |__|  /
Thanks for Fingering Us!
```

Those strange-looking symbols near the end, by the way, are my attempt to create a piece of ASCII art (it's supposed to depict the word Stylus . . . no, really; just back up, and tip your head a bit if you can't see it . . . well, take my word for it!). ASCII art is comprised solely of common symbols found on a computer keyboard, and ASCII art designs are commonly seen in many signature files.

Whether you create ASCII art or not (believe me, it's very much optional), the next step is to save this text file in plain-text only format with a filename extension specified by your ISP. (My provider told me to simply name the file `.plan`.) Publish it on your Web server as described in Chapter 14. Your server may have you call this document FINGER.PLAN or PLAN.TXT.

If you're curious, you can see my own `.plan` file by opening up a Finger program and connecting to `gholden@cluster.interaccess.com`.

An address book card looks like a signature file, but the card is able to provide much more information than just a name, job title, and URL to those people who receive your message using Netscape's e-mail program, Netscape Messenger. Plus, it looks more professional than a plain-text sig file.

The drawback with the address book card is that only the people who correspond with you using Netscape Messenger are able to see it. If, however, you use Messenger regularly (as I do) and want to provide an address book card as an additional option in case your correspondents *can* receive it, follow these steps:

1. **Start Netscape Communicator.**

   You can have any one of Communicator's applications running. If you have Netscape Messenger running, for instance, the Inbox - Netscape Folder window is open on-screen.

2. **From any Communicator window, select E̲dit⇨Pr̲eferences.**

   The Preferences dialog box appears.

3. **Click on the plus sign (+) next to Mail & Groups, and then click on Identity.**

   The Identity Preferences dialog box appears.

4. **Check the box labeled *Always Attach Personal Address Book Card to outgoing messages*. Then click on the Edit Card . . . button.**

   The Card for [Your Name] dialog box appears (as shown in Figure 12-2).

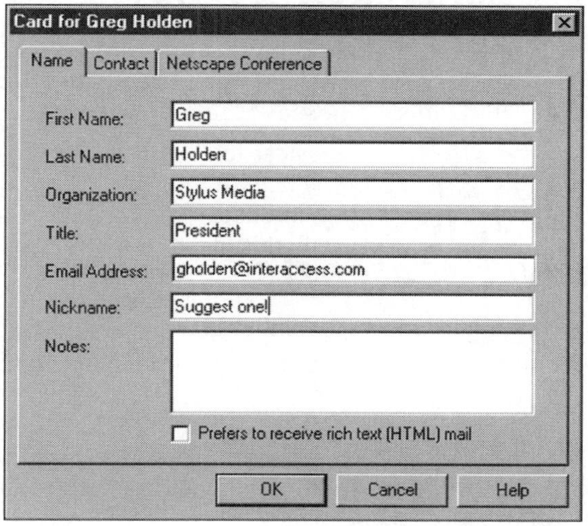

Figure 12-2:
Give your e-mail correspondents lots of business information by using this dialog box to create a Netscape personal address book card.

Card for Greg Holden	
Name	Contact	Netscape Conference

First Name: Greg
Last Name: Holden
Organization: Stylus Media
Title: President
Email Address: gholden@interaccess.com
Nickname: Suggest one!
Notes:

☐ Prefers to receive rich text (HTML) mail

[OK] [Cancel] [Help]

5. **Fill out your personal information in each of the fields, as requested. If you prefer to receive HTML-formatted e-mail, check the box saying so. Click on the Contact tab and fill out your address, phone, and other real world information.**

6. **Click on OK.**

The personal card dialog box closes and the Messenger window you were in previously reappears.

Figure 12-3 shows how an address book card looks when it's received by someone using Netscape Messenger, the e-mail software that comes with Netscape Communicator.

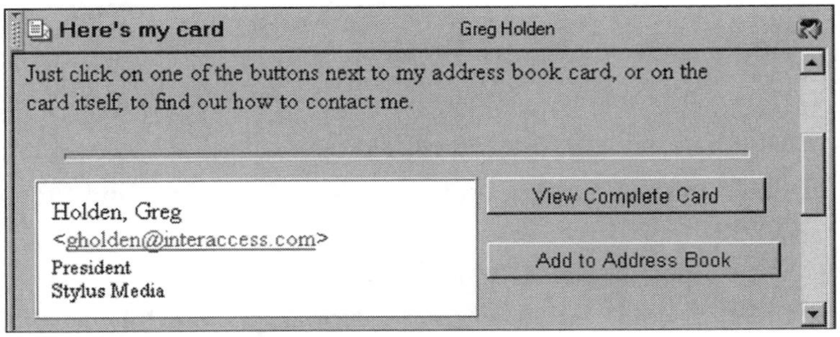

Figure 12-3: An address book card can include personal information, such as your business address and job title.

> **Here's my card**   Greg Holden
>
> Just click on one of the buttons next to my address book card, or on the card itself, to find out how to contact me.
>
> Holden, Greg
> <gholden@interaccess.com>
> President
> Stylus Media
>
> View Complete Card
>
> Add to Address Book

Define your business in 20 words or less

Often, search services, indexes, and shopping malls require you to describe your business in 20 words or so. Invest the time to create an attention-getting description. A well-delivered message makes a difference.

Leave a trail of keywords to help the Net searchers

Write down a list of 10 to 15 words that people may associate with your business. If you sell children's books, you may compile a list that includes

```
Books, Kids, Children, Fairy tales, Mother Goose
```

You can use your word list to increase the chances that Web surfers may find your site in one of the Internet search services.

Give visitors a home page worth returning to

On the Net, your home page is the cornerstone of your publicity program. By *home page* I'm talking about the opening or welcome page that leads visitors into the group of pages that makes up your Web site. All listings can direct people to your home page.

Image-ine your company with a logo

You probably already have a logo that you use on your business cards and stationery. Coming up with a single small visual image for your organization can also help you get more attention when you're publicized on the Web. In most cases, you can simply scan a printed copy of your existing logo.

If you don't have access to a scanner in your office, many local printing services, such as Kinko's Copies, provide scanning services. Remember to pick a good image with high contrast, and to scan it at a low resolution such as 72 dots per inch (dpi) to keep the file size small. Also crop your image — in other words, select that part of the image that you want to appear in the Web page, and leave out any parts of the image that aren't essential.

Think links!

The more links you provide, the more interesting your site is, and the more information you offer visitors. The longer your guests stay on your site the more likely they are to return. Remember, your primary purpose is to build a relationship with your visitors. The best way to do this is to make your site indispensable. Include all the links you can in a Web page that you publish on your Web site. Title this page Links to Related Sites. List all of these on one page so that your visitors can have other places to go to find out about your field of interest. It may seem illogical to send visitors to other Web sites, but do it anyway. Remember the movie *Miracle on 34th Street,* when Kris Kringle sent Macy's customers to Gimbel's and the store generated goodwill, thus paving the way for more return business? When you provide clues to locate other Web sites, you're capitalizing on the same idea.

Where do you find sites that complement your own? Saunter over to your local bookstore and look through the trade magazines that cover the Net. Check out *Yahoo! Internet Life, NetGuide, Internet World,* or *Internet Life.*

How to request a link

Whenever you want to include a link on your page to someone else's Web page, it's good practice to ask permission first. There's no hard-and-fast rule. Just send an informal e-mail message to the Webmaster of the site that you want to link to. It's common practice for the site to reciprocate by adding a link to your Web site on one of *their* pages.

Don't be content with so-so content

Too many Web sites are information dumps — places where information gets planted and never updated. The best way to advertise your business is to provide as much information as possible.

Banner ad

A banner is a rectangular display ad that uses color, graphics, and a few words to advertise a business, and that's commonly seen on many Web pages, such as the ones shown in Figure 12-4.

Figure 12-4:
Link-Exchange's examples of variations on the banner ad — the second ad from the top generated more click-throughs than the others.

If banner ads seem to be approximately the same shape and size, there's a reason: Such ads are often distributed around the Net by ad networks, and these networks require the ads to be a standard size of 440 x 40 pixels, or roughly 5 $\frac{1}{2}$ x $\frac{1}{2}$. Measurements in pixels are commonly used because that's what many computer graphics programs use, too.

Unless you have a staff designer, you may need to hire someone to develop a good eye-catching banner ad for you. Amateurish-looking graphics can't contribute to a positive impression. Plan to invest from $100 to $300 for a designer to create your ad. But the results can be worthwhile.

According to a story on CNET TV (www.cnet.com/Content/Tv/Web/Whatson/ads.html), the Web site for the House of Blues nightclub (www.hob.com) is turning a profit from banner ads alone.

Creating a banner ad

Technically, there's no reason why a banner ad needs to be 468 x 60 pixels (or other sizes like 440 x 40 or 400 x 40 pixels). You can create a circular, oval, or tetrahedron-shaped ad, as long as the site where you publish the ad accepts it.

If you want to create your own banner ad, you need the following:

✓ **A good graphics program.** The most popular graphics programs, the ones used by most Web designers, are Adobe Photoshop and Adobe Illustrator. They're very powerful, but hard to figure out. A good graphics program called Microsoft Image Composer comes bundled with Microsoft FrontPage 97. Another good program called Paint Shop Pro is available for a 30-day trial; after that the program costs $69. You can download it from www.jasc.com.

✓ **A scanner.** Actually, this is optional. You only need a scanner if you plan to use a photo or if you want to copy type or art from your business's logo.

✓ **A look.** Do you want to look businesslike? Cool and dreamy? Revolutionary? All these feelings can be conveyed by the right choice of color and type. (This is where a good designer can help you.)

After you collect your thoughts and resources, you open your graphics program and begin drawing and selecting colors. The following steps give you an idea of how to start creating a simple text-only banner. The steps assume you have downloaded and/or purchased a copy of Paint Shop Pro from the site previously mentioned:

1. **Double-click on the Paint Shop Pro icon to start the program.**

   A blank window appears, ready for you to start drawing.

2. **Select File⇨New.**

   The New Image dialog box appears (as shown in Figure 12-5).

3. **Enter 400 in the box next to Width and 40 in the box next to Height. (400 x 40 is the standard size for LinkExchange banners; other ad networks have different requirements.) Select White as the background color. Leave the option under Image Type set to 256 Colors (8 Bit). Click on OK.**

   The New Image dialog box closes, and a new white image drawing window titled Image 1 appears.

4. **Click on the text button (the one that looks like the letter A) in the Paint Shop Pro toolbar. Move the mouse pointer into the Image 1 window.**

   The arrow turns into a crosshair.

5. Click on anywhere in the Image 1 window.

The Add Text dialog box appears (as shown in Figure 12-6).

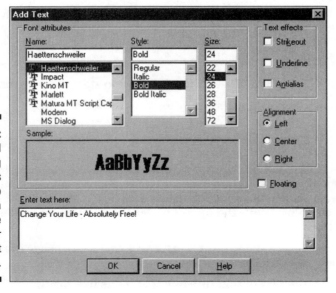

6. **Scroll down the list of typefaces under <u>N</u>ame, and then click on one to select it. Also click on an option under St<u>y</u>le and <u>S</u>ize.**

   A preview of the typeface appears in the area under Sample. If you don't like the option you selected, select another; the sample changes accordingly.

7. **In the text box under <u>E</u>nter Text Here, type a phrase that you want to appear on your banner ad. Click on OK.**

   The Add Text dialog box closes, and you return to the main Paint Shop Pro window. An outline of the text you typed appears in the Image 1 window.

8. **Move your mouse to the color palette that's visible on the right-hand side of the Paint Shop Pro window. (If the color palette isn't visible, select View⇨<u>C</u>olor Palette.) Carefully position your mouse over a color that you want your text to be. Right-click on the color you want in order to select it.**

   The color that you select appears in the lower of the two rectangles under the color palette.

9. **Click on the outline of the phrase you typed and drag it down so it disappears from the Image 1 window.**

   A dialog box appears asking you to confirm if you want to drag the type away.

10. **Click on OK.**

    The type appears in the Image 1 window in the color you selected (as shown in Figure 12-7).

Text tool   Color palette

Figure 12-7: If you're just figuring out how to use graphics programs, a text-only banner is a good way to start.

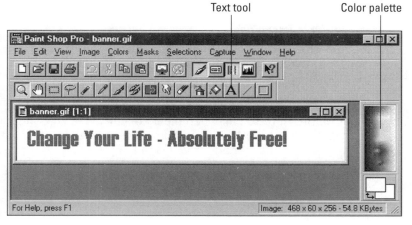

Now that you have some text for your banner, you can use Paint Shop Pro's other controls to add a background color or draw arrows or dividers to spice up the banner. You may also import a scanned image.

Save your image in one of the standard formats that are used on Web pages. For most simple logos, Graphics Interchange Format (GIF) is best.

To save your image in GIF format do the following:

1. **Choose File⇨Save from the Paint Shop Pro menu bar.**

   The Save dialog box appears.

2. **In the text box next to File Name, enter a name for your file, such as banner.gif.**

3. **Click on the arrow next to the Save As Type text box, and select GIF - CompuServe from the list of graphics file options.**

4. **Click on Save.**

   The Save dialog box closes, and you return to the Paint Shop Pro window. You can now select File⇨Exit to quit Paint Shop Pro.

GIF compresses the graphics information in your file so that the file is made as small as possible without losing any essential visual information. (In fact, LinkExchange requires banners to be only 7 kilobytes, or 7K, in size.) The smaller the file, the faster it appears on a Web page.

If you can't reduce your banner to 7K in file size (which is pretty small), LinkExchange suggests using a utility called GIFWizard, which is a simple form that you can fill out at useast.gifwizard.com/linkexchange.html. GIFWizard makes sure the physical size and file size of your banner are okay, and the utility resizes the file if necessary.

Free banner ad services

Unless you're experienced with graphics, don't create your own banner ad for the Web. You may spend hours designing an original that can't come close to what a professional can accomplish in half the time.

A practical alternative is to take advantage of some of the free banner ad services on the Web. You may find plenty of clip art that creators invite you to copy and use on your Web page. You can even find utilities that offer to generate your own banner ad for you, and people who create banner ads for free. LinkExchange collects many of these resources at www.linkexchange.com/members/create.html.

Clip art sites

These sites contain drawings, Web page backgrounds, animated GIF images, icons, and more. Clip art doesn't always mean that the art being offered is absolutely free. The authors hold the copyright, but they let you copy their work, while sometimes asking for a credit or restricting use to nonprofit sites. Be sure to read about use restrictions or fees before you start copying.

- ✔ Barry's Clip Art Server (www.barrysclipart.com)
- ✔ Free Art@Solarflare (www.solarflare.com/freeart)

Banner ad generators

These are Web sites that use special software to generate banner ads for you automatically. You enter some specifications about your banner in a Web page interactive form. You submit instructions to the site for your ad, and the software turns it into an ad for you.

- ✔ The Banner Generator (www.coder.com/creations/banner)
- ✔ Crecon's Banner Creation Site (www.crecon.com/banners.html)

Free banner ad designers

Some businesses that belong to LinkExchange volunteer to create banner ads for other LinkExchange members. Go to www.linkexchange.com to find out more.

Marketing and advertising is a daily activity. The most effective programs are ones that you devote some time to every single day. Set daily or weekly or monthly tasks for your staff.

Delivering Results with E-Mail

People don't usually think about e-mail when it comes to publicity and advertising. But e-mail is one of the effective (not to mention cost-effective) ways to get the word out on the Net. Why? E-mail is perfectly set up to build relationships, one-to-one. You reach lots of individuals with a single mouse click, and those people can respond to you quickly. E-mail can give you more publicity results for lower cost than any part of the Internet.

Keeping an address book

That little black book that holds your important phone numbers, addresses, or business cards has its equivalent in the world of the Net, too. It's called an address book, and any good e-mail program enables you to set one up. Do it! Every time you encounter an e-mail address, save it in your e-mail program's address book. Programs like Eudora, Microsoft Internet Mail and News, and Netscape Messenger enable you to group the e-mail addresses into mailing lists so that you can reach everyone in the list all at once. Messenger's address book is shown in Figure 12-8.

Figure 12-8:
Netscape Messenger's address book enables you to click on a name and click on the New Msg button to open an e-mail window preaddressed to that person.

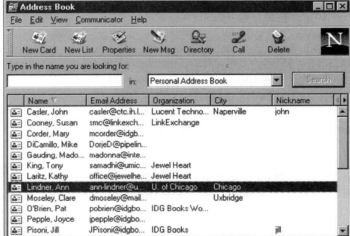

E-mail newsletters

Newsletters don't *look* like ads. They purport to tell you what's going on at a particular organization. But they serve many of advertisements' purposes. Newsletters put your company name before prospective customers, and provide those prospects with lots of information about your organization.

Games and giveaways

People who love the Net often love to play games. Besides that, everyone likes to receive something for free. Take advantage of these to build relationships with both prospective or current customers.

Alerting the media

Check out the e-mail addresses of the media representatives with whom you communicate. You can assemble those addresses in your e-mail program's address book, so you can send them a quick e-mail announcement when you don't have the time or the postage to mail out a press release. It's amazingly easy to send reporters a quick message telling them you're online and adding a link to your Web page.

Columnists who concentrate on the Internet can help publicize your site, too. Many columnists make their living by getting free publicity from people just like you. Find all the reporters and columnists who cover your area of interest, and keep their e-mail addresses in an address book, as explained earlier in this chapter. Then send them a notice when your Web site goes online or if some new and exciting business development occurs. The keys to success in media relations are the same as in other parts of using the Net:

✔ **Targeting.** Find the reporters/columnists who are likely to be interested in you, and concentrate on cultivating a good relationship with them. If you provide investment services, look for the business reporter, not the automotive writer or the general assignment reporter.

✔ **Content.** Do you have a new piece of software that no one else has? Do you find apartments for people who need them? Did you just sell your 10,000th gift basket? Stress what is new and newsworthy about your business, and be as specific as possible.

Make sure that your site is ready to go before you send off that press release. Be sure all your graphics appear correctly and proofread your Web pages for typos.

The most reliable way to find the current staff people at an online newspaper or magazine is to scroll down the Web site, looking for the person's name or e-mail address. However, this can be time-consuming. There are a couple of places on the Web that can make the work easier, such as

✔ Commercial News Services on the Internet (www.jou.ufl.edu/commres/webjou.htm)

✔ Ecola's Newstand (www.ecola.com/news/press)

✔ Yahoo!'s Indices to Media Resources (www.yahoo.com/News_and_Media/Indices)

Start by searching Yahoo! or another popular Internet index such as Excite (www.excite.com) in the category that applies to you. Look for newspapers, TV, radio stations, and magazines. You can also use some Internet resources that charge to make the contacts for you. PR Newswire (www.prnewswire.com) and Business Wire (www.businesswire.com) can send e-mail announcements to the journalists in their respective databases. You can target specific journalists in travel, finance, the southern U.S., and so on. However, these services aren't free: you're required to pay a $100 membership fee, and then $45 to reach a small category of reporters or $600 to blanket reporters around the country.

Keep your message simple in ASCII text format. Few e-mail users can read formatted e-mail. Separate headings with spaces; don't use bold or italic. It's also a good idea to mail yourself a copy of your announcement first to see how it looks before you broadcast it.

Free Publicity on the Web

Yes, Virginia, there is such a thing as a free lunch, at least where the World Wide Web is concerned. Plenty of Web sites are ready and willing to take your business's name, URL, contact information, and other information and publish it online absolutely free.

The next few sections describe the pros and cons of each of these advertising freebies in greater detail, so you can choose the best alternative(s) for you and avoid indigestion from your free lunch.

Search services

Search services are among the greater resources on the Web. They help Web surfers find information about almost any topic. (If you want to discover more about how the search services work, see Chapter 16.) You can be more likely to attract visitors if you follow a few simple steps.

Registering your site

To help potential customers locate your business when they conduct an Internet search, is to register your site with the service. Registration involves filling out a form that tells the service the name of your business, the URL of your Web site, and a short description of what you do. Each search service or index has its own form, and all the forms are slightly different. Instead of traveling from one site to another and filling out form after form, you can go to one of the announcement services such as Submit-It! and fill out a single form (shown in Figure 12-9) that automatically registers you with 30 popular search services.

After you submit the name of your company and the URL of your Web site to a search service, the company then uses a special indexing program called a *spider* or *wanderer* to visit your Web pages and record some of the contents. Those contents are stored in a huge database of Web pages. Telling the search service about your site and providing it with a URL ensures that you make it to the service's database more quickly.

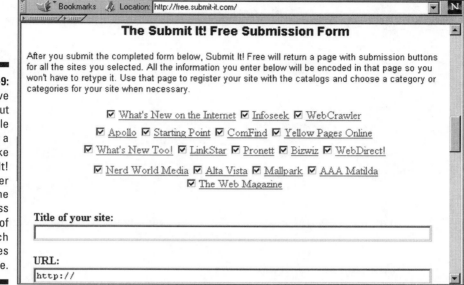

Figure 12-9:
To save time, fill out a single form and a service like Submit-It! can register your online business with lots of search services for free.

Be sure that you at least register your business with search services that focus on helping to find businesses on the Internet: Business Seek (www.businesseek.com) and The YelloWWWeb Pages (yellowwweb.com). These two services limit commercial Web sites exclusively.

Using keywords

If you expect to use the Net to advertise your business, you want to make sure that your company's Web pages show up as often as possible.

> ✔ In the headings used near the top of your Web pages.

> ✔ In the HTML commands that are used to create the page; specifically, between the two parts of an HTML command called META.

If you know HTML and want to pursue this second alternative, add your keywords by editing the source HTML for the home page of your Web site. (You can use a text editor or HTML editor to do this; see Chapter 13 for more on the role HTML plays in formatting Web pages.)

You can even go a step further and add a second META tag to your HTML document in order to add a standard description that the search services can display when they display your page and its URL.

The following example shows some keywords and a description I added to the home page of a small business called Future View Inc. (members.aol.com/realjobs):

```
<HTML>
<HEAD>
   <TITLE>Future View Inc.</TITLE>
   <META NAME="description" CONTENT="Home Page of Future
           View Inc., which handles placement of full-time
           software development/MIS professional/SMT posi-
           tions near Chicago; works with employers and
           applicants; Web site explains in detail how
           placement process works.">
   <META NAME="keywords" CONTENT="computer jobs, employment
           services, software development, MIS, SMT, CNC,
           job listings, high-tech careers, high-tech jobs,
           job placement, placement services, Chicago,
           Chicago jobs, Chicago computer jobs">
</HEAD>
```

If all this HTML scares you, take heart; some Web page editors give you a space in which you can add the keywords yourself.

One-stop search registration

Going from one search service to another and registering with each one takes time. The number of search services that scour the Web is growing all the time. (That fact is a measure of how many people need to find information on the Web.)

Some services enable you to register with many different sites at once. Table 12-1 presents the URLs of a few one-stop registration sites.

Table 12-1	Multiple Search Registration Sites
Service	**URL**
All4One	easypage.com/all4one.html
The Big Page	www.beaucoup.com/engines.html
Excite City.Net	www.city.net/
HotBot	www.hotbot.com/
LookSmart	www.looksmart.com/
StreetEye	www.streeteye.com/
University Toplinks	www.university.toplinks.com/

Internet indexes

Internet indexes attempt to act as a sort of Dewey Decimal System for the Internet. They organize Web pages according to their subject matter, and provide visitors with lists of links to all the sites in a given category.

For small businesses, these indexes are a real gold mine. They're free, they let you reach lots of readers, and your business is categorized on a page where lots of people can find it. Table 12-2 lists some of the major indexes:

Table 12-2	Internet Indexes
Site	_URL_
Yahoo!	www.yahoo.com/
TradeWave Galaxy	www.einet.net/galaxy.html
AOL NetFind	www.gnn.com/search/

Perhaps the only drawback with listing your site with an index is that you appear with lots of other similar businesses and it's hard for viewers to tell why yours is special. The next section, which uses the well-known index Yahoo! as an example, provides suggestions to make your site stand out.

Why Yahoo! Is Good for You

Yahoo! is among the more successful well-established businesses on the Web. If you only list yourself with one index or search service, this is it.

Yahoo! lists can be long. Businesses that begin with the letter A or B definitely have an advantage over the ones at the bottom of a page. Always write a description. Never leave your Yahoo! description space blank.

Write a good Yahoo! ad

Don't waste your Yahoo! space by not putting in any more than the name of your company. Take time to write a great 25-word Yahoo! ad. My colleague John Casler receives plenty of responses with his listing:

```
Casler, John - involved with the Web and Web site design
since 1991. Currently Webmaster for many commercial sites,
including fortune 500 companies. Serious inquiries only,
please.
```

Yahoo! now operates in several metropolitan areas of the country. You're well-advised to advertise with the metro Yahoo! near you. Listing with a regional or local Yahoo! can attract inquiries from people who live right in your area and who are looking for someone local to work with.

To find the current Metro Yahoo! branches, go to the main Yahoo! page (www.yahoo.com) and click on the button labeled More Yahoo!s. At the time of this writing, 11 Metro Yahoo!s are available, as well as 6 Yahoo!s in other parts of the world such as Asia, France, and Japan.

Exchanging links

One of the great ways to advertise yourself on the Net uses tried-and-true one-to-one communications. Simply call or e-mail the owner of another Web site and ask to exchange links with that person. You each put a link to one of the other site's Web pages (or to their e-mail address) on your site.

Making local listings and links

Identify magazines, newspapers, or other publications on the Web that may be interested in your business. Send them an e-mail message and ask if they want to link to your page.

It's not a good idea to exchange links with your hottest competitors. Try to find a group or organization that covers every business in your field.

Concentrate on directories in your local area that will enable you to add links to your business or group for free.

Can we link?

Asking for a link isn't complicated. Just be friendly, brief, and to the point. You may write something like this:

```
Would your office be interested in exchanging a link with
       the Web site for my office, the Housing Bureau
       for Seniors? Our office is actively looking for
       senior citizens in the Ann Arbor-Detroit area
       who are in need of housing options. In return,
       we would be glad to include a link to your site
       on our page as well.
```

LinkExchange

LinkExchange (www.linkexchange.com) is a large, highly regarded ad network on the Web. LinkExchange works like this:

1. You become a member of LinkExchange by filling out a form and submitting to the network's Web site. Membership is free (although LinkExchange has options for members who want to advertise).

2. You need to copy some HTML code that LinkExchange provides, which you then paste onto one of your Web pages. This causes a banner that reads LinkExchange Member to appear on your page.

3. You create a banner ad for your business. Submit your banner ad to LinkExchange. After your ads are approved, you see the LinkExchange banner on your page change. You can now display the banner of another LinkExchange member.

4. You earn advertising credits as soon as the LinkExchange banner appears on your page. Each time a Web surfer views your page, you earn half a credit. When you earn one credit (only two visits), your own banner goes to another LinkExchange member's site displayed. The more credits you get, the more your ad appears on the Web.

If you want to find out more about LinkExchange, read the FAQs at `www.linkexchange.com/members/faq.html`.

Shopping malls

In the vast spaces of the Internet, you may find business by joining numbers of other business people in a place where online shoppers can locate them. These places are called *malls,* the same as in the offline world. If your business generates sales, you may consider joining a mall — it doesn't cost much, and it may attract more business for you.

The Internet Mall (`www.internet-mall.com`) charges $24 for a year's listing in the mall. You get a short description and a link to your Web page.

The Gateway Mall (`www.gatewaymall.com`) comes in either a Virtual Reality version or a plain-text version. If you don't have a Web site, the mall's staff can create one for you.

Making partnerships

Small businesses can earn a bigger bang for each buck they spend on an Internet connection by partnering with a related business. I'm not talking about teaming up with the competition, but with another business whose products or services complement your own. Big players do this all the time. Microsoft signs an agreement with NBC; Yahoo! joins Viacom.

On a smaller scale, Gempler's, a mail-order garden supply business in Wisconsin, joined up with @griculture Online (`www.agriculture.com`) to produce its Web site (`www.gemplers.com`).

Gempler's, the small business site shown in Figure 12-10, is an example of how you can invite more attention by finding an Internet partner.

Case study: Housing Bureau for Seniors

You don't need to have a for-profit business to benefit from exchanging links with others on the Net. Non-profits can profit from making links, too. The Housing Bureau for Seniors in Ann Arbor, Michigan is a small, nonprofit group that tries to locate housing for senior citizens in need. The Bureau's director, Carolyn Hastings, asked me to suggest some sites that she could approach for links to her home page (www.med.umich.edu/whrc/HBS.html). I found a number of local organizations that cover a variety of resources in the Ann Arbor-Detroit metro area, such as

- A free listing with NewQuest City's Ann Arbor community information (www.buyersusa.com/nqc/cities/mi/chamber/0080.htm).

- A listing in the Ann Arbor Area Directory, part of the Ann Arbor Web site (annarbor.org).

- Another free listing in Branch Internet Services, Inc.'s Ann Arbor Web directory (ann-arbor.com).

- A Web page published by the Michigan Aging Services System at mass.iog.wayne.edu/OSAMSRD/MSRDMEPP/msrdme81.html.

- SeniorNet (www.seniornet.com).

- The American Association of Retired Persons Web site (www.aarp.org).

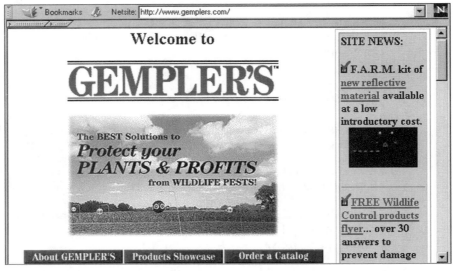

Figure 12-10: By partnering with another organization, your small business can get more attention and reach the audience you want.

Paying for Publicity Help on the Web

Sometimes it pays to call in an expert to help you with marketing. Consider hiring an online advertising agency. The Web abounds with ad agencies and marketing experts who are dying to help you put your name on the Web.

You may want to pay someone to assist with your advertising if

- ✔ Time is short.
- ✔ Staff help isn't available.
- ✔ Online exposure is essential.

Here are some ideas for ways to effectively spend your advertising dollars using outside resources.

Ad agencies

Lots of advertising agencies are waiting out there in cyberspace, ready and eager to promote your services. Some of these companies exist only on the Net. Others are traditional ad agencies that have home pages on the Web. Look for the ones that specialize in your particular business. Some specialize in financial institutions. Others work with newcomers, such as Accel Partners (www.accel.com), which offers advice to first-time entrepreneurs.

Online advertising buzzwords

If you start talking with Internet advertising agencies, it may be helpful to learn a few essential online terms so that you can impress the ad experts with your knowledge of the lingo:

- ✔ **Clickthrough.** The act of clicking on an ad on a Web site and going to the site that is linked to that ad.

- ✔ **Impression.** A visit to a Web page. Some Web sites charge for advertising based on how many impressions (or visits) are made to the page that contains the ad.

- ✔ **Cookies.** A cookie is a bit of electronic information that is generated when someone visits a Web site. The cookie is left on the visitor's computer. The next time the person visits the same site, the site can generate special information based on the information contained in the cookie. Not all Web sites create cookies.

- ✔ **CPM.** Short for Cost Per Thousand (M equals one thousand). Usually, this refers to the cost per thousand impressions.

Announcement services

For a small investment, you can hire a business that can send announcements of your own business or Web site to the various Internet search services and indexes. You submit the name, description, and URL of your site to the service, and the service sends it out to one place after another.

!Register-It! (`www.register-it.com`) can announce your site to 16 indexes and search services for free. For $39.99, it can send announcements to 100 locations, many around the world.

Submit-It! (`www.submit-it.com`) has a free 20-site announcement service. For $60, you can announce two separate Web pages to more than 300 search services and indexes.

PostMaster (`www.netcreations.com/postmaster`) is more expensive than the others, but it includes media outlets and more than 10,000 interested individuals in its announcement service, which costs $249.

Placing banner ads

In traditional advertising, you place an ad in a publication, and the publication delivers readers to you. The price you pay is based on estimates of how many individuals read the publication, based on the number of subscriptions and newsstand purchases.

- ✔ **Impression.** The advertiser is charged for the number of impressions — the number of visitors to the Web page that contains the ad.

- ✔ **Fixed price.** Some Web sites charge a fixed rate such as $1,000 a week; ask for statistical research to show you're getting your money's worth.

- ✔ **Percentage of sales.** Some online businesses, such as bookstores, may place an ad on your site, and then track who visits to determine if an order for a book or other item is placed from a click made on that ad. If an order results from such a clickthrough, you receive a commission.

- ✔ **Partial audience.** If a Web site gets 10,000 visits per month, you don't have to pay for all 10,000. You may pay a rate that's based on only 5,000 visits, while someone else pays for the other 5,000.

- ✔ **Targets.** The search engines and Yahoo!s index sell you narrowly targeted advertising so that your ad only appears if someone searches for a particular keyword. If one of the search terms is the word "book," for instance, Yahoo! displays an ad for an online bookstore on the page that presents the search results.

Ad networks

An ad network is a group of businesses that join together to exchange ads. One ad can go on thousands of Web sites. Usually, these networks have a central *ad server,* a Web site that manages and distributes the ads.

One advantage of ad networks is cost. The cost is lower than if you simply place an ad yourself on a single site that gets a lot of traffic. Another reason for the conservative pricing is that the networks provide customers with reports on how many people click on your ad, and how many visits are made to the page on which the ad appears.

If you're thinking about placing banner ads at all, be sure to visit Mark J. Welch's terrific Web Site Banner Advertising page (`www.markwelch.com/bannerad.htm`). Mark does a great job of explaining the different kinds of online advertising options, and his site includes links to hundreds of useful resources.

WebConnect (`www.wordata.com/webcon.htm`) acts as a broker for Internet ads.

Yahoo! charges for banner ads based on each 1,000 page visits. Rates cost $20 to $50 per 1,000 visits on most pages. That may not sound like a lot, but if you have to pay for 500,000 visits, the ads can cost $10,000 to $25,000. (See the rates at `www.yahoo.com/docs/advertising/rates_yahoo.html`.)

Building Relationships with Usenet

Usenet is a great way to build value for your company, spread your name far and wide among the online community, and build long-term relationships.

Being an expert

A much more effective way to generate publicity with Usenet (or with mailing lists, too) is to show off your expertise in your chosen field. You provide free advise, you answer questions, and you make suggestions in response to questions you read in Usenet messages. Why do you want to give away your knowledge for free? For one thing, it recalls the original purpose of Usenet, which is short for User's Network. Usenet is a community of people who share ideas and help others. By helping others, you get a side benefit: you make yourself more visible, and provide potential clients with a reason for contacting you.

In order to communicate successfully with those users, you have to learn the Usenet lingo. See Chapter 6 for more about Usenet.

Where do you find newsgroups? Try DejaNews. Try a few selected business newsgroups like `biz.marketing.moderated`. Be aware that lots of discussion groups are filled with ads from people trying to give something away for free. It can take some searching to locate some business discussions.

Becoming a Resource with FTP

Using FTP is a great way to build goodwill on the Net, and thus generate good publicity for your site. Often, you don't even see the results of your efforts. Someone makes a link to your FTP site, and you start getting lots of hits. Someone asks to bundle your software with a book or another product, and you strike it rich.

Every Web server keeps track of who visits each page. The techie term for the list of visitors is a *log file*. If you're curious about your own page, ask your Internet provider about counting hits and reporting them to you.

Log files tell you about who visits the page that contains your ad or link, such as

- ✔ The kind of computer each visitor uses.
- ✔ What kind of Web browser each visitor uses.
- ✔ What domain name is used by the visitor (usually, this is the domain name of the visitor's Internet Service Provider, so it may not tell you where they live).

Unfortunately, log files can't tell you each visitor's name, age, hometown, or other useful marketing information. To get that information, you need to set up a *guestbook,* a place where people can sign in and send you comments, or a form that people can fill out and send you.

Lpage's Web site, `www.Lpage.com/wguestbook`, guides you through the process of setting up a guestbook. You can also follow the step-by-step instructions in Chapter 7 of my book, *Creating Web Pages For Kids & Parents,* published by IDG Books Worldwide, Inc.

After you try out some advertising strategies, it's essential to evaluate your results to gauge your success. This is where online advertising gives you an advantage over advertising in traditional media outlets. If your ad, link, or announcement appears on a Web page that's hosted by your own Internet Service Provider, or if you have placed an ad through an ad network, you can obtain reports that indicate exactly how many people have seen your ad, link, or announcement.

Chapter 13

Putting Your Web Site to Work

● ●

In This Chapter

▶ Deciding whether to create your own Web pages or hire a consultant

▶ Envisioning your own site by considering common business Web sites

▶ Finding Web page software to make the job easier

▶ Using GeoCities' and AOL's free Web page creation software

▶ Tips for making Web pages that get responses

● ●

*T*hese days, the Web rules as king over the various domains of the Internet. While it's important to use e-mail, Usenet, FTP, and other parts of the online world to promote your small business, a Web site is becoming pretty much a necessity if you want to have a presence on the Internet.

This chapter assumes that you have an Internet connection and that you know whether you want to serve your own Web site or outsource the serving to an ISP. In that case, you're ready to create a business presence on the Web that gets attention for your company, attracts new customers or clients, and helps your current patrons stay satisfied.

Whether you create your site yourself or decide to hire a Web consultant to do the work, it's useful to know what contents are essential on any Web site, and what kinds of sites you can create. This chapter discusses those topics and also suggests ways to create a business Web site that's effective rather than one that just takes up space on a server and doesn't grab much attention.

As a small business owner or manager, you have two goals for your Web page that may seem to be at odds with each other. On one hand, you want to create a well-designed, professional-looking Web page that can catch the attention of potential customers and give your business credibility. At the same time, you want your page to offer useful information, and look straightforward and simple so that it appears on viewers' screens quickly. You have two choices:

✔ **Simple.** You can make your graphics as simple as possible, which promises to cast the widest net. An uncomplicated appearance takes into account the fact that many Web surfers have slow modem connections as well as widely differing hardware setups, and monitors that vary in image size and resolution.

✔ **High-tech.** You can use more sophisticated technologies like animated GIFs, Java applets, JavaScript or VBScript, style sheets, or dynamic HTML (in case you're wondering what these techy terms mean, see the sidebar "Web page lingo" later in this chapter). You can reach the viewers with fast connections who are more technically sophisticated, and have the knowledge that less Web-savvy readers don't.

You don't have to pick only one of these alternatives; there's a way that you can combine aspects of both approaches in the same Web site. Some sites provide visitors with different levels of Web graphics: The designer presents the visitor with two or sometimes even three ways to view the site's contents graphically. One version of a site is a simple text-only design, with only a few or no graphics; a second version can have simple JPEG or GIF images. A third version might have Java applets, animations, and the proverbial high-tech kitchen sink. The Web site for Berg, Inc., a construction contractor in Shreveport, Louisiana, presents visitors with two alternatives. If the graphical version shown in Figure 13-1 takes too long to appear, the visitor can click on the link "Text-only version available," at the top of the page. The text-only alternate version is shown in Figure 13-2.

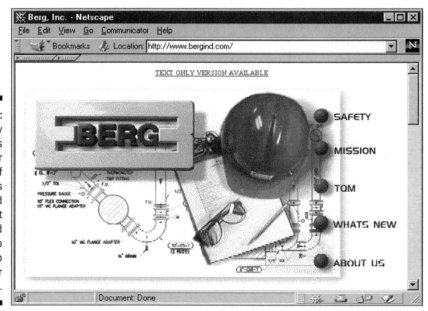

Figure 13-1:
High-quality graphics defeat your purpose if your visitors can't load them fast enough and decide to go to another site.

Figure 13-2:
Offering a
text-only
version of
your Web
site is an
extra-nice
touch for
some
viewers.

Of course, if you create two versions of your Web site, you're likely to do almost twice as much work. A big decision that you need to make is: Who's going to do that work?

When Should You Do It Yourself?

If you're accustomed to doing things yourself and plan to keep your Web page simple anyway, creating your own Web site is certainly a practical option.

For one thing, making Web pages is fun. It's quite a thrill to create your own pages and see them appear on the Web in just a matter of minutes. There are some great software programs, such as Microsoft FrontPage and Netscape Composer, that make the job surprisingly easy.

Be aware, though, that if you decide to create your own Web pages, you need some way of capturing images. If you don't already own a scanner or a digital camera, you have to purchase one, borrow a friend's, or rent time on a scanner at Kinko's Copies. And you need to download and/or purchase a program that alleviates the need to know HTML, which stands for HyperText Markup Language, the set of commands used to format Web pages so that they appear the way you want on someone's Web browser.

Web page lingo

Whether you decide to weave your own business Web or hire someone to do it, it helps to know the basic terms that you can expect to see and hear people throwing around. Here are some essential Web page terms you need to know about.

Animated GIF: An image saved in a special variety of Graphics Interchange Format (GIF) that can consist of a number of separate GIF images. Some browsers can play the images in succession, providing an animation effect.

Background: Every Web page has a background color that appears behind the primary text and graphics. By default, the color is grey, but the designer can assign another color, or use a graphic image that can be tiled (repeated over and over) to appear as wallpaper behind the page contents.

Domain Name: An easy-to-remember name assigned to many Web sites, such as www.mycompany.com.

Dynamic HTML: HTML that is supplemented by Java, JavaScript, and other programming languages to generate Web page content dynamically in response to data input or mouse clicks by the user.

Frames: Frames are subdivisions of a Web page, each consisting of its own separate Web document. Depending on how the designer sets up the Web page, a user is able to scroll through one frame independently of the other frames on the same page. A mouse click on a hypertext link contained in one frame may cause a new document to appear in an adjacent frame.

GIF or JPEG: Two file formats that employ different methods to compress computer graphics with minimal or no loss of image quality. GIF stands for Graphics Interchange Format; JPEG stands for Joint Photographic Experts Group. Compressed files appear faster on the Net. A third format, PNG (Portable Network Graphics), is expected to replace GIF in the next few years.

Home page: Often, people use the term home page generically to mean any Web page. Actually, the term refers to the main point of entry or welcome page to a Web site.

HTML: Hypertext Markup Language, the set of commands used to mark up documents with standard elements so that they can be displayed and read on the World Wide Web by different browsers on different computers.

Java applet: A bit of computer code, written in Sun Microsystems' Java language, that executes in response to mouse clicks and produces sound, video, or other effects in a Web browser window.

JavaScript and VBScript: JavaScript (created by Netscape Communications) and VBScript (created by Microsoft) are two relatively simple computer programming languages that are designed to add functionality to Web pages. The scripts are added to the HTML commands for a Web page.

Plug-ins: Applications that launch and display sound, graphics, or animations within the Web browser window. Plug-ins process graphics or multimedia files that browsers cannot display/play on their own.

Style sheets: Sets of HTML instructions that can affect the appearance of all the headings, body text, and many other elements that appear on a Web page.

Tables: A set of HTML commands that enable you to present tabular data in columns and rows, much like a spreadsheet. A border around the table can be used to separate lots of different information on a page into cells, but the borders can be hidden, too.

URL: Uniform Resource Locator, the address that enables you to find my file or Web page on the Internet. The URL is like the Dewey Decimal number that helps you find one book among all the stacks in the library.

Web server: A computer set up to exchange information with another computer over the Internet using one or more standard protocols, such as HTTP, FTP, Gopher, and so on.

Web site: One or more interlinked documents published on the Web and associated with a particular individual or organization.

At least three different terms are used to describe software that enables you to create Web pages without having to enter raw HTML by hand. Sometimes, they're called *Web page editors* or *HTML editors*. In your travels around the Web, you may also see references to *Web authoring tools* or *Web authoring programs*. This chapter uses the terms *editor, program,* and *tool* interchangeably, but each of the terms refers to the same thing: a program that allows you to format text, add graphics, and design Web pages without having to look at the HTML instructions that make the pages work.

If you don't have the time to climb the learning curve and figure out how to create a Web page, hire someone. If your Web page is going to play an important role in promoting your business or making sales, by all means spend the money up-front to hire an expert. Your investment can return important time-savings and a more professional, inviting page.

The Web is booming; competition is getting fierce, and it's becoming more and more difficult to stand out from the crowd. Network Wizards (www.nw.com), in its January 1997 survey, reported more than 828,000 unique domain names on the Internet, compared with only 488,000 only six months before. You need someone who knows the field, who can do the job right the first time, and who agrees to maintain your site.

Hiring a Web page designer requires the same care as enlisting help from any other contractor. Call around and get at least three prices. Be sure the consultants send you URLs of sites they designed, and references of satisfied customers. These days, Web page consultants are popping up all the time, and few of them have been in existence for more than a couple of years, so be sure that you're working with a vendor you can count on.

Web Site Models to Follow

When you start thinking about what sort of Web site you want to create for your business, it's a good idea to consider exactly what type of Web site can best serve your business needs. Here are some suggestions.

An online store

Many businesses make their Web debut to increase sales. Marketing merchandise on the Net is advisable primarily if the goods or services you sell are distributed by mail order or have a potentially wide customer base, like an online bookstore or CD mail order house, as opposed to a business that only attracts local customers, like an auto repair shop.

Often, sites that conduct commerce on the Web provide visitors with a catalog of items for sale. Some sites use electronic commerce software to enable customers to place orders online using credit cards. It's always a good idea, though, to take into account visitors' concerns about security on the Net and provide alternatives to entering credit card numbers online — options like toll-free phone or fax numbers.

An online store doesn't have to *look* like a store, either. The Chicago Gourmet Steaks site shown in Figure 13-3, for instance, is tasteful and clean and doesn't oversell itself.

Figure 13-3:
This site provides for ordering by phone, fax, mail, or filling out an online form.

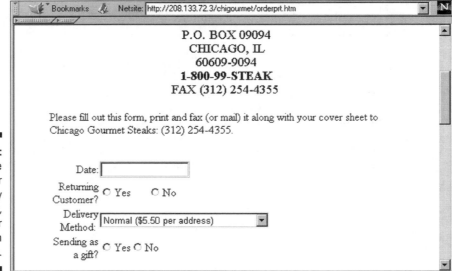

A "just the facts" Web site

Many commercial Web sites are not created with the primary goal of actually selling goods and services online. Rather, the Web site serves to explain what the company does, promote its services, and supplement personal contacts. As stated in Chapter 15, the best way to keep people returning to your Web site is to make it a useful resource. The more information you provide, the more reasons people have to stay.

Future View, Inc., a recruitment firm located near Chicago, limits its customer base to the immediate metropolitan area. Most of its recruitment work involves lots of phone calls with prospective employers and employees. Future View, Inc. doesn't expect to gain many new customers through its Web site.

However, the Web site *is* a good way to invite individuals who have some experience with the company to find out more about the recruitment process and how it works. The Web provides plenty of space to put out a set of Frequently Asked Questions (FAQs), as well as a set of current job opportunities. A site of this sort acts like an online press release that provides visitors with current news, an e-mail address for inquiries, and background information about the company.

Customer service site

The Web is a great place to provide your current customers with a way to contact you and ask questions or find answers 24 hours a day. The Customer Solutions page on the visually attractive and complex Garden Escape Web site (www.garden.com), shown in Figure 13-4, provides a wide range of information, including

- Hours of operation
- Phone numbers
- Feedback forms
- A way to obtain your password to the site if you forgot it
- A way to check the status of any orders that you placed with the company
- A statement of the company's policy on returns, and instructions on how to return items

Figure 13-4:
A customer service page is an integral part of many business Web sites.

An E-zine

Speaking of customer service, the Customer Service Review site (www.csr.co.za) shown in Figure 13-5 is an example of another kind of Web site that you can create if you're inclined toward news and publishing. It's an e-zine, or electronic magazine, a publication that exists only on the Internet, and that presents news and views on a particular subject. (Electronic newsletters and magazines are discussed further in Chapter 15.)

Figure 13-5:
Create an e-zine to give online visitors the latest news in your field.

An intranet site

The Web pages that you create may only be visible on your corporate intranet, but they're important, too. You can do a lot of team building by creating a page or pages devoted to the group of people you work with. My friend John Casler designed a series of pages for the Web Team at Lucent Technologies. The pages helped create an identity for the group and gave the members a place to track the progress of current projects. An internal Web site can

- ✔ Provide employees with a way to access training and human resources information.
- ✔ Distribute updated versions of software.
- ✔ Give staff people a way to access discussion groups and bulletin boards.
- ✔ Deliver company-wide announcements from management.

Weaving Your Site on the Web

Now that you have ideas about how you want your Web site to look, feel, and communicate — and you know who is actually going to design it — you can get down to work.

It's advisable to start small and work up instead of trying to undertake a 30- or 50-page Web site all at once. You may only create half a dozen pages to begin with. Starting small gives you an opportunity to focus on making your pages look good; you can always add more pages later on.

Draw a map of your site. You won't catch a house builder starting to pour concrete without having a good blueprint that shows exactly what goes where. You're making your own construction, too. I tend to diagram Web sites in the shape of a triangle. The welcome page of the site is at the top, and the second-level pages are beneath it. The third-level pages fall beneath those. An example is shown in Figure 13-6.

Don't worry about HTML

If you're contemplating creating your first Web page, you may be intimidated because you think that you have to learn HTML. Not true! Although it helps to know a little about HTML and what it does, you don't have to learn every nuance of the language. Yes, it's true that HTML resembles a computer

Figure 13-6:
Draw a map
of your site
before you
start
creating
pages so
that you
can keep
track of
links and
URLs.

programming language in that you have to use special symbols in the right
places so that text and images can appear a certain way. But don't be
intimated. There are two reasons that HTML is easy to work with, even for
nonprogrammers:

✔ **It's a markup language.** Like the name says, HTML is a markup language, not a computer programming language. You use it in much the
same way that old-fashioned editors marked up copy before they gave
it to typesetters. Anyone can learn how to use HTML instructions
because they resemble English.

✔ **HTML software does the work.** A number of software programs are
available that make it possible to mark up documents with HTML
without having to enter HTML commands. All you have to do is click on
buttons and select menu items to format text and images on a Web page.

You don't need to be acquainted with every nuance of HTML before you can
create your first Web document. But it's very helpful to be somewhat
familiar with the structure of HTML documents and individual commands.

If you really want to know more about HTML, a good place to start is *HTML
For Dummies,* 3rd Edition, by Ed Tittel and Steven N. James (IDG Books
Worldwide, Inc.). There are also some very good HTML tutorials on the Web,
such as the Beginner's Guide to HTML, (www.ncsa.uiuc.edu/General/
Internet/WWW/HTMLPrimer.html) and the Forty Five Minute HTML Primer
(www.grossmont.k12.ca.us/HTMLClass/Primer.html).

Rely on your Web page software to make the job easier

The most important thing that you can do to simplify the task of creating a Web is to pick the right software. Spending a few extra bucks on the best program can save you time in the long run and make your life easier.

Rules for good tools

There are qualities common to all Web page tools:

- ✔ **Previewing.** Most Web page creation software enables you to preview your work so that you can see what to expect when it appears in a Web browser.

- ✔ **Formatting.** You get an assortment of menus and toolbar buttons to change selected text to bold, italic, or another style.

- ✔ **Linking.** Web page tools enable you to create both internal links (links that move from one part of a single document to another) and external links (links that take you from one page to another on a single Web site, or to another Web site altogether).

Web page tools differ in one way. Some tools keep the HTML commands transparent; others make them visible on the screen as you work with the document. If you are an HTML-phobe at all, try one of the transparent programs like Netscape Composer, Adobe PageMill, and Microsoft FrontPage.

The joy of WYSIWYG

If you want to build your Web page piece by piece and see how the final product is going to look, I highly recommend that you try one of the WYSIWYG HTML editors mentioned earlier. You have to purchase FrontPage either through an online store like PCConnection (www.pcconnection.com) or from a retail computer store in your area.

Netscape Composer is part of the standard version of Netscape Communicator, which you can download from Netscape's Web site (home.netscape.com/comprod/mirror/client_download.html). You can download the software and use it for free, but in order to get technical support or receive discounts on future releases, the company asks you to become a registered user and purchase the program. You can order Communicator for $59 from Netscape's online store (merchant.netscape.com/special/netstore/clients/communicator.html).

You can download a 30-day trial version of Adobe PageMill, which is available for both Windows 95 and Macintosh computers, from the Adobe Systems Incorporated Web site (www.adobe.com/prodindex/pagemill/main.html). Mac users may consider a related Adobe product, SiteMill, that includes PageMill's features and adds some tools that help you organize and maintain a set of Web pages.

Each of these programs comes with instructions on how to use them. The following example uses Microsoft FrontPage, but the same general instructions apply to the other programs as well. The procedure of selecting text and assigning styles is the same; the specific menu options and toolbar buttons are different:

1. **Double-click on the program's icon or select its name from the Program Manager to start it. For this example, I launched FrontPage Editor, the Web page creation program that comes with Microsoft FrontPage 97.**

   A new blank document appears on the screen. The text cursor (a single vertical line) appears at the top of the working area (the big blank area just below the toolbars), ready for you to begin typing. You can import an existing plain-text document if you have one ready (see Chapter 15). This example follows the steps involved in creating a document from scratch.

2. **Start by typing the name of your Web site's home page (the page that you want visitors to go to first). For this example, I typed** Welcome to Aquatic World.

   In the final version, you may actually have a logo or graphic at the top of the page, but this message can serve as a placeholder for your work-in-progress.

3. **Click and hold down the mouse button, and drag across the words you just typed to select them (you can also click in the invisible selection gutter in the left margin of the window to select an adjacent line; double-click to select an adjacent paragraph).**

   The line of text becomes highlighted.

4. **Click on the little triangle next to the paragraph styles drop-down list in the bottom left-hand corner of FrontPage's toolbar area.**

   Right now the style is set to the default style for body text, which is simply called Normal. When you click on the triangle, a list of HTML styles drops down. HTML formats text by assigning generic styles so that the text appears the same no matter what kind of computer or Web browser is used to view the page.

5. Scroll down the list and select the style Heading 1. Six levels of headings are provided in HTML: from H1 (the most important and biggest heading) to H6 (least important, and very small).

6. Press Enter or Return to insert a blank space, and type a subheading or a paragraph of descriptive text that describes your company or organization in a nutshell. To format the subheading, select the text and choose Heading 3 from the paragraph styles drop-down list. With the text still selected, click on the Italic button (the one that looks like an italic letter A).

The selected text becomes a small, bold italic subheading.

7. You can create a list of items by typing Press or Enter after each item, and then scrolling across the series of items to select them all at once. Then click on the Bulleted List toolbar button.

The series of items appears as a bulleted list (shown in Figure 13-7).

Figure 13-7:
The slicker Web page tools enable to you concentrate on the content, not the HTML.

8. It's always a good idea to change the default grey background of a Web page to something more interesting. When in doubt, choose white. Select Format⇨Background . . . .

The Page Properties dialog box appears with the Background tab in front.

9. **Click and hold down on the triangle next to the Ba<u>c</u>kground box.**

A list of background colors pops up.

10. **Select white, or whatever color you want. Then click on OK.**

The Page Properties dialog box closes and you return to the FrontPage Editor window, where your new background color appears behind your text.

11. **It's important to save your work and name your page. FrontPage Editor enables you to do both in one easy step. Select <u>F</u>ile⇨<u>S</u>ave.**

The Save As dialog box appears (shown in Figure 13-8).

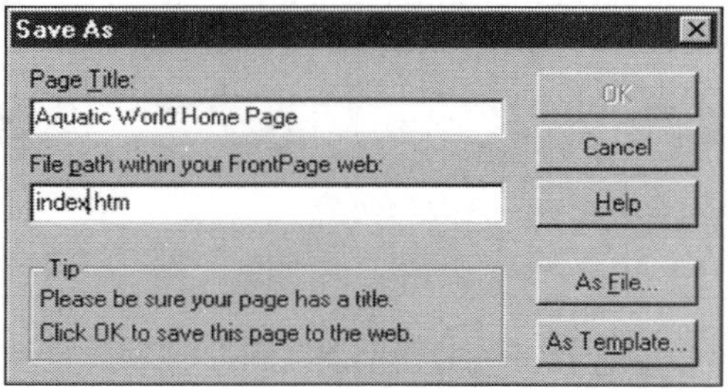

Figure 13-8:
It's a snap
to create a
simple Web
page with
headings, a
bulleted list,
and a
background
color using
FrontPage
Editor.

12. **In the text box beneath Page <u>T</u>itle, enter the title that you want to appear in the title bar at the very top of the Web browser window. In the text box beneath File <u>p</u>ath within your FrontPage web, enter a filename for this Web page.**

Because this is the home page for your site, it's a good idea to enter one of the standard filenames `index.htm` or `default.htm`, which most browsers recognize as a site's default page (the page to visit first). Subsequent pages can have names that describe their content, like `links.htm` or `catalog.htm`.

13. **Click on As File . . . .**

The Save As File dialog box appears.

14. **Select a location on your hard disk in which to save the file, and then click on <u>S</u>ave.**

Your file is saved, and you return to the FrontPage Editor window.

15. **Choose <u>F</u>ile⇨E<u>x</u>it.**

The program quits and you return to your desktop.

FrontPage Editor gives you many more functions so that you can add all sorts of Web page goodies like links, forms, and images. See the program's documentation for more detailed instructions on how to use the program. The next section continues the process of creating this Web page with a different type of Web page tool, so that you can get an idea of which one you may prefer.

See your food HTML editors

There's a cafeteria-style restaurant in Chicago that's locally famous for its neon sign, which proclaims that you have the chance to "see your food" before you order it. One type of HTML editing program enables you to see your HTML before you publish your Web page. If you want to understand how Web pages are put together by actually seeing the HTML being added as you choose menu options or click on buttons, you can use this watch-it-as-you-work kind of HTML editor. Many Web page consultants (like Debbie Levitt of As Was) use software that provides visual updates so that they can see the HTML and edit the commands themselves if they want to.

One of the more popular of these programs is HotDog Professional. You can download a trial version (Windows 95 only) at the Sausage Software Web site (www.sausage.com). Follow these steps to open the document created in the previous example and continue working on it:

1. **Double-click on the HotDog icon to start the program.**

   The Welcome to HotDog screen appears, presenting you with options to learn more about HTML or to start using the program.

2. **Click on the button labeled Use Hot Dog Now.**

   A new blank HotDog window appears.

3. **Click on the close box in the Document Window area on the right half of the main HotDog window.**

   The Welcome to HotDog document closes.

4. **Select File⇨Open (or press Ctrl+O).**

   The Open File dialog box appears.

5. **Locate the** index.htm **file you created in the earlier example, and then click on Open.**

   The file opens in the Document Window area of the HotDog window. The Web page looks much different than it did earlier; now you can see the HTML commands behind the formatting (shown in Figure 13-9).

6. **Scroll down the HTML document in the Document Window and position your mouse at the point in the Web page where you want an image to appear. Click at that spot.**

   The text cursor is inserted in the HTML for the document.

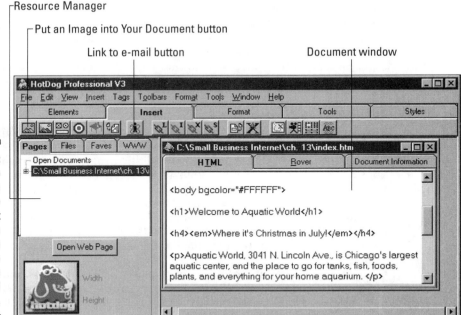

Resource Manager

Put an Image into Your Document button

Link to e-mail button

Document window

Figure 13-9:
Many Web
page
editors, like
HotDog, lift
the curtain
and let you
glimpse the
HTML while
you build
a page.

7. **Click on the Image tab to bring it to the front, and then click on the toolbar button at the extreme left, the Put an Image into Your Document button.**

   The Insert Image dialog box appears.

8. **Click on the button that has an open folder on it, next to the Image File box.**

   The HotDog Professional - Select Image File dialog box appears.

9. **Locate a GIF or JPEG image on your hard disk.**

   Such a file has the filename extension .gif or .jpg/.jpeg, respectively. If you don't have a scanner and don't feel confident drawing an image in a computer graphics program, go to a clip art site such as The Clip Art Universe (www.nzwwa.com/mirror/clipart) and copy a picture. Be sure that you read the restrictions on use — some sites don't let for-profit businesses copy their artwork for free, but charge a nominal fee instead.

10. **Click on the file's name and click on Open.**

    The image file is added to your document. You only see the HTML for this file when the HTML tab is active in the Document Window. If you click on the Rover tab, you see a preview of your Web page with the image added.

Adding a Mailto link

Another common task in Web page design is adding links. A good HTML editing program like HotDog makes it easy to create hypertext links. Begin by opening your document in HotDog as described in Steps 1 through 5 in the previous section. Position your cursor in your document where you want your link to appear (see the preceding Step 6). Then follow these steps to create one type of link that's an important part of every home page: a `mailto` link that enables visitors to send you e-mail easily.

1. **Click on the Image tab to bring it to the front.**

   The Image set of toolbar buttons appears.

2. **Click on the Link to email/news/ftp and more button.**

   The Insert an Internet Object dialog box appears (see Figure 13-10).

3. **Click on Email, and then click on OK.**

   The Enter Mail Address dialog box appears.

4. **In the text box beneath Mail Address, enter your e-mail address. In the text box beneath Description of Link, enter a few words that describe what the link does (**`send e-mail to our Webmaster`**, for instance).**

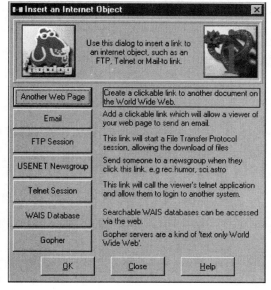

Figure 13-10:
This dialog box enables you to enter links, images, and all kinds of goodies to a Web page.

5. Click on OK.

The Enter Mail Address dialog box closes and you return to the main HotDog window. You can preview your link by clicking on the Rover tab in the Document Window. Then scroll down the page until your link appears.

When you're done with HotDog, select File⊅Exit to quit the program and return to your desktop.

Building Web pages on the Web

Some sites on the Web can help you build a Web page for free. You don't have to download any software; rather, you connect to the Web site and use the software tools provided there. One such site is called GeoCities. GeoCities enables people to make Web pages and get e-mail addresses for free. The site makes money by selling advertising.

Go the welcome page for GeoCities (www.geocities.com) and then click on the link Free Home Pages & Free E-mail. Follow the instructions on the Web site to become a member of GeoCities (it's free) and get a username and password. This process is described in detail in Chapter 1 of my book *Creating Web Pages For Kids & Parents* (IDG Books Worldwide, Inc.).

After you become a GeoCities member, you set up a homestead on one of GeoCities' Web servers and create a Web page with a GeoCities service called the Basic HTML Editor (see Figure 13-11).

Figure 13-11: GeoCities' online editor enables you to create simple home pages using its Web site software.

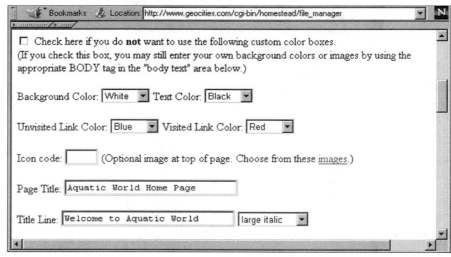

The big advantage of GeoCities is cost: You pay nothing to set up your own Web site and e-mail service. The drawback is that the Basic HTML Editor is not even remotely as powerful as HotDog, for instance. (Another GeoCities utility, the Advanced HTML Editor, enables you to format your page by entering your own HTML commands.) However, for $5 to $10 per month, you can sign up for the company's GeoPlus program, which gives you a virtual domain name (www.mycompany.com) and lots of space for a big business Web site.

The online services' Web page software

If you use America Online or CompuServe to connect to the Net, you can use the Web page tools that are supplied with each of those services.

America Online's My Home Page/My Place

AOL has lots of resources for any of its members who want to create Web sites. You can use an online form called My Home Page, which resembles GeoCities' Basic Home Page Editor, to create a simple home page. AOL also gives members free Web server space where you can post Web pages that you create with a program other than My Home Page, like HotDog. These pages can be for business or personal use. AOL also provides its members with Frequently Asked Questions and step-by-step tutorials that lead you through the process of creating and publishing Web pages.

The place to start is by connecting to AOL and following these steps:

1. **Select <u>G</u>o To⇨Keyword or press Ctrl+.**

   The Keyword dialog box appears.

2. **Type** Personal Publisher, **and then click on Go.**

   You go to the Personal Publisher welcome page.

3. **Scroll through the list of options, and double-click on the option To Access Personal Publisher 1.**

   The Personal Publisher page appears (shown in Figure 13-12).

Click on the button Create/Edit My Home Page to use AOL's My Home Page service. Scroll down the list of pages; you can go to HTML tutorials, tips on creating Web pages, and assorted assistance with Web publishing in general. Select Go to My Place if you already created a Web page and want to upload it to America Online so that everyone can enjoy it (see the section "Getting Your Page Online" for more information).

Figure 13-12:
Follow
along with
the
characters
Roger and
Byte, who
can help
you create a
Web page
on AOL.

Tips for Making Great Web pages

What makes some Web sites more successful than others? It's no mystery. Basically, the key is to do the same things that make your business successful: Devote as much time and energy as you can to the project, and keep updating your pages to make them more and more useful.

This section presents a few tips for creating great Web pages. Instead of offering only one opinion on the subject, I asked some successful Web site consultants to give a few tips of their own on how to create an attractive, attention-grabbing Web page. In particular, thanks to Debbie Levitt (info@aswas.com) for contributing lots of useful advice.

Case study: As Was Web site design

Debbie Levitt is the owner of As Was (www.aswas.com/info.html), a small business in Long Island, New York that she formed in 1995. She started with just two staff people, but now she employs eight, and Debbie's in the process of hiring 20 salespeople around the world. As Was has two dial-up connections to the Internet: a 28.8Kbps and a 33.6Kbps modem which, Debbie says, are much more affordable than direct connections. She adds: "Since I'm a Web site designer, I like to have an average system. That way, I know how fast my sites really appear on most peoples' computers."

Tip #1: Give people a reason to (re)visit

The most successful Web sites not only give people a reason to visit in the first place, but also provide an incentive for people to return. Simply telling people that your site updates every week or two can help encourage users to bookmark your site and come back later on.

One way to encourage visits is to capitalize on your existing customer base. If you regularly place an ad in a newspaper or magazine that already draws visitors, add a reference to the URL of your Web site somewhere on that ad. Bill Cameta, the owner of Cameta Camera (see Chapter 15) tells people in his *Shutterbug* magazine ad that they can find more up-to-date information on his company's Web site, for instance.

Tip #2: Remember your audience

The most successful Web sites take their audiences into account and make allowances for their visitors' computer equipment, time constraints, and need for information. Use standard colors and keep your site clean. Don't try to do too much on any one page. Use Java applets, forms, and animated images sparingly. Keep your Web pages clean and uncluttered so that people won't mind looking at them.

Tip #3: Remember your other publications

Be conscious of the rest of your company's printed material and publicity outlets when you create your Web page. Be consistent in your graphics; use the same logo that appears on your letterhead, and the same kind of writing style that's found on your other business materials.

Coordinate your Web page with other forms of communication. Put your URL on all your ads. Let people order brochures from your Web page. In turn, the printed brochures can refer to your Web page for more timely or detailed information than you can provide in print.

Tip #4: Do one thing at a time

Lots of Web pages take the kitchen sink approach to graphic design. All their contents are packed into a single document, complete with plenty of graphics. Be sure to divide your text and images into several pages, and include no more than one or two topics on each page.

Whenever possible, it's best to keep Web pages short, perhaps only one or two screens in length. When that's not possible, it's helpful to provide a table of contents that people can click on. Often, the contents are presented on the left side of a Web page screen in a narrow column.

Tip #5: Care and feeding of your Web pages

Like a garden or a pet, a Web site benefits from constant care and feeding. Once you create your graphics and design your Web pages, your work is by no means unchangeable, as it would be after it's printed on paper. On the Web, revising and republishing your work is simply a matter of transferring some files from your computer to the Web server, the computer that presents your documents on the Internet, and possibly revising some links to those graphics.

The image on the left side of Figure 13-13 shows a site that Stylus Media created originally. The image on the right shows how the site was redesigned a few months later. The first layout used frames; the second was simplified to make the page appear more quickly in a browser window. Stylus wanted to provide the client with a cleaner, simpler layout as well as a more generic graphic, one that didn't seem oriented solely toward female visitors. Don't be afraid to get feedback from visitors and colleagues, and revise and improve your work.

Figure 13-13:
Don't be afraid to rehab your Web page to give it a new, improved appearance.

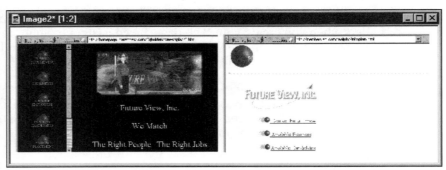

Tip #6: Don't send visitors away

Be careful about adding links and ads that encourage people to leave your site. They may never return. It's hard enough attracting visitors in the first place. Banner ads may get you more visits, but they can lead people away from your site, too. If you really want to invest in banner advertising, make sure you try sites that work, like Yahoo! (Debbie Levitt also suggests Double-Click, www.doubleclick.com).

Tip #7: Proofread, check, and test your page

A key point in creating a Web page is not something you *do* but something you *don't* do: make spelling errors and grammatical blunders. A single typo at the top of your Web page can ruin the professional appearance you tried so hard to create. Find someone in your office who has an eye for detail to go over your text. (It's easier for outsiders to find mistakes than for the authors who are close to their work.) Many HTML editors like HotDog have built-in spell-checkers. Use them!

Be sure to test your page to see how it looks and how fast the graphics appear. All your work can go wasted if your viewer gets impatient, presses the Escape (Esc) key, and goes to another site. It's also a good idea to load your Web page(s) in different browsers — if more than one is available — to make sure that they look the way you want: Different browsers display colors differently, and some older models don't display goodies like Java applets or JavaScript at all.

Dressing Up Your Web Page

Often, a page with only one image is more effective than one with five or six because it gets the viewer's attention and invites mouse clicks to explore the site further. Place a graphic next to the most important element on a page, or the element where you want the reader to click next. The important elements on a crowded page can be further highlighted by creating white space around them.

Adding images and colors

Graphics can go a long way toward creating the look and feel of a Web site. The most effective sites use graphics to retain their existing corporate logos, typefaces, and other elements that make up their organization's identity, while still creating a presence that's unique to the Web.

Line art versus photos

Much can be done with simple line art rather than scanned photos. A designer who has artistic ability should feel free to draw his or her own original art. This sort of graphic can be more effective than a photo because the style of the drawing can convey the style of the designer. The drawings can be wacky, restrained, classic, or anything in between, and can help give the site graphic flair and style. Some of the better illustrations on the Web appear in the online magazine Salon (www.salon1999.com).

Good design, bad design

Visit sites that exhibit good design to get ideas for your own Web pages. A number of sites recognize Web designs that they consider good or cool in some way. You can stop in at the Webby Awards site (`www.webbyawards.com`), (`www.iNetCity.Net/inetcool.htm`), or the Speared Peanut Design Awards (`web.wt.net/~sprdpnut/winners.html`). Cool Site of the Day (`cool.infi.net`) picks a site every day judged tops in design or content.

Sites chosen for their good use of typography, color, and composition are recognized by the IPPA Award for Design Excellence (`www.ippa.org`).

At the other end of the spectrum are sites that provide you with examples of what *not* to do, such as Web Pages that Suck (`www.webpagesthatsuck.com`) or Mirsky's Worst of the Web (`mirsky.com/wow`).

 The Web abounds with sites full of images whose creators generously provide them for others to copy and use on their Web pages. Use the search services (see Chapter 16) to find clip art sites. However, if you're looking for a particular image and you need it fast, here's a suggestion for finding it: Search services simply try to find Web sites in their databases that contain whatever keywords you submit. If you're looking for an image of a particular object or scene, you can find it by entering a filename. If you're looking for an image of a tree, for instance, you can send the following keywords to the search service:

```
tree.gif
tree.jpg
```

The search service returns links to Web pages that contain files called `tree.gif` or `tree.jpg`. (Keep in mind that some services don't accept the period in a search query, so you may end up with hits on every page that contains tree, gif, or jpg.) The identified pages don't necessarily hold clip art images, so you cannot use them in your own Web pages without permission; however, the images that you find may help by serving as a starting point for you to draw your own image.

Getting Your Page Online

After you or your consultant has prepared your Web pages, the next step is to get them online so that people can start visiting you. This involves moving your HTML documents and graphics files to a Web server, a computer that remains connected to the Web all the time and serves up Web pages. The following sections describe what to look for.

Finding a host

If you're operating your own Web server in your office, you have no problem. Just have your Webmaster do the work. If you don't have a server, you need to find one.

Many Internet Service Providers can give you space on one of their servers where you can publish your pages. However, the company that provides you with access to the Internet is not always the best option for providing you with a place to publish your Web pages so that people can see them. Why? For one thing, some ISPs charge you extra for business Web sites. You may find it much more economical to locate a host that's specifically set up to host business sites online.

If you're on the Internet, investigate several services and compare prices to get the best deal. There are many, many services to choose from, and it's impossible to provide a representative sample here. The following Web pages list lots of hosting services:

- ✔ Yahoo! index (`www.yahoo.com/Business_and_Economy/Companies/Internet_Services/Web_Services/Hosting`)
- ✔ The List (`thelist.internet.com`), arranged by area code or individual country
- ✔ budgetweb.com list of Budget Internet Providers (`budgetweb.com/budgetweb/index.html`)

A good rate for Web hosting is less than $30 per month for the following:

- ✔ A virtual domain name (`www.mycompany.com`). You have to pay registration fees to InterNIC, however, above and beyond the monthly rate.
- ✔ 25MB of disk space.
- ✔ Five e-mail addresses.
- ✔ Support for Microsoft FrontPage extensions, so that you can publish your pages directly through FrontPage.
- ✔ At least 20MB of File Transfer Protocol (FTP) space.

GeoCities offers one of the better deals on Web space. If you use the GeoCities Web site (`www.geocities.com`) to create your own Web pages and send and receive e-mail, you already have some space where you can publish your pages. If you pay a small monthly fee for the company's GeoPlus program, you can get lots more space and a unique domain name as well. For $4.95 per month, you get 5MB of disk space, which holds lots of Web pages. To get a unique domain name, you pay a $5 set-up fee and $5 per month, plus fees to InterNIC (see the next section).

If you subscribe to America Online, you can get a domain name as well as other benefits for a business Web site by enrolling in AOL's PrimeHost program. You pay $99, plus the InterNIC registration fee (see the next section). You also get a software package called AOLPress to help you create Web pages.

Getting a domain name

These days, having an easy-to-remember virtual domain name for your business site, such as `www.mycompanyname.com`, is pretty much a require-ment. A longer name just doesn't have as much credibility, in my opinion at least.

Choosing your own domain name for your Web site can be even more fun than getting one of those vanity license plates for your car. A domain name is an easy-to-remember word or phrase that you can use in the Internet address (also called the URL) for your Web site. Not only does it look cool to have a simple domain name, but it's easy to remember. Instead of a URL like

```
http://www.cactusnet.com/~/)username/index.htm
```

you can have an address like this:

```
http://www.company.com/
```

The virtual in virtual domain name means that the welcome page of your Web site can be accessed by sending a Web browser to a short URL, which is actually an *alias* for your usual, long URL. Although your Web site may be one of dozens or hundreds on a Web server, the short address makes it seem like you *are* the server.

With all the companies and individuals getting their own Web sites these days, someone has to keep track of domain names in order to avoid dis-putes. An organization called InterNIC performs that function. To get a virtual domain name for your company's Web site, you have to pay a $100 application fee to InterNIC. This organization keeps your name registered for two years. After paying the initial application fee, InterNIC charges a yearly $50 maintenance fee thereafter. You may not have to deal directly with InterNIC yourself. Some service providers help you apply for a domain name. On the other hand, some providers don't allow customers to have their own domain names at all. Ask your provider for the current policy.

The number of possible domain names is dwindling every day. The place to start is to search for the name that you want to use and see if anyone is using it already on another Web site. InterNIC lets you perform a domain name search on its Web site, `rs.internic.net`.

Transporting files through FTP space

Another question to ask when you're shopping for Web server space is this: Can you upload and download files easily using FTP (File Transfer Protocol)? Can your friends access files that you want them to download? On AOL, the process is hardly straightforward; with other providers, it's a no-brainer.

Transferring files with FTP

When you work with an ISP, you need to use some type of FTP software to move your files to the server. Sometimes your ISP provides the software. Otherwise, you can download one of the programs from the Web, as I describe in Chapter 4. If you use a Mac, you need a program like Fetch; if you're on Windows, you need IFTP or WS_FTP.

Some Web page tools enable you to publish your pages on a Web server directly from within the same program that you used to create the pages. One big advantage of direct publishing is that you can send all the graphics at once, instead of laboriously moving one file at a time to the server. The server that you use has to support the software's publishing feature, however. Netscape Composer has a one-step publishing feature that sends your files to a directory on a server with a single mouse click. Microsoft FrontPage has a set of extensions that publishes your files as well, and a growing number of hosting services supports this feature.

AOL's My Place

If you're on America Online, whether you use Personal Publisher or another Web page tool to create your Web pages, you move your pages to your Web site on AOL by using software called My Place. In fact, when moving pages to AOL, you *must* use this software, which is provided for free by AOL, to upload your files; you can't use other programs. You don't have to copy the software to your computer; you connect to AOL and then use it.

CompuServe's Web Publishing Wizard

CompuServe provides its users with a simple program that helps you move your Web page files to your directory on CompuServe's Our World service. It's called Microsoft Web Publishing Wizard. You find it by clicking on the Internet button in the main CompuServe Interactive window. The Internet window appears. Click on the button labeled Build Your Own Home Page. The Download Publishing Utilities window appears. Click on the button that applies to your computer platform (Windows 3.1, 95/NT, or Macintosh). The program is loaded to your computer.

After you create a Web site, test it carefully to make sure that everything works. Go from page to page and check to see that all the graphics show up and do not appear as broken image icons, which indicate that the browser can't find the image file that's supposed to be there. Fill out any forms on your site to make sure they work correctly, too. Ask your friends and coworkers to evaluate your pages. Sometimes the best feedback (though not the easiest to hear) comes by word of mouth.

Many hosting services let you add a *counter* to one of your Web pages. A counter is a utility that records the number of visits that are made to a Web page — that is, how many times the files on your page are accessed. This utility resides on the Web server, but you can make a link to it on your page so that a counter shows up and provides you with a visual record of how many people have visited you. America Online and GeoCities provide these to their members.

By all means provide a mailto link on your Web page so that people can respond to you. Another way to get feedback is through a Guest Book (see Chapter 15). Probably the best way to get information from your visitors is through a Web page interactive form. The interactive forms, an important aspect of online customer services, are discussed in Chapter 14.

Chapter 14

Customer Service on the Internet

● ●

In This Chapter

▶ Learning how to make customer service effective

▶ Providing customers with around-the-clock information on the Net

▶ Creating interactive forms to get feedback

▶ Offering easy ways for customers to find and reach you online

● ●

*F*or many small businesses, the key to competing effectively with larger marketplace players is superior customer service. Remembering names, listening to questions and problems, and working to address those individual concerns quickly builds loyalty.

If your business exists solely on the Web, customer service plays an essential role in building credibility. Web surfers may wonder if you're a real, live, serious business. Providing a timely and receptive response to an e-mail inquiry can be the key to making a sale later on.

The Internet, dominated by technology and machines, may not seem like the place for the personal touch. But *people* created the Internet and all of its content. In fact, the Internet is an outstanding medium in which to provide your clients with excellent service, and to promote a customer-friendly attitude among employees and customers alike.

Having an Internet connection enables customer service specialists to accomplish some things that may pose an impossibility otherwise, including

✔ Providing a place for clients to find information and ask questions at any time of the day or night.

✔ Using e-mail, toll-free phone numbers, and chat rooms to submit comments, questions, and complaints.

✔ Using computers to keep track of customers' names, previous purchases, and other pertinent information to provide better service in the future.

In addition, small business managers can use Internet technologies like e-mail and Web pages to set policies and procedures for dealing with customers.

Case study: Customer Service Review

Customer service is so important a topic that an online publication is devoted solely to the topic. Customer Service Review (www.csr.co.za) is an electronic magazine (or e-zine, a publication with five staff people that exists solely on the Internet and not in print) that started in January 1997.

"Customer service is a major concern for individuals across all industries and there is very little written about it, especially on the Internet, besides complaints," comments Leigh McLean, Managing Director.

CSR typically contains articles about trends in customer service, customer loyalty, and how technology can help businesses provide better service.

"Customer service on the Web is one-on-one and very easy," says McLean. The customer dictates the pace and frequency of the interaction via e-mail requests and feedback. "The CSR includes a comment form on its site, as well as feedback buttons at the end of each article so that," McLean explains, "we can get a feel for what kinds of information our subscribers are looking for."

Like many new businesses, Customer Service Review is growing slowly. It has been operating in the red but the owners hope to turn a profit eventually. In six months, the magazine had 25 subscribers paying $44 for six months or $79 for a year to receive the zine by e-mail. Its subscriber base was growing at a rate of about four per month.

Online Customer Service Must-Haves

When Garden Escape Inc., an Austin, Texas based full-service garden resource, began to develop its Web site (www.garden.com), the company realized early that customer service needed to play an integral role.

"Ever since we started (in spring 1996), we have invested heavily in customer solutions, where we feel a heavy amount of investment is needed," says Garden Escape's CEO, Cliff Sharples. "We are an online brand; we don't exist off the Web, and customers want to know that it is a real business. With our 1-800 number and our Web site, they can get to us 24 hours a day."

The Garden Escape Customer Solutions page, shown in Figure 14-1, provides a good example of one aspect of customer service on the Internet: the ability to give your visitors lots of options.

The page gives visitors a place to contact the company by e-mail, a toll-free number, or a feedback form. Another customer service page answers Frequently Asked Questions (FAQs). Responsiveness and interest are the basics of customer service on the Internet.

Figure 14-1:
Garden
Escape
gives
customers
different
ways to talk
back or ask
questions.

E-mail is the most popular way for customers to ask questions and give feedback, Sharples says. Garden Escape is inundated with e-mail inquiries; a customer support group of nine staff people works on a rotating schedule to respond to all the inquiries.

"We really feel like that is an important thing. On the Web, things are imperfect: software goes down, the network goes down, and glitches can happen, and our customer service group smoothes things out," Sharples says. Customer service is particularly important for Garden Escape because live plants can be affected by crop failures and cold weather, which can delay deliveries by a week or two. In this case, customer service does damage control in advance.

Garden Escape also goes beyond the basics to provide extras that you can expect to see on the Net, like live chat sessions with garden experts.

Live chats are certainly feasible for any businessowner; you only have to announce a time when you can be available to answer questions on an Internet Relay Chat server or an Internet Phone online directory. These and other real-time communications options are described in Chapter 9.

However, small businesses that are just starting out are wise to concentrate on the basics, which are described in the next few sections.

Making it easy for customers to find you

These days, there are lots of possible alternatives to a Plain Old Telephone Number and an e-mail address. A Web page enables you to make use of some of those alternatives so that potential clients can find you.

Be a URL-y bird

On the Net, the simplest URL gets the worm. First and foremost, go for a URL that's as easy to remember as possible. If your company's name is Acme Corporation, request the domain name www.acme.com. If that's not available, try to get something close, like www.acmecorp.com. (See Chapter 13 for more about choosing a virtual domain name for your company's Web site.)

Send mailto yourself

After you obtain a good URL, put a link on each of your Web pages so visitors can send you e-mail without having to enter your address. In the language of Web page creation, this is a *mailto* link. When a user clicks on a link, an e-mail message window opens with your e-mail address already in the To: line. You create a mailto link by adding this line of HTML to your Web page source code:

```
Send mail to <A HREF="mailto:name@acme.com>Webmaster@acme.
       com</A>
```

When viewed on a Web page, the HTML commands that are contained within the < and > brackets don't appear. Instead, your visitors see this:

```
Questions? Send e-mail to Webmaster@company.com.
```

 You can find lots of great resources focusing on customer service at The Right Answer, Inc. (www.therightanswer.com). The site includes training tips, chat sites for discussing customer service issues, and examples of Internet businesses that offer good customer service.

Go by the numbers

Include your general phone number on your customer service page. Your Web site becomes available to worldwide visitors, so include your area code. If you have a toll-free number, include it — customers may be more interested in trying to reach you.

Provide FAQs and figures

Brainstorm with your staff to come up with a set of Frequently Asked Questions about your individual company or (if you don't get that many questions) about your general line of work. Emphasize in your answers what customers can expect if they encounter any problems with your products or services; note your eagerness to quickly resolve customers' concerns.

Even if you don't know about creating Web pages, Microsoft FrontPage makes it easy to set up a discussion area on your Web site where customers can talk about your products. It's a little risky to provide this feature on pages that are intended to discuss customer service, because people may feel encouraged to bring up problems they have experienced.

You can also sign up with a mailbot or autoresponse service. The service can send a document or e-mail message automatically to anyone who sends an inquiry to a specific e-mail address (info@company.com).

Paging from the Net

An e-mail address and a phone number are essential parts of any customer service effort on the Internet. But you can take some additional unusual and high-tech measures to help customers reach you — among them, making yourself available by Internet telephone. As described in Chapter 9, a user who has Internet telephony software can call you up and speak to you through his or her computer, thus saving long-distance charges.

You can also provide a way for customers (and coworkers, spouses, and so on) to page you, not only by telephone, but also through your Web site. A company called PageNet (www.pagenet.com) enables its customers to receive e-mail messages from the Internet through a program called e-WORX.

My colleague John Casler, who's a technical whiz, set up his own Web page (www.manaburger.com) so people can type messages to him there, as shown in Figure 14-2. The messages end up on his pager in seconds.

Figure 14-2:
Dedicated Internet users can page you by sending e-mail messages or through a Web page interface like this.

This Web page paging area is set up as an online form of the sort described in the following section. Messages are posted to a URL on the PageNet Web site, `www.pagenet.net/pagenet`. An invisible or hidden field in this form contacts John's pager through his PageNet PIN number.

To find out more about customer service concerns for businesses, check out *Customer Service For Dummies,* by Karen Leland and Keith Bailey (IDG Books Worldwide, Inc.).

Building Relationships with Online Forms

Something as straightforward as a fill-out form can work wonders. Forms give you essential marketing information about where your customers live, how old they are, how they found your business, and so on. They also give customers a place to sound off and ask questions. The speed of the Internet enables you to send a response right away. Because you have background information about the person making the request, you can tailor your response to that person's individual needs and interests.

How Web page forms work

Some Web pages feature forms that permit two-way communication between the owner of the page and individual visitors. Forms enable Web users to make purchases on the Internet, fill out surveys, subscribe to publications, or submit other data to remote Web servers. Federal Express, whose Web site (`www.fedex.com`) is frequently praised for its usefulness, demonstrates forms that support customer service. Customers can fill out forms on the site, such as the one shown in Figure 14-3, that track their packages.

Forms consist of two parts. You only see one part, the visible part, when you fill out a form on a Web page:

✔ The visible parts are the text entry fields, buttons, and check boxes that an author creates with HTML commands.

✔ The part you don't see is a computer script that resides on the server that receives the page. This script, which is typically written in a language like Perl, AppleScript, or C++, processes the form data that a reader submits to a server and presents that data in a usable form so the owner or operator of the Web site can read and use it.

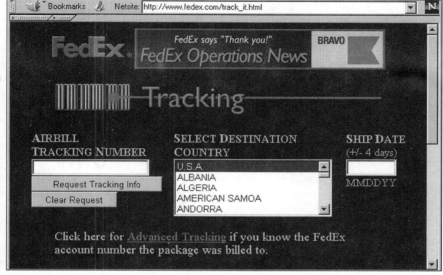

How forms take form

When you create a form, you set up elements that visitors can use to send you data. The most common form elements are

- ✔ **Text Boxes.** These are simple one-line text fields in which a user can type his or her name, e-mail address, or any sort of textual information.

- ✔ **Comments.** These are larger text fields that enable the visitor to enter extensive comments or questions about a site.

- ✔ **Radio Buttons.** Radio buttons are used when you want the user to choose a multiple-choice alternative. By clicking on a button, the user locks out alternatives.

- ✔ **Check Boxes.** Check boxes are similar to radio buttons, but they enable the user to choose more than one alternative in a list.

- ✔ **Selection Menus.** These drop-down lists enable the user to choose items; the format is familiar to Windows and Macintosh users.

- ✔ **Passwords.** These are boxes that enable the user to submit a password in order to access a Web site.

- ✔ **Submit and Reset Buttons.** These buttons enable the user to submit the form data to your Web site or reset all the form elements to fill them out again.

Forms can also contain images and hidden fields that perform functions after the data is submitted, such as returning a Web page to the user that says *Thanks*.

How the data gets to you

When someone fills the form out, the following takes place:

1. Your customer fills out the text-entry fields, radio buttons, and other areas that you have set up. That person then clicks on a button marked Submit or some other designation in order to transmit or post the data from the remote computer to your Web site. (In the course of creating the form, you designate a URL or e-mail address where the data is to be sent.)

2. A computer script called a Common Gateway Interface (CGI) receives the data submitted to your site and processes it so that you can read it.

3. An optional next step is to rely on a computer script to send the user a Web page that acknowledges and delivers a thanks for the feedback.

Writing the scripts that process form data is definitely in the province of Webmasters or computer programmers and is far beyond the scope of this book. But you don't have to hire someone to write the scripts: You can use a Web page program that not only enables you to create a form but also provides you with scripts that process the data for you.

Using Web page tools to create forms the easy way

Lots of Web page editors enable you to create the visible parts of a form, such as the boxes that contain your customers' names, addresses, and other information. Not all these programs include the invisible part, the script that's essential for the form to actually work.

Forms aren't easy! They take longer to set up than simple Web pages that contain text and images. Small business managers with limited resources and a do-it-yourself spirit may choose to use Microsoft FrontPage 97 or World Wide Web Weaver to create simple forms. But actually getting the forms to work may require some time-consuming troubleshooting or trial-and-error.

Microsoft FrontPage 97

Microsoft FrontPage 97 is a versatile suite of applications that enables you to design Web graphics, Web pages, and entire sites full of interlinked Web pages. FrontPage's wizards and scripts help you create sophisticated Web page contents without programmers and consultants.

Another set of built-in goodies are scripts that Microsoft calls *webbots*. These scripts perform lots of functions, one of which is to process data that customers submit to your site using interactive Web page forms.

You can find out more about Microsoft FrontPage by visiting Microsoft's Web site (www.microsoft.com/frontpage). You may find a new beta version of FrontPage to download on a trial basis. Beta software is software that's still being developed. The program has bugs (mistakes, that is), but people can evaluate the product and report any problems they encounter. However, Microsoft doesn't normally provide trial versions of FrontPage. You probably have to purchase the program from a software outlet. I've seen FrontPage advertised for $139 with a $40 mail-in rebate. Front Page is available for Windows 95 or Macintosh computers.

After you create a form, you need to publish it and any associated images and webbots on a Web server so that people can use it and send you their feedback or other information. You can test your pages by filling out the form yourself and submitting some data to see how it works. To publish your pages, follow the steps described in the sections "Publishing Your Pages" and "Testing Your Pages" in Chapter 8.

World Wide Web Weaver

Dedicated Macintosh users can benefit from a shareware program called World Wide Web Weaver that includes a Form Editor utility for processing data that visitors submit to your Web site. The following steps show how to create a simple form using World Wide Web Weaver, assuming that you have a trial version or your own copy from the manufacturer, Miracle Software, Inc. (See the following Tip for more on where to get the program.)

You can download a trial copy of World Wide Web Weaver or purchase it directly from the Miracle Software, Inc. Web site (www.miracleinc.com). The program comes in a commercial version for $89 that includes free upgrades as new versions come out. You can purchase a version without upgrades for $59, or a Lite version for $25. You can also find a copy of the program on the CD that accompanies my book *Creating Web Pages For Kids & Parents* (IDG Books Worldwide, Inc.). World Wide Web Weaver is only available for the Macintosh and requires either a 68000 Macintosh with 3.5MB of RAM or a Power Macintosh with 5.5MB of RAM, plus 7.5MB of available disk space. It works on any Macintosh with System 7.0 or later.

Check with your Internet provider before you start running forms and scripts on the ISP's server, to make sure the kind of form that you want to run can work there.

Low-tech alternatives

Let's say that you aren't exactly burning to tackle Web page forms and the scripts to handle them. You have a form that you want to put online quickly. Is there a low-tech way to put forms on the Internet and have your customers submit them to you? Of course.

Faxing forms

Simply type your form on a Web page using any Web page editor. This form doesn't have to be elaborately formatted — it's more important that it be brief so that your customers can fill it out quickly and fax it to you economically. Try to keep the form to a page. Include a note on your Web site that asks your customers to print out the form using their Web browser. Include an address or phone number so they can fax or mail the form to you.

E-mailing forms

If you have e-mail correspondence from a customer or client, you can send that individual a form by e-mail. The easiest way to transmit the form is to do the following:

1. **Open the form document in the word processing or page layout program in which it was originally created.**

2. **Select the entire contents of the form.**

3. **Paste the form into the body of an e-mail message that you send to the customer.**

Ask the recipient to fill in the form and simply return the e-mail. The customer can type a capital X in order to check an option that you provide. You can also ask the client to enter a number from 1 to 6 to rate your services.

Exit surveys

One simple form that can be transmitted easily by e-mail is a client or customer exit survey. This sort of survey is sent after a sale is made or a project is completed. You may ask questions like the ones that follow, and include 1 to 6 ratings as shown:

How well did we do on your job?

(Poor) 1 2 3 4 5 6 (Excellent)

What could we have done better?

How do you rate the service you received from us?

(Poor) 1 2 3 4 5 6 (Excellent)

How would you rate our Web site?

(Poor) 1 2 3 4 5 6 (Excellent)

Another part of Internet customer service is responding to e-mail messages. Deerfield Communications Company, the creator of the WinGate proxy server for small businesses (see Chapter 10), offers an e-mail collaboration server called Adanté. Among other things, Adanté enables groups of staff to keep track of customer e-mail messages and their profiles. Incoming messages can be queued up and shared by several users so that a response can be given more quickly. Find out more at `www.adante.com/index.htm`.

Customer Service = Information

You can help customers help themselves on the Internet by providing as much information as possible about your company. That way, customers can find answers for themselves, instead of approaching you personally.

One of the masters in conveying information is Ben & Jerry's, Inc. Their Web site (`www.benjerry.com`) provides lots of great customer service information, and is generally user-friendly and fun, too.

Ben & Jerry's gives visitors plenty to peruse on the Web through its library of press releases and its Study Hall, shown in Figure 14-4.

The Study Hall contains lots of good ideas about information that any business can make public, including a company history, a mission statement, annual reports, employment opportunities, and much more.

Figure 14-4: Help your customers by providing data so that they can answer their own questions, as shown on this Web site.

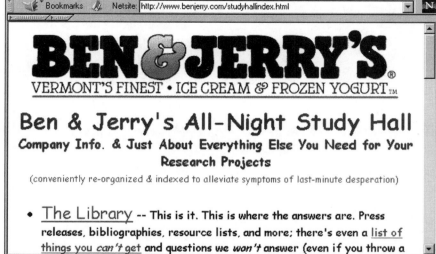

Some other ideas you may consider are described in other chapters, including "Setting up your own FTP site" (see Chapters 4 and 15) and "Creating an electronic newsletter" (see Chapters 7 and 15).

Customer service on the Internet can be measured by the number of e-mail messages or forms submitted to your Web site. The comments that you receive on forms can be invaluable, and can indicate exactly what you're doing well and what you need to improve upon. Sometimes, if your online customer service is good, you may not receive direct evidence of that fact. If you provide enough information about your company and your goods and services, customers can answer questions themselves, without having to contact you — that is, until the next time they want you to provide them with help or sell them your products.

Ideally, you begin to experience the success of Garden Escape, the company mentioned earlier in this chapter. "We get a lot of e-mail feedback to the effect of, 'I love your site, my order came in on time,' or 'The person who works on the 1-800 number helped me beautifully,'" says CEO, Cliff Sharples. "We get a lot of e-mail feedback, and not all of it consists of issues or questions."

Chapter 15

Creating Online Catalogs and Other Publications

*G*oing online seems to bring out the latent publisher in all of us. If you ever wanted to speak your mind, teach, or simply spout off, the Internet provides you with plenty of opportunities. With an Internet connection and the right software, you can create Web pages and other documents that visitors can read, download, or open with their e-mail software.

For businesses that are connected to the Net, the opportunity to publish announcements, updates, documentation, or sales catalogs can be a great supplement to existing brochures, catalogs, and other printed matter.

Publishing is even more than a supplement, however. The quality and quantity of the information you provide can mean the difference between a business Web site that attracts lots of visitors and one that's basically a dud. The way you present information can also be a way to offer customer service and build productive relationships, not only between you and your customers but among those who visit your Web site. The goal is to create an attractive Internet community for your clients and customers where you are an available and trusted resource.

Exactly what sort of publication is right for you? The way to answer that question is to take a moment and do some good old-fashioned goal-setting. Publishing takes work, after all, so be sure that you are clear on what you want to accomplish before you start devoting your own or your staff peoples' energy to the project. Here are some possible goals of providing information online:

✔ **Commerce.** You want to increase sales by providing customers with another place to find out about what you have to offer, so you put out a list of items for sale.

✔ **Publicity.** You want to spread your company name far and wide, and you know that the more information you put on the Net in the form of press releases, newsletters, and documentation, the more reasons people have to visit you.

✔ **Communication.** You know a lot about your field, and you have something to teach people. As an indirect result of sharing your expertise and being available to answer questions, you realize that you may get more inquiries or sales.

Creating publications, putting them online, and keeping them up-to-date takes work, but clear goals and a genuine commitment to providing useful information can mean the difference between an Internet presence that works and one that doesn't.

Getting Your Catalog Online

One of the most common reasons businesses connect to the Internet is to get their catalog online. A catalog doesn't necessarily have to be a list of items for sale. It can also be a description of other goods and services you provide. Here are some examples:

Just the facts, ma'am

Cameta Camera (www.cameta.com/) is just one of several camera companies that offers an online catalog of long lists of both new and used equipment. The simple format makes it easy for customers to find what they want because an index page contains a list of links to each type of camera for sale (see Figure 15-1).

Bells and whistles

The Go2WhatsNew site (www.go2whatsnew.com), shown in Figure 15-2, does a lot of different things, but mainly it lets people know about new sites and merchandise they can find on the Net. The layout is clean and professional and uses lots of images. This site is one of many on the Web that uses software to output information from a database to Web pages *on the fly* (when people connect to the site).

Case study: Cameta Camera

Bill Cameta, owner of Cameta Camera in Amityville, New York, says putting his company's sales catalog on the Web was "one of the best things I have ever done." Cameta stresses the importance of using his Web site (www.cameta.com/) in conjunction with advertisements placed in a well-known camera magazine called *Shutterbug.* Some customers find his business through the URL for the Web site that is in the magazine ad and others find his Web site by using search engines or indexes. One advantage of publishing on the Web is timeliness. "We can be more up-to-date on the Web than in *Shutterbug,* which only comes out once a month," says Bill. " Many of our customers have made bookmarks so they can check out new merchandise as soon as it comes out."

Cameta periodically outputs a text file containing about 300 new items for sale, and e-mails it to Web consultant Deborah Levitt, who does copyediting and cleanup, and then formats the text and puts it on the Web using a popular HTML editor called HotDog Pro 3. Levitt comments: "Bill's site is an example of something that *works.* Why does Cameta's site work while others don't? In my opinion, it's the commitment of the owner to provide useful information and use the Internet to communicate. Cameta answers all of the company's e-mail inquiries promptly, for instance — an activity that occupies every Thursday morning. Cameta puts it succinctly: "You have to give something on your Web site that has value or people don't go back to it."

Figure 15-1:
Simple but effective: Cameta Camera's online catalog has been a big success.

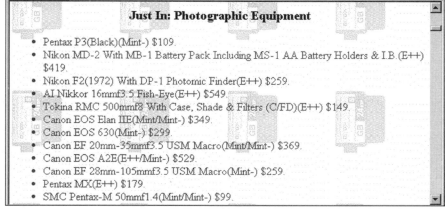

Bookmarks   Netsite: http://www.cameta.com/just-in.html

Just In: Photographic Equipment

- Pentax P3(Black)(Mint-) $109.
- Nikon MD-2 With MB-1 Battery Pack Including MS-1 AA Battery Holders & I.B.(E++) $419.
- Nikon F2(1972) With DP-1 Photomic Finder(E++) $259.
- AI Nikkor 16mmf3.5 Fish-Eye(E++) $549.
- Tokina RMC 500mmf8 With Case, Shade & Filters (C/FD)(E++) $149.
- Canon EOS Elan IIE(Mint/Mint-) $349.
- Canon EOS 630(Mint-) $299.
- Canon EF 20mm-35mmf3.5 USM Macro(Mint/Mint-) $369.
- Canon EOS A2E(E++/Mint-) $529.
- Canon EF 28mm-105mmf3.5 USM Macro(Mint-) $259.
- Pentax MX(E++) $179.
- SMC Pentax-M 50mmf1.4(Mint/Mint-) $99.

Figure 15-2:
More
elaborate
online
catalogs
use images
and color
to sell
products.

This kind of programming is not the kind of thing you want to tackle yourself unless you are really into computing. It is more likely to be something you discuss with the person that you hire to create or administer your Web site.

You don't have to put your entire catalog online. One alternative demonstrated is to highlight items from your printed catalog on your Web site.

Preparing content

Where do you start? A good first step is to decide how much material you want to publish, and how you want to deliver it to readers. You have two alternatives which you can use to deliver your information:

- ✔ **A Web page.** This is the obvious choice, but not the only option.
- ✔ **E-mail.** E-mail mailing lists are a versatile way to deliver information. You can set up an *announcement list* that sends news to subscribers; you can take that a step further and create a newsletter that you e-mail to people who subscribe to it; you can also set up a system that automatically e-mails documents to people who request them.

You don't have to decide on one method or the other right now. Often, the best approach is to combine the graphics and interactivity of the Web with the immediacy of e-mail in a two-phase marketing strategy. No matter which alternative you choose, you have to get your data from its present form into a format that can be put online.

Let your fingers do the typing

Well, *somebody's* fingers, anyway. If you've got time to burn (I hear you chuckling) and you love to create Web pages, take a few hours or so to type up some simple catalog listings. If your material is contained in a database, export it to a plain-text document. If the material is formatted as a word processing document, choose File➪Save As and save your material in plain-text format.

After you have a plain-text document, you can either clean the text up and format it yourself, or you can hire someone to do the work.

If you want to do the work yourself, get one of the HTML editors mentioned in Chapter 13, and import your plain-text document. Usually, importing is a simple process:

1. **Double-click on the program's icon to open it.**

2. **Choose File➪Open.**

   A dialog box appears that enables you to locate the file on your hard disk.

3. **Double-click on the file name to open the file.**

   The text appears in your editor's main content window without any formatting and with additional strange characters that are likely to have been added from the ASCII text conversion.

Some HTML editing programs (such as Netscape Composer) only open HTML documents, not plain-text documents. If that is the case, save your document in plain text format but add the filename extension .htm, which fools the editor into thinking the text is actually an HTML document.

Or borrow someone else's fingers

If time is short, you can hire one of the many Web site consultants who are only too happy to format your text and publish it on the Web for you. I want to point out that this is one of the services offered by my company, Stylus Media, before I proclaim that you are likely to find it more cost- and time-efficient to hire a consultant.

How much does this cost? In my experience, it can take from six to twelve hours to design the original graphics for a Web site and come up with some basic page layouts. After the ground work is done, you can reasonably estimate that each additional page costs from $100 to $150. If the pages are pretty simple, the price is likely to stay under $100.

Try to include internal links — the top of the page to locations farther down the page. Any Web page that's more than three or four computer screens in length can be broken into smaller, separate pages and joined by links. Include a link to your home page and an e-mail link on every one of your catalog pages.

Using conversion programs

These days, so many software programs are available to help you create Web pages that you don't have to type everything from scratch.

If you're a Macintosh user, one program you can download freely from the Net, called rtftohtml, does the job well. This program has been around for several years so the bugs are worked out of it by now.

If you use Microsoft Office 97 Small Business Edition, you can process files created with Word or PowerPoint in HTML format by using the Web Page Wizard.

Get some assistants

If you use earlier versions of Access, Excel, PowerPoint, Schedule+, or Word, you can download free add-ons that output HTML. You can find links at www.microsoft.com/msdownload/default.asp

Convert your database to Web pages

Often, a company's list of items that are available for sale or use is kept in a database. Databases enable you to sort and print out the information in lots of different ways. You may have your database in Access if you use Office 97; if you're on the Macintosh, you may use FileMaker Pro.

If your catalog information is contained in a database and you are looking for a less laborious alternative to exporting the contents to plain text, consider a powerful suite of tools called Cold Fusion by Allaire Corp. Among many other things, Cold Fusion enables you to select data from a database and output the data in HTML format.

You can find out more about Cold Fusion at Allaire Corp.'s Web site (www.allaire.com/). The Workgroup version of Cold Fusion 3.0 costs $495; this version works with databases, such as Microsoft Access, dBASE, and Microsoft FoxPro. The Professional version of Cold Fusion 3.0 costs $995 and works with enterprise servers, such as SQL Server and Oracle.

Office 97 is a great tool for converting databases or text files to Web pages. See *Office 97 Small Business For Dummies* by Dave Johnson and Todd Stauffer, published by IDG Books Worldwide, Inc.

No matter what program you use, the basic principle is the same. First, you need a database that accepts computer scripting in some way. Then, you identify the fields in the database that you want to export to Web pages.

Next, you associate each field with an HTML tag and tell the program how to format the results (that is, in what order you want the tags presented).

Some visitors may go directly to your catalog by clicking on a link provided by one of the Internet search services. These visitors may spend a lot of time looking through your offerings without ever knowing who you are or where you are located. For that reason, remember to include a copyright notice and your company name on each of your Web pages.

Then, input the plain text file into an HTML editor. Two that I use often are Netscape Composer (part of the Netscape Communicator suite) and FrontPage editor (part of the Microsoft FrontPage suite of tools).

Netscape Communicator can be downloaded for free from the Web. The software can be used free for nonprofit and educational purposes. However, Netscape asks that for-profit businesses pay a license fee to keep using the program. Microsoft FrontPage must be purchased; it's available for less than $100 from most computer discount warehouses.

After the catalog, the follow-up

A study by Jupiter Communications, Inc., a new media research company, cautions that simply putting a catalog online is not enough to boost sales on the Internet. Here are three recommendations for using the Net more effectively:

✔ **Update your Web site.** Keep your information fresh by revising it on a regular basis. If sale items are sold out or unavailable from the manufacturer, delete them so as not to frustrate online shoppers. You don't have to redo the complete catalog every time, however. Like Bill Cameta (see the sidebar "Case study: Cameta Camera"), you can put new products on a separate Web page. Create a link to a page that is entitled "Just in!" or "New Products."

✔ **Keep visitors informed.** Tell visitors when information was last updated so they don't waste time looking through listings they've reviewed already. Also, tell people how often this page is updated — every week, every two weeks, or some other interval. That way, you encourage your best customers to check in on a regular basis.

✔ **Use e-mail.** Be sure to give customers an easy way to contact you by e-mail. E-mail gives shoppers who are squeamish about conducting online transactions a way to place orders or make inquiries more safely. Set aside one day or one afternoon each week to handle all your e-mail correspondence.

All three of these follow-up techniques add credibility and usefulness to your catalog. Remember, most people are still getting used to the concept of shopping online, so it's in your interest to build their confidence.

Capture images

Whoever said an image is worth a thousand words never tried to view those images over a dialup modem connection. On the Web, images are a great supplement to descriptions, prices, and other information, but they aren't the most important thing.

If you *do* want to include images with your catalog, you have these options:

> ✔ **You can scan printed photos.** Take traditional print or slide photos of your merchandise, and convert the images to computer format by scanning them and saving the scans in GIF or JPEG format.

> ✔ **You can get a digital camera.** You can connect images directly to your computer and eliminate the need for scanning or photo processing.

If you take photos with a digital camera, be sure that the image is well-lighted. Look for cameras that support 24-bit color (each pixel in the image can contain 24 bits of digital information). The better cameras can produce images with resolutions of 640 x 480 pixels or higher. (The more pixels an image has, the more detailed the image.)

Creating an Electronic Newsletter

An electronic newsletter that you create, publish on your Web site, or distribute by mailing list is a great way to gratify the part of you that has always wanted to impress people with how much you know. It's also an effective way to deliver information about what your company does.

Newsletters take a lot of work to create and update. Whether yours comes out every month, every quarter, or just once a year, you are required to re-create your publication with every new issue.

For that reason, keep your newsletter simple and make sure that you have the resources to do it.

To find out more about starting an e-mail newsletter, see *Marketing with Newsletters* by Elaine Floyd.

Just as the benefits of using newsletters are great, the work that is required to produce them is also substantial. Your budget needs to reflect not only the cost of getting the premiere issue to your audience, but also the cost of regular issues and updates. Some areas to investigate include

- ✔ **Sources of free content.** Identify industry magazines so that you can quote articles and get on the mailing list for press releases that you can scan.

- ✔ **Staff.** Assign an editor and other contributors. Determine the role that you want to play.

- ✔ **Format.** You want to send out a plain text version so everyone can read it, but you may want to send an HTML version to those who can read formatted e-mail.

- ✔ **Audience.** The better you identify your readers, the more focused and useful your content is for them.

The pitfall with adding Internet Information Provider to your list of other business hats is that you don't have enough time to do a really good job with it. Designate a staff person (or persons) to help you create content.

If you need help with your newsletter, the Net abounds with writers and editors who are looking for freelance work. Take out an ad with the National Writers Union Web site (www.nwu.org/nwu/). Also advertise on newsgroups where writers lurk, such as alt.journalism.freelance.

Becoming a news hound

Start by writing down a list of stories you want to include in your newsletter. Here are some suggestions that can apply to many kinds of businesses:

- ✔ **Your opinion.** Haven't you always wanted to say what was really on your mind without being censored? Now you can. Tell people what you think about your industry. Provide tips, advice, and suggestions based on your experience.

- ✔ **FAQs.** Have your staff report what they get asked most often, and write a question-and-answer column.

- ✔ **Letters.** A newsletter is a great place to give your customers a place to talk back. Invite letters that provide opinions and criticism.

- ✔ **What's New.** Include new products and employees.

- ✔ **Reviews.** Explain how some products work and recommend what product you think is best to fill a particular need.

- ✔ **Help Wanted.** You never know — you may save yourself some money in print advertising by putting a notice online.

- ✔ **About the Company.** Introduce yourself by providing a company history and a mission statement.

Start typing!

Set your contributors' (including your own) deadline, and give them an idea of how long their stories need to be. Even just three or four paragraphs take up most of the average computer screen which is a natural stopping point for an electronic article.

On the other hand, if you have a lot to say, don't hold back. You aren't constrained by space requirements online as you are in print. (That's one of the best things about writing for the Web, as a matter of fact.)

You can include graphics only with the formatted HTML version of your newsletter, if you decide to create one. If you distribute only a plain text newsletter, you can include a plain text link to your sponsor's Web site. Graphics make your e-mail file bigger and slower, so use them sparingly.

Format your newsletter

Like Netsurfer Digest and a growing number of Internet newsletters, you may decide to take your visitors' personal preferences into account by creating both an ASCII and an HTML version of your newsletter.

If you are going to format your newsletter to put it on the Web anyway, you may as well send a formatted version by e-mail. The transition doesn't take that much extra work.

Case study: Netsurfer Digest

The electronic newsletter, Netsurfer Digest, has been around for several years and is still a good source for information on what's going on in the online world in many areas, including business. Editor Arthur Rebak puts out both an ASCII text and a formatted e-mail version. Some of the stories are only one-paragraph notices of new Web sites or other tidbits of information. Art Rebak, by the way, is the co-author of *Creating Web Pages For Dummies*, published by IDG Books Worldwide, Inc.

Netsurfer Digest begins with something else you may consider for your own newsletter if you start to get a number of subscriptions (Netsurfer Digest has more than 50,000): a sponsor. A link to the sponsor's home page and an ad are shown in Figure 15-5.

The ASCII version

ASCII text isn't going to win any awards for beauty, but plenty of Internet users don't care. They simply want information fast. They are happy to get tips, news, and suggestions without having to wait for graphics' lengthy e-mail messages to arrive.

Just because your newsletter is in plain text doesn't mean it can't be formatted, either. Here are some suggestions that emphasize or separate one section from another:

- ✔ **All caps.** This is always useful for the name of the newsletter.
- ✔ **Rules.** A row of equal signs, hyphens, or asterisks can be used to separate sections.
- ✔ **Blank spaces.** Who says you can't divide plain text into columns? You can if you use blank spaces carefully.

How big is too big when it comes to e-mail? 30KB is about the limit for a simple e-mail communication: The smaller you make the file, the better for both you and your readers.

Many of these elements can be seen in the plain-text version of Debbie Redpath Ohi's newsletter Inklings (`www.inkspot.com/inklings/`), which has more than 14,000 subscribers (see Figure 15-3).

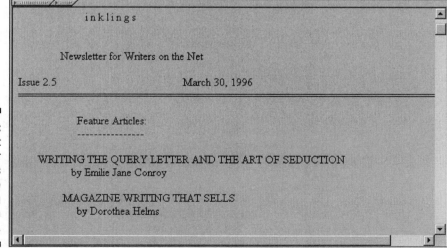

Figure 15-3: A plain text newsletter that uses single formatting to create a masthead.

Case study: Kenny's Bookshop & Art Galleries

Kenny's Bookshop & Art Galleries Ltd. (`www.iol.ie/kennys/Review.html`), a small bookstore located in Galway, Ireland, publishes an electronic newsletter called the *Kenny Review*. The *Review* tells subscribers about new books that Kenny's has obtained and profiles authors who are likely to be of interest to the store's customers. Their newsletter is a great example of how a company's Web site can work with other parts of the Net. This example shows that you don't have to put out every single bit of information in your newsletter, but instead you can refer back to your company Web site for more information.

The HTML version

If you plan to publish your newsletter on the Web in addition to sending subscribers an e-mail version, you only need to prepare the Web pages once. Simply attach the HTML document and associated graphics to your e-mail message when you send it out. Readers with e-mail software that supports HTML e-mail messages can see the formatting and graphics in the body of the e-mail message.

Keep your HTML version simple, too. Remember that your newsletter appears through your readers' e-mail software, not their Web browser. Stay away from fancy stuff like frames, tables, or style sheets.

Don't forget to proofread your newsletter thoroughly before you send it out. Have someone on your staff who has not worked on the text (or a friend or your spouse) read it with a fresh pair of eyes.

Sending your newsletter

After you're done creating your newsletter, follow these steps to get your publication out:

1. **After you format your newsletter, save your file with the usual filename extension — ".htm" if you are sending an HTML version and "." for a plain-text version.**

2. **Attach the file to an e-mail message by using your e-mail program's procedure for sending attachments.**

   You may want to break your newsletter into several pieces if it's very long, as a courtesy to your readers.

3. **Address your file to the recipients.**

   (See the section "Starting Your Own Mailing List," in this chapter, for more information on this step.)

4. **Send your newsletter out.**

   Instead of sending the newsletter to all of your recipients at once, you may want to divide the transmission into bunches of 25 or 50.

If you have lots of subscribers to your newsletter (hundreds, or perhaps thousands), send it off late at night or on a weekend when network traffic is light and your publication can get where it needs to go much faster.

Get an ISSN number

ISSN stands for International Standard Serial Number, an internationally recognized code for identifying a serial publication (that is, one that comes out in a series). You can apply for a free ISSN number for your publication if you plan to publish it for a number of years and if you have chosen a fairly common name that may be copied by someone else.

An ISSN number uniquely identifies your publication, which makes tracking your publication easier for libraries and copyright agencies. ISSN numbers are sometimes used in bar codes, too.

After you get an ISSN number, you can add a notice to your publication like this:

```
Industry News (ISSN 1826-3610) is a free electronic news-
letter posted on the Web site industry.com and e-mailed to
subscribers. To apply for an ISSN number, call the National
Serial Data Program of the Library of Congress at 202-707-
6452.
```

Starting Your Own Mailing List

You can simply keep track of the names by using your e-mail program, and send them out manually whenever you are ready to send out a mailing.

Hire a mailing list service

If you don't plan to run your own Web server, it's much easier to hire a company to run your mailing list for you. One such company is SkyList, and it's offered by SkyWeyr Technologies (www.skyweyr.com/skylist/index.html). SkyList charges only $25 per month for a list that has 100 or fewer members, and $250 per month for a list with 500 to 1000 members. This service is useful because it performs the time-consuming task of setting up the list, keeping the software and computers running, and dealing with messages that bounce back because they can't be delivered. You still need to monitor the content of messages to make sure that they are suitable, however.

Picking a type of mailing list

A mailing list, popularly called a *LISTSERV,* is a versatile and cost-effective way to communicate to your customers and possibly get your customers talking to one another. You can set up two types of mailing lists:

- **A discussion list.** This is the most common type of list. Users subscribe to the list; after subscribing, they can send e-mail messages to one another. Each message sent to the list goes to everyone in the group. Each person can reply to a message, and replies can be sent either to the original sender or to everyone in the group, too. The resulting series of messages on a topic is called a *thread.*

- **An announcement list.** This list provides only one-way communication. Subscribers get a single message from the list administrator. That list announces any sort of news or current events.

Because this chapter is about providing information on the Internet, this section concentrates on announcement lists. Some of the largest mailing lists on the Net consist of a series of announcements about a Web site, such as CNET's Digital Dispatch, which provides subscribers with information about what's new on the CNET Web site (www.cnet.com).

After you have a mailing list, what do you actually do with it? Your mailing list can be a great marketing and publicity tool for your company. The list also has substantial benefits in the area of customer service, as described in Chapter 14. Visitors to the 1-800-FLOWERS site can make use of a Gift Concierge Service. They submit the important dates of up to five friends or relatives, and the service sends them an e-mail reminder of when each event occurs, plus gift ideas, five days before the recorded date.

Case study: Computer Book Publishing List

One mailing list that I'm personally familiar with is run by my agency, Studio B Productions, which is itself a small business Internet success story. David Rogelberg, president of Studio B, says that the mailing list has had great benefits. David started the list himself by using ListSTAR software for the Macintosh, and the list now has 625 members. These days, the list is maintained by Skyweyr (see the sidebar "Hire a mailing list service"). "Most of my clients have come from the mailing list or through referrals," Rogelberg says. "Our revenues are in excess of $1.5 million now, largely due to the marketing value of the list."

Finding a host

Unless you have your own mail server connected to the Net all the time, you have to consult with an Internet Service Provider *(ISP)* before you start up a mailing list. Operating a mailing list means that, depending on how busy your list is, more e-mail messages are going through your ISP's machines. Then again, different ISPs use different list management packages. You need to make sure that the available features match your needs.

Setting up a list with ListSTAR

If you want to host and run your own mailing list, you don't have to pay maintenance fees to a mailing list service. On the other hand, you have to set up the list (which requires that you operate your own Internet server and some kind of special mailing list software) and take the responsibility for administering the list. To make the job easier, you need a *good* software program.

Two mailing list programs that I've seen highly recommended are:

- ✔ **SLMail 2.5:** A program for Windows 95 or NT users by Seattle Labs (www.seattlelabs.com/slmail). The program is available for $199, and you can download the program and try it out for 14 days.

- ✔ **Majordomo:** A freeware mailing list program for the Macintosh by Michele Fuortes. Majordomo is available at hofdi.med.cornell.edu.

However, the special mailing list software that I personally know and recommend is ListSTAR for the Macintosh, which is produced by StarNine Technologies, Inc.

You can obtain ListSTAR from the Quarterdeck/StarNine Web site (`www.qdeck.com/liststar/liststar.html/`). You can either pay for a copy right away for $199 from Quarterdeck's Web site, or download a 30-day trial version.

E-mail on demand

One thing you can do with a mailing list after you set it up is to provide e-mail on demand. This function is the online equivalent of Fax-on-Demand. Users send an e-mail message to your mailing list with a special word in the subject or the body of the message. The list server software recognizes the word and responds by automatically sending a file to the user by e-mail.

One common document you can provide by automatic e-mail response is a Help file that tells users how to subscribe, unsubscribe, and perform other functions with your mailing list. Another is a set of FAQs. You can provide any sort of information you want: tips, customer service numbers, or documentation, for instance. The Computer Book Mailing List provides instructions for how to obtain the list's Help file at the end of every daily digest of messages (see Figure 15-4).

Figure 15-4:
If you have a mailing list, you can publish information by having the list server automatically send documents to subscribers.

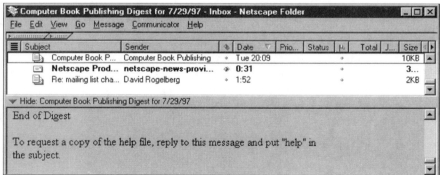

Using Netcasting to Push Your Content

Netcasting is one of the hottest topics on the Internet and, like many hot topics, it has its own buzzwords in its vocabulary. Before the people who created Netcasting software came up with "Netcasting," they used to call it "server push."

Netcasting takes Web pages (which Netscasters call *channels*) and updates them at regular intervals. Users who subscribe to a channel can either revisit the page when it is updated, or have the Web page download in the background to their computers at preset times. The latter alternative makes it possible for users to read the content offline — that is, when they're not connected to the Net.

Starting Your Own Channel

You can set up your own Web site as a channel without a problem. If you already publish information that is updated regularly, having your own channel can be an efficient way to deliver that information to subscribers. Netscape makes the process easy by providing a utility called a Channel Wizard.

To set up your own channel, go to Netscape's home page (home.netscape. com) and click on the link *Add Channel Wizard*. If this link isn't available (after all, Netscape's home page changes all the time), go directly to devel-oper. netscape.com/library/examples/examples.html and click on the link *Netcaster Channels* in the left-hand frame. The section entitled Add Channel Wizard is visible in the right-half frame.

Follow the steps on Netscape's Web site to copy and paste some JavaScript code to your page. The JavaScript is used to tell visitors the name of your channel, how often it is updated, what size it is, and other facts. After this, you need to copy some HTML commands to add the Subscribe button to one of your Web pages.

Better check with the technical support people at your ISP before you start operating as a channel, just to make sure that it's okay with them.

The catch with this system is that it only works if your users have installed the add-on application Netscape Netcaster, which works with Netscape Communicator. As with so many other Web-related innovations, Microsoft is backing its own brand of push technology, called Channel Definition Format (CDF). You may want to wait until the two companies (hopefully) agree on a standard protocol for Netcasting before you start providing channels.

You know if your Internet publishing efforts are successful by the amount of feedback you get from visitors on the Net. You want to also pay attention to the quality of that feedback. The longer and more serious and earnest your questions are, the better your project is working. Respond quickly and thoroughly, and you can achieve benefits in the long run.

Chapter 16

Market Research — and More — on the Internet

- -

- -

*I*f information is the treasure you seek, the Internet is without parallel for the wealth and range of data and the speed with which you can retrieve the data. The challenge is in finding the time to locate the databases that are most useful to you.

As the owner or manager of a small business, you wear lots of different hats, and you have to use your time wisely. This chapter suggests ways that you can use your Internet connection to gather information about your own business, your competitors, and your customers with just a few clicks of a mouse.

When you use the Internet for research, you want to find the people and information sources that you need when you need them. That way, you know exactly where to go on the Web when you need background informa-tion on another company, or advice on a business problem. If you have a legal problem, a tax question, or a personnel dilemma, you'll know where to turn. Here are some goals to consider when you research your Internet resources:

▸ **Market research.** Who out there on the Net may want to use your goods and services? Who are the customers that are most likely to purchase what you have to offer?

> ✔ **Competition.** Who, in your industry, is online already, and what are they doing? What do your customers like about your competitors?
>
> ✔ **Legal help.** How can you get advice on rules, regulations, laws, and disputes you may encounter in your day-to-day activities? Can you get advice without going through the expense of hiring a lawyer?

This chapter gives you an overview of the best utilities and services for searching the Internet — not just the Web, but other, lesser-known services, such as Gopher and FTP. You can also follow the provided, step-by-step instructions for using some of those resources.

Becoming an Internet Power Searcher

If you've been online for any length of time, you probably have a favorite way of finding out about a particular topic or site. The search site is the first page you see when you take that first sip of coffee and open up your Web browser in the morning.

The indexes and searchers are great, but relying on them exclusively is like groping around a dark room with one hand tied behind your back.

Hmm . . . where do I start?

When you need to find something, use the part of the Internet with which you are most comfortable. Here are some suggestions for starting points:

> ✔ **If you use AOL,** sign on and enter the keyword **Reference**. You are sent to AOL's Reference page, from which you can find the specific types of information you want.
>
> ✔ **If you use the Web,** you can't go wrong with Yahoo! (www.yahoo.com). If Yahoo! feels too big and gives you too many results, try a more specialized index that gives you a selected list of resources, such as the Internet Research Plaza (www.catalog.com/expdata/irp).
>
> ✔ **If you use FTP,** connect to an Archie server, which is a machine set up specially to catalog the contents of FTP sites.

If you're short of time and need to find important information, consider hiring a research service, such as CompuServe's IQUEST service.

The place to start is with the Web, which is the hottest part of the Net and the place that's the most fun to search if you don't have a lot of experience.

Understanding Web search engines

A Web search engine is a computer program that searches for documents on the World Wide Web that contain keywords or phrases that interest you. Manually browsing the Web is an impossibility given the sheer number of sites. So, these software programs do the work for you and retrieve the information you have requested in the form of a list of Web sites that you can access, one-by-one, from your computer.

How the searchers work

You simply enter a word or phrase (such as the name of a business or individual) in a search service's text box, such as the one shown in Figure 16-1. You then click on the button that activates the search.

Figure 16-1:
WebCrawler, like many Web search services, enables you to enter search terms in a simple text box. Click on Search, and you get results.

In a few seconds, a new page appears containing your search results. Look through the URL and description of each site to see if any cover the subject(s) you are looking for.

- ✔ **AltaVista** (altavista.digital.com). AltaVista is run by Digital Equipment Corporation. They have one of the largest indexes of all the search engines, and this search engine delivers search results particularly fast.

- ✔ **Excite** (www.excite.com). Excite is more than just a search service. It has indexes to categories of information on the Net. Excite also has channels, which push current information to your Web browser. Under the heading Channels by Excite, click on the link <u>Business & Investing</u>, and your browser goes to the channel shown in Figure 16-2.

Figure 16-2:
You can find current stock quotes and business headlines on Excite's Business & Investing channel.

✔ **InfoSeek (**www.infoseek.com**).** One thing that's notable is that, when you receive a set of search results, you have the option of constricting your next search to cover only the results you just received. That way, you can narrow your search down rather than searching the entire Web over and over again.

✔ **Lycos (**www.lycos.com**).** It started out as a search engine created by a professor at Carnegie-Mellon University, and has since turned into a big operation, with sites in several foreign countries, many licensing partnerships, and stock offered on NASDAQ.

✔ **WebCrawler (**webcrawler.com**).** WebCrawler was one of the first Web searchers, and it often brings back very accurate information.

How to do a multiple search

Internet searchers are habit-forming. After you get used to a particular search service, you tend to stick with it for a while. Conducting random searches for mysterious quotations you are trying to identify or the home pages of old friends you haven't seen for a while can be addictive.

A good way to break the habit of using a single search service is to check out one of the *meta-search engines.* These engines are search services that access several search engines simultaneously. An example is shown in Figure 16-3.

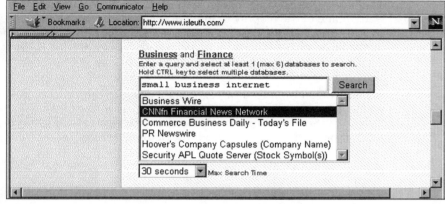

Figure 16-3:
This is a list
of the
Internet
Sleuth's
Business
and Finance
databases
that small
companies
find helpful.

To get the results from one of these places takes longer than it does from an individual service. But you get many more options from which to choose, and you can compare search services to see which one tends to give you the best results.

Some examples of meta-search engines are:

- ✔ **Internet Sleuth (**www.isleuth.com**).** One nice thing about this service is that it enables you to target your search: You can search the Web, Usenet, business databases, or software archives.

- ✔ **MetaCrawler (**www.metacrawler.com/index.html**).** If you want to track stocks, this is a good place to go.

- ✔ **SavvySearch (**www.cs.colostate.edu/~dreiling/smartform.html**).** SavvySearch has interfaces in foreign languages from Norwegian to Esperanto.

InterNIC, an organization that keeps track of domain name registrations and other things related to the Net, maintains a set of links to all of these services at ds2.internic.net/tools.

Web search tips

Sometimes, you have to look through many different pages of search results before you find the site you're looking for. In that case, try some advanced techniques to make your searches more accurate.

Each search service has its own way of refining or focusing your search terms so you're more likely to find what you are looking for. Usually, you find a link on the main page labeled Help or Tips that shows you how to target your search more precisely.

The following sections present some general tips to help you find what you want. Some of them apply to most of the services, while others apply only to one service. Check each searcher's Help pages to get more specific information.

Combining specific terms

Generally, you want to *string* together a group of specific nouns related to your topic rather than a single word or two. If you're looking for the Housing Bureau for Seniors located in Ann Arbor, Michigan, don't just type **Housing Bureau** or even **Housing Bureau for Seniors**. Instead, enter this:

```
Housing Bureau for Seniors Ann Arbor
```

If you don't find the exact page you're looking for, you'll at least find some Ann Arbor Web sites related to the topic that may lead you to the page you want.

Using Boolean operators

Most search services recognize *Boolean operators* — a high-tech term that describes words such as *and* and *or* that enable you to refine your search in different ways. If you use *and,* you tell the search service to look only for pages that look for the two words together. A search for **business *and* law** turns up pages that contain both words together. In contrast, a search for **business *or* law** turns up any pages that contain either the word *business* or the word *law*. A search for **business law *not* copyright** excludes the word *copyright* from any results.

Using quotation marks

If you add quotation marks around the word or phrase you are seeking, you tell the search service to look for the exact combination of words you are looking for, rather than a concept related to the words. For example, a search for **"Pathfinder Mars Mission"** is more focused than simply entering **Pathfinder Mars**, which may turn up articles about the popular Pathfinder (www.pathfinder.com) Web site, companies called Pathfinder Corp. or Pathfinder Inc., and so on. (AltaVista enables you to *glue* words together by using semicolons as well, like this: **Pathfinder;Mars;Mission**.)

Excluding a word

If your search results turn up too many pages that contain a word you're not interested in, try to use Lycos and exclude the word by adding a minus sign (-) before it, for example, **Microsoft -"Bill Gates"**.

Excluding a Web site

You often get pages and pages of references to the same Web site when you submit a search. AltaVista enables you to exclude one of these sites by making a reference to its URL. For instance, say you submit these search terms to a service: **Auto Repair Shop in Chicago**.

Assume that the search service returns six pages worth of URLs, all from the same site with the address www.garage.com. However, garage.com isn't the site you are looking for; you want to find another repair service in Chicago. Most search services enable you to constrain your search so that you can exclude any sites with garage.com in the URL. In AltaVista, you want to enter the following in the text box: **Auto Repair Shop in Chicago host:garage.com.**

Concentrating on one Web site

If you are looking for a document or software program that you know is contained on a particular Web site, you can tell AltaVista to limit its search only to those pages that contain a particular domain name in the URL. For instance, if you are looking for a list of search services and you remember reading somewhere that there's a list on the InterNIC Web site, which has the domain name internic.net, you enter the following: **Internet search services host:internic.net.**

If you know the name of a document, you can tell AltaVista to look only for that name. For instance, if you are looking for a document called business.htm, you can enter **url:business.htm**. This line tells AltaVista to only look for documents with the name business.htm in the URL.

Looking for variant spellings

Some services enable you to add an asterisk (*) at the end of a word in order to search for variations on a particular word.

You can easily get lost or sidetracked in the process of doing a search. One subject leads to another, one Web page leads to another, and before you know it, you (or an employee) have suddenly spent an hour or two with ten new topics and no information on the original topic that you wanted to research. Employ the art of *bookmarking:* keeping track of sites that seem of interest and that you may want to visit later on.

Setting up a personal Internet index

If you use a Web browser as your main tool for navigating the Net, you can save time if you set up your own custom Web page full of links to the information sources you use most frequently.

In Netscape Navigator, these storage sites are called bookmarks; in Microsoft Internet Explorer, they're called Favorites.

Bookmarks and favorites do the same thing: They store the URL and the title of a page in a special list that you set up. When you want to revisit a page, you choose its name from one of your browser's menus.

In Netscape Navigator, you choose Communicator⇨Bookmarks and then select Add Bookmark from the pop-up menu (or press Ctrl+D).

In Internet Explorer, you choose Favorites⇨Add to Favorites when you are at a Web page that you want to add to your Favorites list.

Using personalized/customized news services

One of the best aspects of the Internet is the availability of personalized news services. These services are sites that save you the time of wading through newspapers and listening to the entire evening news looking for information that may not even be there that day. You specify the types of information you want to receive, and the news service retrieves that information and delivers it to you, usually in the form of a custom Web page with content arranged according to the categories you requested earlier.

Finding people and businesses

The Internet is beginning to give the venerable Yellow Pages and other phone books a run for their money. A number of services on the Web can help you find phone numbers, e-mail addresses, street addresses, and other information about businesses and individuals. Here are some suggestions for places you can go, especially when you are looking for someone in another state or even another country.

If you want to find someone's Web page . . .

If the search services don't turn up an individual's Web page fast enough, try InterNIC. InterNIC will help you find Web pages associated with organizations at ds2.internic.net/ds/webfinder/WebFinder.html.

If you want to find the name of a company . . .

One of the big advantages of searching on the Web is that you don't have to look through lots of phone books in the library or run up directory assistance charges. Here are some resources for finding individual companies online:

- **Companies Online** (www.companiesonline.com). This site provides an on-line database of U.S. companies on the Web.
- **BigYellow** (s15.bigyellow.com). This is just one of several Yellow Pages services on the Web that can help you locate millions of U.S. businesses.

✔ *MapBlast* (www.mapblast.com). If you want to pinpoint a company on a map before you travel, this site enables you to locate a detailed street map from almost any street address in the U.S. You can also e-mail a map to somebody or add a map to your home page.

If you want to find someone's e-mail address . . .

Looking for a long-lost friend, old business adversary, or president of a company that you want to do business with? Try one of these personal directories:

✔ **Four11** (www.Four11.com). Four11, one of the oldest and most popular Internet white pages directories, enables you to find e-mail addresses and phone numbers of individuals.

✔ **Switchboard** (www.switchboard.com). This service enables you to find real world information as well as e-mail/Web information for individuals and businesses.

If you're on AOL, be sure that you check out AOL's Phone and Address Directories page (keyword: **PhoneBook**), which contains the American Yellow pages as well as the Switchboard list of phone numbers and e-mail addresses.

Searching Other Parts of the Net

The Web is the part of the Internet that gets all the attention these days, but some sources of information, like government archives or University records, are contained on other parts of the Net, such as Gopher. Software programs are still made available by File Transfer Protocol *(FTP)*. And you can find a wealth of information on the online services America Online, CompuServe, and Prodigy, including some discussion forums and current publications that you can't find on the Internet. This section gives you an overview of ways you can search the non-Web part of the Net.

Digging for FTP riches

FTP is used to send data from one computer to another, and a primary use is in providing software that you can download from an *anonymous FTP site* — a site that enables anyone to log in and copy files.

You have two ways to find something on FTP sites:

✔ **A Web front door.** Software repositories like Shareware.com and Jumbo enable you to search through FTP sites from the comfort of your web browser, by entering search terms in a simple Web page interactive form that resembles an Internet search service form.

✔ **An Archie search.** An Archie server compiles the contents of anonymous FTP sites around the world into a database that you can search quickly if you are looking for a particular program or file.

If you're in a hurry and want to stick with using your Web browser, go to one of the shareware sites with an easy Web interface, such as the highly recommended Stroud's Consummate Winsock Apps List, which is a great source for Windows 95 and 3.1 shareware programs. This site is so popular that it has several *mirrors* (alternate locations, that is) on the Net. If one location is busy, try another:

```
http://cws.internet.com/
http://cws.icorp.net/
http://www.icorp.net/stroud/
http://cws.iworld.com/
```

As shown in Figure 16-4, interacting with Stroud's is easy: Just send your Web browser to the home page. You can then search through indexes that contain many categories of software by clicking on the buttons labeled *16-bit Apps*, *Introduction*, or *32-bit Apps*. Or, you can enter the name of the program you want in the search box shown at the bottom of the screen.

Figure 16-4:
If you search a software archive from the Web, you don't have to download or launch special FTP software.

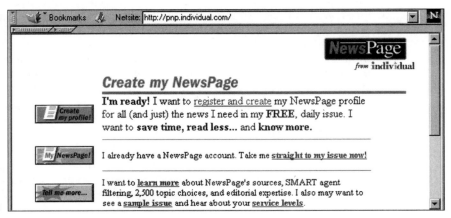

Stroud's is only one of several sites that provide shareware and freeware programs you can download. Some of the other sites I've used include:

- **Shareware.com** (www.shareware.com).
- **The Jumbo! Download Network** (www.jumbo.com).
- **Tucows**, the Ultimate Collection of Winsock Software (www.tucows.com).

These three sites all provide software for the Macintosh as well as Windows 95 and 3.1 and other platforms.

Using Anarchie

If you're a dedicated Macintosh user, you have a cool alternative when it comes to searching FTP sites for software. It's a program called Anarchie, which is available as shareware for just $10, and which was created by an Australian computer whiz named Peter Lewis.

Using Archie takes longer than the Mac Search option, but you get lots of locations from which you can download the application. (My search for NetPresenz returned a list of thirty different FTP sites that contain the program.) That's all there is to it.

Don't forget that although shareware is easy to download and use, it's not necessarily free. Be nice to the programmers who have made the software available to you, and send them the nominal shareware fee they request.

Fun with Gopher, Veronica, and Jughead

Sounds like a cartoon, doesn't it? Actually, as you can find out in Chapter 4, Gopher is a program that provides access to Internet resources by using a menu-based search system. It includes databases, library catalogs, and bulletin board systems all over the world. Although the Web has now replaced Gopher as the most popular way to navigate the Net, you can still find lots of information on Gopher.

What, exactly, can you find using Gopher? Lots of libraries and library catalogs can be accessed by connecting to Gopher servers. Plenty of electronic books and journals can be accessed through Gopher, too.

After you get to a Gopher site you're likely to see an option that begins with the words "Search the Site...." This is a local search option that only works with the site in question; double-click on the folder with the question mark (a standard Gopher graphic that means Search), and a simple dialog box appears with a single text box in which you can enter a keyword you're looking for (see Figure 16-5).

Home Gopher

📁 Information About Gopher
📁 Computer Information
📁 Discussion Groups
📁 Fun &
📁 Inter
📁 Libra
📁 News
📁 Other
📁 Phone

Find what?

[   ]

[Cancel] [**Find**]

▓ Search Gopher Titles at the University of Minnesota
❓ Search lots of places at the University of Minnesota

©1991–95 University of Minnesota.

Veronica is a type of server that performs the same function for Gopher sites as an Archie server does for FTP sites. Veronica, in fact, stands for "Very Easy Rodent-Oriented Net-Wide Index to Computerized Archives." It is an application that works by searching the contents of Gopher sites around the world and compiling the contents into a database.

Only a few Veronica sites can be found around the world, but you can access them pretty easily. Just follow these steps:

1. **Launch your Gopher software and connect to the University of Minnesota home Gopher site.**

   The Welcome to Gopher window opens.

2. **Double-click on the folder icon next to Other Gopher and Information Services.**

   Another gopher window opens.

3. **Double-click on Search titles in Gopherspace using Veronica.**

   A Gopher window opens with lots of search options. You see directories that, when you double-click on them, enable you to search three Veronica servers, which are located at: PSI Net, SCS Nevada, and UNAM.

Veronica only works for words in the titles of documents. It doesn't search the full text of a site's contents. You can use the Boolean operator *and* with the asterisk (*) as a wildcard to narrow a search.

Business resources on the online services

If you like to participate in online chats, or if you just want to listen in on discussions, not just about business issues but virtually any topic, the online services provide lots of opportunities. If you subscribe to America

Online or another commercial online service, you are able to participate in chat sessions. After you enter a chat room you can read the messages posted by others and post your own if you like. You have the option to post to everyone in the chat room or privately to one of the participants.

When you get to a Web site that offers a chat, you are asked to register and you can use your real name or one you make up. By using a *screen name* (a name that you make up for yourself) you offer yourself some privacy and it is important not to give out personal information to strangers online, such as phone numbers, addresses, or credit card numbers.

Here are brief summaries of some ways in which you can use the online services for research.

America Online

America Online *(AOL)* has a wealth of information, some of which is still not available on the wider Internet. A business can use America Online exclusively for business research and get along quite well (see the sidebar "Case study: Sense and Nonsense," in this chapter).

Be sure that you click on the button labeled Tools and Reference at the bottom of the Your Business Front Page. The Tools and Reference page appears, with links that enable you to do company research, find business profiles, get stock quotes, and find other business data. You can also go to the Company Research page directly by typing the keyword: **Company Research**.

Case study: Sense and Nonsense

Sense and Nonsense (sensenon@aol.com) is a small company in Chicago that does writing, editing, proofreading, and other book development services for educational publishers. Two of the company's four computers are equipped with modems so they can make dialup connections to America Online. "We only have one personal phone line, and our other line is for the fax, so when both computers are connected, people just get a busy signal," says Jan Gilder, president of the company.

Although Sense and Nonsense had only made use of the Net for a few weeks when Gilder spoke, she said that the Net had already made a big difference in the company's daily research needs. One employee, Kerri Hatcher, searches America Online's reference materials full-time. She has used AOL for fact-checking, information gathering, and solving problems with software. Kerri especially likes Grollier's Multimedia Encyclopedia, which is available to AOL members. "It beats the heck out of going to the library all the time," she comments.

Prodigy

Prodigy's resources for small business owners can be accessed by jump (Ctrl+J) **small business**. If you operate a small business from your own home, you may enjoy Prodigy's Your Business Bulletin Board, a forum where home-office workers can commiserate and collaborate. Jump (Ctrl+J) **your business** to get started. When the Your Business Bulletin Board opens, click on the button labeled Choose a Topic. You see a list of current discussions that you can pick up. The topics change all the time, but typical ones include:

- Marketing a Business
- Healthcare/Insurance
- Accounting/Finance/Taxes

If you want to join in an ongoing discussion, you can post a question to the participants by clicking on the Go To Chat button. Then you can type a message and submit it to the group.

If Your Computer's on the Fritz . . .

The Internet is a good place to turn if you need help with your computer or a particular software program fast. It can be faster to download a patch (a software program that is created to fix a *bug,* or a flaw, in another program) or an updated version of software you use frequently than to order it from a computer store. You can even get tips on obvious or simple fixes you can try with your computer, which can come in handy on the weekend when the repair shop is closed.

Of course, if one of your computers is down, you need access to another computer that is connected to the Net in order to *use* the Net. Nonetheless, small businesses like Sense and Nonsense (which is mentioned in the sidebar "Case study: Sense and Nonsense," in this chapter), which has four computers, commonly turn to the Net if they have a computer-related problem.

Software resources

If you encounter a software glitch, turn first to the Web site for the company that made the software. Often, you are able to download an updated version or a patch for the program with the problem.

Here are some of the biggest and most popular sites for software:

✔ **Adobe Systems Incorporated (**www.adobe.com**).**

✔ **Microsoft Corporation (**www.microsoft.com**).**

✔ **Apple Computer (**www.apple.com**).** Much of their software is made available on their FTP site (ftp://ftp.apple.com).

Hardware problems

If something is seriously wrong with your computer, take your machine to a good repair person. However, you may find answers to some of the simpler problems at these sites:

✔ **Macintosh Crash Tips (**www.zplace.com/crashtips**).** This site offers extensive information on application freezes, extensions conflict/bugs, but the best feature is a huge list of troubleshooting links for the Mac.

✔ **Computecraft Reference Library (**www.computercraft.com/docs/refmenu.html**).** An eccentric site on how to repair PCs, which includes links to other sites.

✔ **The Hand-Me Down PC (**www.daileyint.com/hmdpc/repair.htm**).** An online version of a book by the same name. This site includes a troubleshooting and repair section and links to other PC resources on the Web.

✔ **The Tech Support Site (**www.bway.net/~realty**).** This site provides links to Hardware and Software Support, for both Macintosh and PC.

✔ **The *Washington Post's* Your Computer site (**www.washingtonpost.com/wp-srv/tech/computer.htm**).** This page enables you to enter questions or search terms and returns answers to your computer questions.

Where to buy hardware

You can find plenty of places to buy hardware on the Net. The following are a few resources that I've used myself:

✔ **Onsale (**www.onsale.com**).** A Web site that conducts online auctions not only of computers and peripherals but also for consumer electronics as well.

> ✔ **PCConnection (**www.pcconnection.com**).** An online computer discount store that includes both Mac and PC products.
>
> ✔ **comp.infosystems.www.---- for sale.** This newsgroup is set aside specifically for advertising computer equipment for sale.

Business Information You Can Find Online

All of these search services and tools are great, but what can you actually find using them? Take a look around and you can see that the Internet is full of useful information for any business, large or small. Here are suggestions for some resources you may want to consult.

U.S. Small Business Administration Home Page:

```
www.sbaonline.sba.gov
```

The National Small Business Council is a nonprofit, membership organization promoting small business interests. It produces on-site, one-day technology expositions at government facilities for large and small businesses and conducts small business seminars and conferences on various topics.

```
www.nsbc.org
```

The International Small Business Consortium has 11,000 members from 90 countries and defines itself as a center for business collaboration, helping businesses build relationships.

```
www.isbc.com
```

SoHo Central is an acronym for Small Office/Home Office. SoHo Central is also the official Web site for the Home Office Association of America, the national and local organization for full-time, home-based professionals, telecommuters, and millions of others who use a home office so they can spend more time with their families. Working at home represents one of the fastest-growing business trends of the 90s.

```
www.hoaa.com
```

The Business Education and Training site, maintained by the Cranfield University School of Management, provides an extensive list of links to every major business school in the U.S. and some in Europe.

```
www.cranfield.ac.uk/som/cclt/links.html
```

If you're looking for business consultants, this site includes the *Guide to the Small Business Administration: Starting, Financing and Operating a Small Business,* an excellent nongovernment resource on the Small Business Administration (SBA) and includes information on SCORE, the SBA's free business consultant program.

```
www.geocities.com/WallStreet/2172
```

The *Money$Search Real Estate Connections* page offers links to national real estate resources.

```
www.moneysearch.com/docs/realestate.html
```

If you need accounting help, the following Web page contains the Tax and Accounting Site Directory, a good resource maintained by a professor at the University of Northern Iowa.

```
www.uni.edu/schmidt/sites.html
```

Idea Cafe's Financing Your Business is a great site that covers everything you want to know about borrowing money and getting investors, including pages of self-examinations to find out what kind of financing is right for you.

```
www.ideacafe.com/getmoney/FINANCING.shtml
```

The Smart Business Supersite offers a page of great marketing and advertising resources.

```
www.smartbiz.com/sbs/cats/mktg.htm
```

Telecommunication Information Sources offers a comprehensive listing of telecommunications companies, providers of telecommunications hardware, software, and consulting services, and other information.

```
www.telstra.com.au/info/communications.html
```

Human Resource Management Resources on the Internet provides a huge and comprehensive resource on the topic.

```
www.nbs.ntu.ac.uk/staff/lyerj/hrm_link.htm
```

LawCrawler Legal WWW Search allows you to search any kind of legal information imaginable for every state in the Union.

```
www.lawcrawler.com/index.html
```

The Workplace Rights Center, part of the Business Strategies Forum on America Online has both an Employer's Guide and an Employee's Guide, and provides an attorney you can contact if you need help with a dispute.

keyword:**strategies**

The Business Law Site covers federal and state statutes, cases and agencies, legal research sites, business and high-tech law, and tax forms.

members.aol.com/bmethven/index.html

The IRS publishes *The Digital Daily,* a humorous publication with not so funny tax laws and information that can help you stay informed of changes.

www.irs.ustreas.gov/prod/cover.html

If you're planning business travel, S.E.T.I.I., Search Engine for Travel Information on the Internet, does just what it says.

www.setii.com

Federal Express as well as many other shipping companies offer complete services online.

www.fedex.com

The results of research on the Internet depend on your reason for doing the searching. Generally, though, you can be more up-to-date and credible with the information you pass along to customers. You can plug concrete data into proposals and reports. Your staff can save time looking up facts and figures. And you may even save time running to the computer store or other store to make a purchase. Perhaps the nicest benefit is the knowledge that you have a new resource to turn to whenever you need a question answered or a fact found fast.

Part VI
The Part of Tens

"THE IMAGE IS GETTING CLEARER NOW... I CAN ALMOST SEE IT... YES! THERE IT IS — THE GLITCH IS IN A FAULTY CABLE AT YOUR OFFICE IN DENVER."

In this part . . .

Lists are great tools when it comes to getting things done, whether in the office or on the Web. Lists help remind you of top priorities and focus on essential tasks that need to get completed.

Part VI, in fact, consists solely of lists that you can look through whether you're brainstorming for business ideas or looking to upgrade your Web site. You'll find a collection of tips and stories that sum up what it means to get your small business online. You'll read descriptions of both high-tech and simple features that can add zest and fun to your Web pages which, after all, are the centerpiece of any Internet marketing effort. You'll also hear about more businesses that are prospering online, and learn how to apply what they've done to your own fledgling cyber-venture.

Chapter 17

Ten Ways to Make Your Business Site Sizzle

As more and more businesses go online and make investments in their own Web sites, you need to develop a strategy for standing out from the crowd.

Choosing between a simple or a fancy Web page isn't a clear-cut decision. To beat your competition, you need to make sure that your Web pages have bright colors, original art, snappy headings, or programming tricks to grab the attention of those fidgety surfers before they zoom by your site.

The most effective features add to your page without requiring lots of additional processing power that makes your computer and browser slow down to a crawl. This chapter describes ten such features that are commonly found on effective business Web sites.

Ten Cool Web Page Eye-Grabbers

Here are ten suggestions for words, images, and utilities that can encourage visitors to return again and again. Some of these are a little more techy, which means that you or someone you hire needs to have advanced knowledge of HyperText Markup Language (HTML) or a scripting language such as JavaScript. Others are doable as long as you have the right software — and often, you can download programs for free or for a nominal fee from the Net.

Presentation is everything

The best Web sites take into account the fact that the individual user controls the size of the browser window used to view pages. Users can also configure background colors and typefaces that may be quite different from the ones that you choose for your printed brochures.

An official typeface

If your company has an official typeface that you use in your printed materials, you can specify it using a *style sheet*. The viewer's browser displays the typeface that you have chosen if two conditions are met:

- ✔ The viewer's browser recognizes style sheets.
- ✔ The viewer has the specified typeface installed in his or her computer's operating system.

Because you can't control what typefaces are installed in your visitors' computers, it's a good idea to specify two or three possible typefaces — a first, ideal choice, followed by two backups that are more common and, therefore, more likely for your viewer to have.

Discussing everything you ever wanted to know about style sheets is beyond the scope of this book. But, if you want to give it a try, here's a very simple exercise. Paste the following in the HEAD section of the Web page where you want the special typefaces to be displayed:

```
<HTML>
<HEAD>
<STYLE TYPE-"text/css">
<!--
body (font: 10pt "Verdana, sans-serif");
h1 (font: 36pt "Univers. sans-serif";
font-weight: bold;
color: purple)
p (font: 10pt/12pt "Verdana. sans-serif";
color:black;
-->
</style>
</HEAD>
<BODY>
--body of document goes here--
</BODY>
</HTML>
```

In this style sheet, the font that's chosen as the first choice for body text is 10-point Verdana. The additional designation, sans-serif, specifies that if the reader does not have the typeface Verdana installed, another sans serif font can be substituted. Each Heading 1 HTML heading is supposed to be purple 36-pt. Univers (or another sans serif typeface such as Helvetica).

An online catalog

Many small business owners have a variety of products to sell or various bits of information to convey. In other words, you want to get the contents of your catalog on the Web — a likely job for your Webmaster or Web page consultant. Note that software is available to convert the contents of your database to HTML documents that can be published on Web pages. You can use either a database program that automatically outputs its contents to HTML, such as Microsoft Access 97, or you can extract the data using a product such as Allaire Cold Fusion.

A shopping cart setup

Several sales options are mentioned in Chapter 11, including credit cards and electronic cash. In addition, if you have an extensive catalog of goods for sale on your Internet site, you may consider installing a shopping cart program. Shopping cart software keeps track of items that customers pick as they browse your catalog on the Web. By clicking on a button labeled Add Item to My Shopping Cart, the selected item is stored for the shopper until he or she is ready to check out by actually purchasing the goods from you. At check-out time, the selected items are displayed to the shopper so that he or she can make a final decision to buy them.

Many commercial shopping cart applications are available, but before you spend money on them, you may want to try out a program called Powercart Lite that's put out as freeware by Oakland Group, Inc. The CGI scripts included with this program keep track of the names and prices of items selected and even calculate sales tax for the shopper, based on the tax rate that you tell the program to use.

Although Powercart Lite costs nothing to install and use, you can have Oakland Group install the program for you for a $50 fee. This can be money well spent because the CGI scripts have to be configured to use data that's specific to your business. Call 800-448-2772 to find out more. Powercart Lite is a simple program that doesn't have all the features of more sophisticated software. Visit Oakland Group's Web site (www.oaklnd.com) to explore more powerful shopping cart programs.

If your commercial site is published on the Web by a Web hosting service or ISP, be sure to verify that it's okay to be running CGI scripts on your provider's Web server.

A Netcasting channel

The electronic broadcast can be used by any company that has frequent updates about its products and services that are appropriate for subscribers, such as product announcements, stock prices, or personnel information.

You can set up your own Netcasting channel easily by using a program called WebCast Professional by Astound, Inc., as shown in Figure 17-1.

A 30-day trial version is available for Windows 95 and NT. Find out more at www.astound.com/products2/wcpro/wcpro.html.

Search engine helpers

What's a great way to attract new visitors to your Web site? When someone is doing a search, one of the Internet search engines returns a list of links to them. It's really nice when a link to your Web site is on that list. The idea is pretty simple. The user enters a keyword or phrase and submits the request to the search service so that the service can scour its database for Web pages that contain the word or phrase. Obviously, you benefit if your Web pages appear in as many lists as possible. The way to accomplish this goal is to add some text to the HTML for the page using the META tag. This command goes in the HEAD section of the HTML document, like this:

```
<HTML>
<HEAD>
<TITLE>Welcome to Golf Distributors</TITLE>
<META NAME="keywords" CONTENT="golf, golf ball, tee,
           driver, woods, iron, putter, wedge, caddie, PGA,
           tournament, sand trap, greens, links, 18 holes">
</HEAD>
```

Many of the computer programs that the search services use to scan and index Web page contents register the keywords included in the HTML for a Web page. The more keywords that you include on your site, the more likely you are to have your Web page returned when someone does a search for one of those words. The more often you turn up in a list of search results, the more visitors you get.

An FTP site

File Transfer Protocol (FTP) isn't as glamorous as the Web, but it helps many companies take care of business on the Internet. Many of the best-known software archives on the Internet, such as Tucows (www.tucows.com) or Shareware.com (www.shareware.com) get thousands of visitors each month.

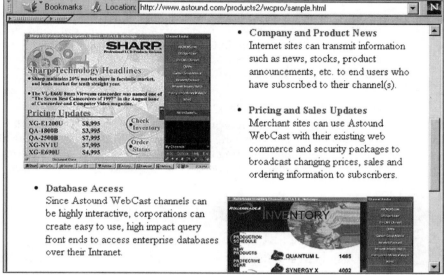

Figure 17-1:
Netcasting enables businesses to send updated information to users.

You don't have to offer software on an FTP site. A program can be used simply to send files from one computer to another — a great way for employees, designers, or suppliers to exchange documents with your office.

Improving communication

Here are some suggestions for Web site features that may help users talk to one another, whether they're working with you or buying from you.

A feedback form/thank you note

Inviting responses from customers on the Web is much easier than setting up a suggestion box in the real world. The user can then type a quick e-mail message and automatically send it to the Web site.

Another nearly painless way to get feedback from your visitors is to supply them with a form they can fill out and send to you. Forms are more complex to prepare than a simple mailto link, but the payoff can be pretty impressive. They can be used to gain valuable marketing information like a visitor's name, address, gender, age, and so on. In addition, a field in the form that gives the visitor a place to type his or her opinions about the site strongly encourages people to send comments that are more detailed, and thus more valuable, than a quick e-mail message.

An extra flourish is to create a CGI script that causes a Web page thank-you note to be sent back to the person submitting the comments. A thanks for the thanks lets people know that you received your data and will respond to them as soon as you can. In the computerized world of the Internet, any additional bit of personal contact with your visitors is likely to elicit good-will that may result in return visits.

An employee discussion group

Internet-style discussion groups encourage serious collaborations on issues or projects in the office. One person can put out a call for ideas about an important business meeting or a community service project, for instance. Colleagues can then compose messages that deliver their ideas.

Some JavaScript tricks

JavaScript is a relatively simple programming language that's designed specifically to add functionality or to create graphic effects in Web pages. It's a good language for either you or your Web page designer to know. Here are a couple of specific JavaScript tricks that you can add to your Web pages.

Be sure to enclose the JavaScript commands within the HTML comments symbols <!– and –>. That way, the script itself doesn't appear in the body of the Web page; your viewers see only the effects. The rest of your Web page contents, however, can be viewed without any trouble.

A pop-up notice

You've probably picked up a glossy magazine, eager to find an article you're interested in, when your attention is diverted by something. Perhaps some coupons that were tipped in to the magazine (not stapled, but just inserted loosely between the pages) fall at your feet. Or a thick fold-out page unfolds as you flip for the table of contents.

These elements that grab your attention before you explore a publication in detail have an equivalent in the world of Web pages. The attraction is a little window that pops up near the upper-left hand corner of the main Web page window. This mini-window contains late-breaking information that the company wants you to see right away.

In order to create a pop-up notice, you or your Web page consultant need to paste the following lines of JavaScript into the source HTML instructions for the Web page where the window is supposed to pop up. Paste the script between the <BODY> and </BODY> tags.

Be sure to substitute the path leading to the document that you want to display in the pop-up window for the path shown in the script below. For instance, if your pop-up window text is a file called news.html and this file is contained on your Web site in the folder news, you can type the path leading to the document like this:

```
/news/news.html
```

The width and height can be varied to suit your taste. In this example, the height and width are 300 pixels; you can make them bigger or smaller, if you prefer. Be sure to use a smaller-than-usual heading size to take the smaller window size into account.

The rest of the script looks like this:

```
<HTML>
<HEAD><TITLE>Golf Unlimited</TITLE>
</HEAD>
<BODY>

<SCRIPT LANGUAGE="JavaScript">
<!--
newsWindow = window.open("/news/news.html", SaleSaleSale!",
          "menubar=no,directories=no, scrollbars=yes,
          resizable=yes,width=300,height=300") ;
-->
</SCRIPT>
</BODY>
</HTML>
```

To find out more about JavaScript, check out *JavaScript For Dummies,* 2nd Edition, by Emily A. Vander Veer (IDG Books Worldwide, Inc.).

A toggling navigation bar

Another cool JavaScript technique causes another image to pop up when the user's mouse passes over an image. Often, this is used in a series of links: When the mouse passes over a link labeled <u>Home</u> or <u>Contact</u>, the word seems to light up.

How does this work? A JavaScript script included in the HTML for the Web page causes a second image to appear when the mouse passes over the first image.

Here's the JavaScript for a simple mouse-over effect like the one shown in Figure 17-2. The script that follows isn't for the effect shown in Figure 17-2; it's much simpler. When the user passes the mouse over the first image, which is called `test1.gif` in the script that follows, a second image called `test2.gif` appears. When the mouse leaves the first image (this is called MouseOut in the script below), the first image, `test1.gif`, reappears. Remember to substitute your own images for the example images `test1.gif` and `test2.gif`.

The first part, the actual script, goes in the HEAD section of the Web page:

```
<html>
<head>
<script language="JavaScript">
function toggle1() {
document.images[0].src="test1.gif"
}

function toggle2() {
document.images[0].src="test2.gif"
}
</script>
</head>
```

The second part causes the two images to appear on the Web page and allows them to toggle from one image to the other. This second part goes in the BODY section of the HTML for the Web page:

```
<body bgcolor="ffffff">
<a href="" onMouseOver="toggle2(0)"
          onMouseOut="toggle1(0)"><img
src="test1.gif" border=0></a>
</body>
</html>
```

You know that your bells and whistles are working if you get increased hit counts, as reported in the log files sent to you by your ISP. You can also be proactive: Instead of waiting to see if more people visit you, ask your visitors to send you feedback on your site, paying particular attention to user-friendliness and practical worth of your site content.

The goal of adding visual goodies and interactive features to your small business Web site is simple — you want to

✔ Attract more visitors to your online business.

✔ Give visitors a reason to stay on your site and explore it instead of surfing to your competitors' sites.

✔ Encourage return visits to your site.

Chapter 18

Ten Small Business Internet Success Stories

*T*he primary purpose behind creating a Web site to promote your small business is the chance to write text and create designs that reflect your unique identity. However, you don't have to reinvent the wheel.

Look at some of the spotlighted Web sites, along with others that you find along the way. When you discover a general approach that seems relevant to you, put your own spin on it.

Big-Time Internet Success Stories

Not every seed that's planted by a small business on the Web grows into a huge flowering profit margin. But success stories *do* happen.

The personal touch: Virtual Vineyards

Virtual Vineyards, an online marketer of fine food and wine, has gained plenty of attention from those who examine businesses that are successful on the Internet. Coincidence? I don't think so. Look at the extensive and professional-looking Web site shown in Figure 18-1.

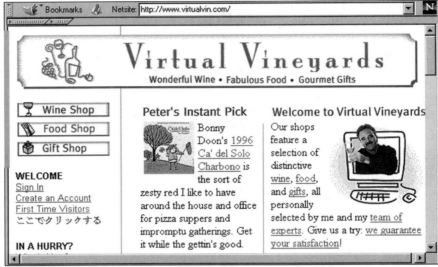

Figure 18-1:
Simple
graphics
plus useful,
interactive
contact
equals
success for
this online
marketer.

Virtual Vineyard's outstanding marketing features include

✔ **Support for international visitors.** Visitors come from far and near. They may be looking for something that they can't get in their own countries; they may also be looking for something particularly American.

✔ **Lots of information.** On the Internet, information sells. This is particularly true when that information is provided to individuals who are already passionate about your area of interest.

✔ **Credibility and authority.** Small businesses can outperform larger competitors on the Internet by providing authoritative information with a professional presentation.

Since first going online in January 1995, Virtual Vineyards has won lots of awards and has been the subject of many laudatory articles in the press.

Competing effectively: Auto-By-Tel

The Internet enables shoppers to browse through lots of options quickly without driving from one auto dealer to another. Because overhead costs are low, prices are better on the Internet than in many real-world dealerships. Shopping for many options is easy because Auto-By-Tel provides extensive search facilities on its Web site, www.autobytel.com.

Building a brand: Amazon.com

Amazon.com, the well-known online bookstore, is achieving an important goal: The company has made its brand name synonymous with online bookstores.

The bookstore's Web site establishes a personal touch that enables shoppers to browse and search for titles based on their reading preferences. The Web site's home page (www.amazon.com) provides a link to a special welcome page designed especially for first-time visitors. A Recommendation Center enables visitors to keep track of books that they purchased from the site in the past, and receive book recommendations that are tailored to their reading habits or their moods as identified on interactive forms.

Casting a Wide Net

No matter how unusual the service or product you sell, there's bound to be someone in the world who's interested in it. The Internet provides you with a way to reach your most promising customers, around the corner or around the world. Here are some examples of Internet businesses that are thriving because they're exposed to an international audience.

Rounding up cowpokes: Ranchweb

Ranchweb (www.ranchweb.com) was named best small business Web site by *Home Office Computing/Small Business Computing Magazine* in 1997. However, other small businesses may be interested in the fact that Ranchweb didn't achieve its present status overnight.

"The first pass of Ranchweb went online in January of 1995," says Joel MacIntosh, Ranchweb's Technical Director. "At that point the site offered basic company information and real estate listings."

MacIntosh, who is also chief manager of WolfNet Technologies, LLC, a Web development firm in Minnesota, worked with Ranchweb's owner Gene Kilgore to develop the site. The site was completely redesigned during the second half of 1996, and had its grand opening in January 1997. Ranchweb now receives about 8,000 visitors each month.

Kilgore Ranch Company, which has only two full-time employees, developed Ranchweb as a service that matches travelers in search of adventure vacations with dude ranch owners in the western United States. Each rancher pays a service fee to be included in the site (shown in Figure 18-2).

Figure 18-2: Consider developing your Web site in stages, as Ranchweb's creators did.

When asked if the Web site has been a success, MacDonald says, "Absolutely! First, Kilgore Ranch Company has been able to offset the production costs of Ranchweb via revenue from the ranchers, while building brand recognition in the marketplace. This has become a fairly significant avenue for promoting this industry. Ranchers and travelers alike have come to trust the Kilgore name. We think it would be fair to say that Ranchweb has helped generate somewhere between 150 and 300 bookings for the industry since January 1997."

An online authority: Gregory Siskind, Attorney

When attorney Gregory Siskind created his first Web page in 1994, he had just left a law firm to start his own practice, and had no partners or clients. Because immigration law is a federal practice that's not restricted to a single country, he thought that the Internet may help him attract clients from all over the world.

He was right. Having targeted his audience, he developed an electronic newsletter, Siskind's Immigration Bulletin, on immigration law.

Today Siskind and his fellow attorneys at Siskind, Susser, Haas, and Chang are a leading online resource in the area of immigration law. The main Web site (www.visalaw.com) includes the Immigration Forms Center, which has lots of forms visitors can download and view.

One-to-one dialogue: Charter Sailing Unlimited

Dennis Dori, owner and sole employee of Charter Sailing Unlimited, uses his presence online only as a starting point. He follows up with personalized communication based on the initial contact — which, on the Internet, is almost always made by the customer, not the merchant.

The Charter Sailing Unlimited Web site (`www.sail-csu.com`) includes a couple of features that other small businesses can follow:

✔ **Detailed interactive forms.** The forms on the Charter Sailing site are designed to discourage visitors who aren't serious about wanting to charter a Caribbean cruise. They invite the user to provide lots of specific information about the kind of trip that's desired.

✔ **A mailing list and newsletter.** Visitors are given the chance to subscribe to a regularly updated newsletter. This not only helps potential customers keep up with travel opportunities, but also gives the business a way to keep in contact with them.

Give 'Em What They Want

By casting a wide net on the Net, you can enlarge your customer base significantly. People who use the Internet consistently are often obsessive about it: They visit the same discussion groups and chat with like-minded individuals, they visit the same Web sites, they search for information going from archive to archive until they find it. This is music to the ears of the businesses who have products or services that these users want. Here are some examples.

Do one thing, do it well: SkyWeyr Technologies

If your business involves providing computer services that are difficult to set up or maintain and that are in demand, now's a great time to be online. Computer programmers and Web site designers are hot commodities. If you're a high-tech expert, identify a field that you know well and promote your abilities in that one area.

SkyWeyr, the small Indianapolis company described in Chapter 7 (`www.skyweyr.com`), identified one single function — setting up and maintaining mailing lists — and is doing it well.

You can do market research with mailing lists and discussion groups. But there are other ways to interact with your visitors online: You can also provide 24-hour-per-day customer service; become an authority by answering questions; or get feedback from online forms.

Target passionate interests: Cameta Camera

The Internet is a vast playground for collectors, hobbyists, and people with passionate interests of all kinds.

One of those stores, Cameta Camera (`www.cameta.camera`), has targeted camera enthusiasts of all kinds, and particularly collectors of high-quality vintage cameras.

In order to create its regularly updated listings of cameras and accessories, Bill Cameta did something that can benefit many other small businesses: The company struck a partnership with a good Web developer. The developer, Debbie Levitt, not only created Cameta's Web site, but also updates it on a regular basis, saving Cameta lots of time and effort.

No business too local: Scaife's Butcher Shop

You may think that a small-town butcher shop in the British countryside could not possibly be a success on the Internet. Don't say that to Chris Battle.

Battle and his wife, Barbara, own a butcher shop in Keighley, Yorkshire, England that was started by Barbara's grandfather 90 years ago. Even Chris Battle was surprised at the number of orders that have streamed in to the Scaife's Butchers Web site (`www.classicengland.co.uk/gourmet/scaife/scaife.html`) since the business went online in November 1996.

Why does this Web site work?

- ✔ **It promotes unusual, regional products.** Where else can you order ox tongue and English puddings and sausages? Lots of British expatriates and Anglophiles around the world order their favorite foods.

- ✔ **It's informative.** The site includes sections such as Making Bacon and Meet the Crew that provide some background about the business and the people who work there.

- ✔ **It's fun and personal.** This family operation has a family portrait, as shown by the Happy Butchers in Figure 18-3.

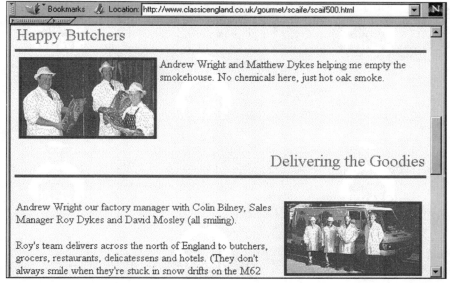

Figure 18-3:
The
personal
touch helps
on the
Internet, as
does a
sense of
humor.

If you have unusual products, take a chance and expand your business to the Internet. You may be surprised at the results.

Making connections: Garden Escape

Garden Escape's Web site (www.garden.com) is described extensively in Chapters 6 and 14. I'm mentioning the site again here because it provides an example of some important techniques for success on the Internet:

- ✔ **Getting a fast connection.** Garden Escape shares a T-1 line with other businesses; it gets a fast Internet connection at a fraction of the cost.

- ✔ **Getting the right address.** The company paid a nominal fee for the virtual domain name garden.com. This simple, easy-to-remember name guarantees lots of visits by garden enthusiasts.

- ✔ **Connecting employees and suppliers.** Staff members in offices that are in different states can collaborate by gaining access to the main internal Web site from their remote locations. They can work together on projects even though they're geographically far apart.

Perhaps most importantly, Garden Escape, Inc. has made a commitment to its online business. The company has backing from several investors, and continually revises its Web site to provide more useful customer service and other information.

If you don't meet with instant success, keep working at it. Revise your Web site, find new ways to market your company with e-mail and discussion groups, and focus on your target audience. Eventually you're sure to find success.

Part VII
Appendixes

The 5th Wave By Rich Tennant

"I'm always amazed at the technological advances made at ad agencies and PR firms."

In this part . . .

The last part of this book explains how to install and use the software on the accompanying CD. You'll find detailed descriptions of programs that have been chosen because they are cost-effective and reliable tools that have been used successfully by many businesses. You'll also get a round-up of databases and groups that can lend support to your Internet business site.

Appendix A

Online Resources for Small Business

• •

Connecting to the Internet is like walking into a huge library that contains lots of business information among its extensive resources. Although the sites listed here were current when the book was being written, some sites have no doubt changed or disappeared altogether. So don't be surprised if your browser cannot find a Web address you type or if a Web site listed in this appendix is no longer at the given address. You may have to search for something similar. You may also try looking for a "missing" site by shortening the address — deleting everything after the `.com` (or `.org` or `.edu`).

General Business Information

@Brint Research Initiative

```
http://www.brint.com/
```

This site, which bills itself as the Ultimate Business, Management and Technology Resource, offers access to a massive amount of business information. A must-see site.

The Jumbo List of Business Sites

```
http://www.clark.net/pub/dbasham/homepage.html
```

Yahoo! Small Business Links

```
http://www.yahoo.com/Business/Small_Business_Information/
```

The Entrepreneur's Bookstore

```
http://kwicsys.com/books/
```

This Nevada-based online bookstore provides more than 600 inexpensive reports on various business topics.

Money Words

http://www.moneywords.com/

Want to learn to speak like your clients do? Money Words provides an on-line glossary of words used in business, finance, and real estate.

U.S. Chamber of Commerce Small Business Institute

http://www.usccsbi.com/

This site provides an on-line catalog offering over 200 books, audio programs, software, and videotapes that will help build your business. The collection is designed specifically to serve America's entrepreneurs.

Minorities in Business

These Web sites are targeted at minority business owners as well as staff people.

Black Business Web: The Black Business Directory

http://www.blackbusiness.com/

Opportunities for Women in Small Business

http://www.mindspring.com/~higley/project.htm

Financial Calculators

http://www.centura.com/formulas/whatif.html

You can find online calculators for personal loans, auto loans, home loans, and investment/savings.

Taxes

If you haven't got an accountant or a tax lawyer, you can find a good number of resources online that will help you at tax time.

State Forms & Instructions

http://www.maxwell.com/tax/state/state_index.html

Social Security Tax

```
http://shell5.ba.best.com/~ftmexpat/html/taxsites/
         ssa.html#regulation
```

Digital Daily

```
http://www.irs.ustreas.gov/
```

International Business

The *Inter* in Internet doesn't stand for *international,* exactly, but the Net *is* ideally suited to communicating, transferring files, and providing information to overseas customers and colleagues. These online resources will help you get started with conducting business around the globe.

Japan Internet Communications Service

```
http://www.jics.com/
```

Webtrade Directory (Hong Kong and China)

```
http://www.webtrade.com.hk/
```

AAMA, the Asian American Manufacturers Association

```
http://www.3wc.com/aama/
```

Freelancers and Consultants

The technical aspects of connecting to the Net, designing Web pages, or extracting data from databases can be time-consuming, and it can be cost-effective to hire consultants to help you. Here's one place to start.

World Wide Freelance Directory

```
http://www.cvp.com/freelance/
```

Federal, State and Local Government

The Federal Web Locator

```
http://www.law.vill.edu/fed-agency/fedwebloc.html
```

Municipal Codes Online

http://www.spl.lib.wa.us/collec/lawcoll/municode.html

Small Business Support Organizations

The Web abounds with sites targeted at small business owners. These are some good sites to visit:

The National Association for the Self-Employed (NASE)

http://www.membership.com/nase/

The Young Entrepreneurs' Organization

http://www.yeo.org/

Institute for Business and Professional Ethics

http://www.depaul.edu/ethics/

West's Legal Directory

http://www.wld.com/ldsearch.htm

The Internet Public Library

http://www.ipl.org/

Compare Net

http://www.compare.net/

Compare Net: The Interactive Buyers Guide, is a good place to research products and services on the Internet, including home office products and express mail carriers.

Patents and Trademarks

If you need to research a trademark or apply for a patent or trademark, you can get started using the Internet. Here are some places to visit:

Easy On-Line Trademark Search

https://storefront.sirius.com/~kdc/trademark/index.html

Questel/Orbit

http://www.questel.orbit.com/patents/patres.html

U.S. Patent and Trademark Office

http://www.uspto.gov/

Travel Information and Weather

If you're traveling on business, you can go online and get the weather or other travel information in a flash from these sites.

The Weather Underground

http://www.wunderground.com/

NITC Travelbase Internet Travel Planning

http://www.travelbase.com/

U.S. State Department Passport Services

http://travel.state.gov/passport_services.html

Center for Disease Control Travel Information

http://www.cdc.gov/travel/travel.html

Industry.Net Tools and Resources Center

http://www.industry.net/c/mn/_sw

This is a shareware library specific to business and technology.

Sales Leads USA

http://www.abii.com/

This free service from American Business Information, Inc., offers sales leads and downloadable mailing lists, business profiles, credit ratings, and customer analysis.

Marketing

If you need more suggestions about marketing your products or services, whether online or off, check out these helpful sites.

The Direct Marketing Association

http://www.the-dma.org/

The DMA is the largest and oldest organization dedicated to evolving the practice of direct marketing.

Advertising Age

http://adage.com/interactive/

The online version of this well-known magazine features articles and hyperlinks on Internet marketing, and especially on the developing, promoting, and advertising of Web sites.

Home-Based Businesses

If you work at home like me, you'll welcome these resources that put you in touch with others in the same situation.

WAHM: The Online Magazine for Work at Home Moms

http://www.wahm.com/

This is the online version of a newsletter available through the mail which provides business ideas, opportunities, advice, and entertainment.

The Home-Office Association of America

http://advgroup.com/links.htm

This is the national and local organization for full-time home-based professionals, telecommuters, and the millions who use a home office so they can spend more time with their families. This site offers a bookstore and links to other sites.

Guides for Internet Beginners

If you're looking for even more beginning Internet information than this book provides, you can consult these sites on the Internet itself.

The Cyberpreneur's Guide to the Internet

```
http://asa.ugl.lib.umich.edu/chdocs/cyberpreneur/Cyber.html
```

A good guide to Internet-accessible resources of use to someone involved in entrepreneurial uses of the Internet.

Best of the Internet Tutorials

```
http://www.bgsu.edu/departments/tcom/tutors2.html
```

You can find plenty of links here to online tutorials covering the Internet in general and the World Wide Web in particular.

Beginners Guide to HTML

```
http://www.ncsa.uiuc.edu/General/Internet/WWW/
            HTMLPrimer.html
```

This is the classic starting point for learning HTML (HyperText Markup Language), as prepared by the University of Illinois' National Center for Supercomputing Applications (NSCA).

CyberAtlas

```
http://www.cyberatlas.com/index.html
```

This site offers reference information specific to the World Wide Web, including demographics, usage patterns, advertising, intranets, site building, and a glossary.

The List

```
http://thelist.internet.com/
```

The List: The Definitive ISP Buyer's Guide lists over 3,000 Internet Service Providers and news about ISP's around the world.

Web Page Graphics

Presentation counts for a lot on the Web. If you want to make a good impression but don't have the time or resources to create elaborate Web page graphics or designs, consult these pages for help. If you are copying "clip art" from the Web, be sure to read the usage restrictions first: sometimes the art is free for use, sometimes the creators request a small fee or ask that you give them credit.

AGL Free Animated GIFs and Postcards

```
http://www.arosnet.se/agl/
```

The nice thing about this site is the interface: You can search a database of animated GIFs to find the one you want.

The Netscape Background Sampler

```
http://home.netscape.com/assist/net_sites/bg/
          backgrounds.html
```

This site has some very nice simple backgrounds that you can use not only with Netscape's software but other Web page programs, too.

Nifty Internet Tools

These are a couple of simple utilities you might find useful when you're using the Web or other parts of the Internet.

E-Minder Web Page

```
http://www.netmind.com/e-minder/e-minder.html
```

This service will send you automated e-mail to remind you of important meetings or occasions customized for your own personal needs, and it's free!

Url-Minder

```
http://www.netmind.com/
```

Url-Minder keeps track of Web pages (and other Internet resources) and sends you e-mail when the pages you register change. It's another free service.

Appendix B

About the CD-ROM

● ●

*T*he ability to obtain low-cost software is one of the best reasons for a small business to branch out to the Internet. You can download trial or demo versions of programs and, by paying the owner a moderate shareware fee, you can keep the program if it seems right for you.

The CD-ROM that accompanies *Small Business Internet For Dummies* is even better. It provides you with software you don't have to wait minutes (or sometimes even hours) to download. You can install and use the programs right away. Some are even free. We've gathered programs that are geared toward the needs of a small business that wants to connect to the Internet.

Here's some of what you can find on the *Small Business Internet For Dummies* CD-ROM:

- ✔ AT&T WorldNet Service, a popular Internet service
- ✔ Paint Shop Pro, a great shareware graphics program for Windows
- ✔ BBEdit Lite, a freeware text editor for Mac OS computers that is useful for HTML editing
- ✔ SLMail, which lets you set up your own e-mail server on one of your office computers
- ✔ Internet Phone, software for making telephone calls with your computer

System Requirements

Make sure your computer meets the minimum system requirements listed below. If your computer doesn't match up to most of these requirements, you may have problems in using the contents of the CD.

- ✔ A PC with a 486 or faster processor, or a Mac OS computer with a 68030 or faster processor.
- ✔ Microsoft Windows 3.1 or later, or Mac OS system software 7.5 or later.

✔ At least 8MB of total RAM installed on your computer. For best perfor-
mance, we recommend that Windows 95 or NT-equipped PCs and Mac OS
computers with PowerPC processors have at least 16MB of RAM installed.

✔ A CD-ROM drive — double-speed (2x) or faster.

✔ A sound card for PCs. (Mac OS computers have built-in sound support.)

✔ A monitor capable of displaying at least 256 colors or grayscale.

✔ A modem with a speed of at least 14,400 bps.

If you need more information on the basics, check out *PCs For Dummies,* 4th
Edition, by Dan Gookin; *Macs For Dummies,* 4th Edition, by David Pogue;
Windows 95 For Dummies, by Andy Rathbone; or *Windows 3.11 For Dummies,*
3rd Edition, by Andy Rathbone (all published by IDG Books Worldwide, Inc.).

How to Use the CD Using Microsoft Windows

To install the items from the CD to your hard drive, follow these steps.

1. **Insert the CD into your computer's CD-ROM drive.**

2. **Windows 3.1 or 3.11 users: From Program Manager, choose File⇨Run.**

   Windows 95/NT users: Click on the Start button and click on Run.

3. **In the dialog box that appears, type** D:\SETUP.EXE.

   Most of you probably have your CD-ROM drive listed as drive D under My
   Computer in Windows 95/NT or the File Manager in Windows 3.1. Type in
   the proper drive letter if your CD-ROM drive uses a different letter.

4. **Click on OK.**

   A license agreement window appears.

5. **Since I'm sure you'll want to use the CD, read through the license
   agreement, nod your head, and then click on the Accept button.
   Once you click on Accept, you'll never be bothered by the License
   Agreement window again.**

   From here, the CD interface appears. The CD interface is a little program that shows you what is on the CD and coordinates installing the
   programs and running the demos. The interface basically lets you click
   on a button or two to make things happen.

6. **The first screen you see is the Welcome screen. Click anywhere on
   this screen to enter the interface.**

   Now you are getting to the action. This next screen lists categories for
   the software on the CD.

7. **To view the items within a category, just click on the category's name.**

   A list of programs in the category appears.

8. **For more information about a program, click on the program's name.**

   Be sure to read the information that appears. Sometimes a program may require you to do a few tricks on your computer first, and this screen will tell you where to go for that information, if necessary.

9. **To install the program, click on the Install button. If you don't want to install the program, click on the Go Back button to return to the previous screen.**

   You can always return to the previous screen by clicking on the Go Back button. This allows you to browse the different categories and products and decide what you want to install.

   Once you click on an install button, the CD interface drops to the background while the CD begins installation of the program you chose.

10. **To install other items, repeat Steps 7, 8 and 9.**

11. **When you're done installing programs, click on the Quit button to close the interface.**

    You can eject the CD now. Carefully place it back in the plastic jacket of the book for safekeeping.

How to Use the CD Using the Mac OS

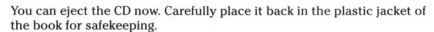

To install the items from the CD to your hard drive, follow these steps.

1. **Insert the CD into your computer's CD-ROM drive.**

   In a moment, an icon representing the CD you just inserted appears on your Mac desktop. Chances are, the icon looks like a CD-ROM.

2. **Double-click on the CD icon to show the CD's contents.**

3. **Double-click on the Read Me First icon.**

   This text file contains information about the CD's programs and any last-minute instructions you need to know about installing the programs on the CD that we don't cover in this appendix.

4. **To install most programs, just drag the program's folder from the CD window and drop it on your hard drive icon.**

5. **Some programs come with installer programs — with those you simply open the program's folder on the CD and double-click on the icon with the words "Install" or "Installer."**

Once you have installed the programs that you want, you can eject the CD. Carefully place it back in the plastic jacket of the book for safekeeping.

What You'll Find

Here's a summary of the software on this CD. If you use Windows, the CD interface helps you install software easily. (If you have no idea what I'm talking about when I say "CD interface," flip back a page or two to find the section, "How to Use the CD Using Microsoft Windows.")

If you use a Mac OS computer, you can enjoy the ease of the Mac interface to quickly install the programs.

AT&T WorldNet Service, from AT&T (Mac OS and Windows)

In the Internet Access category. In case you don't have an Internet connection, the CD includes sign-on software for AT&T WorldNet Service, an Internet Service Provider.

For more information and updates of AT&T WorldNet Service, visit the AT&T WorldNet Web site: www.att.com/worldnet

If you already have an Internet Service Provider, please note that AT&T WorldNet Service software makes changes to your computer's current Internet configuration and may replace your current provider's settings.

BBEdit Lite 4.0., HTML Web Weaver Lite (Mac OS) and Allaire HomeSite (Windows)

In the More Cool Stuff category. Each of these programs helps you create your own business or personal Web site without having to learn everything there is to know about HTML, the programming language for making Web pages.

BBEdit Lite 4.0., from Bare Bones Software, Inc., is a Macintosh freeware text editor with powerful features that make creating HTML scripts for your Web pages easy. The commercial version of this program, BBEdit 4.5, has even stronger HTML editing features. If you are familiar with HTML already, BBEdit is a good program to use. BBEdit is ideally suited for marking up text. When you are ready to design a Web page, you can use another program such as HTML Web Weaver or HomeSite to combine your text with images, colors, and other graphic elements. You can find out more about BBEdit at `www.barebones.com/products/products.html`.

HTML Web Weaver by Miracle Software, Inc. is one of the best Web page creation programs around for the Macintosh. This is a good program for learning HTML. As you format headings, lists, or other parts of a Web page, you see the HTML commands added to your document in the World Wide Web Weaver window. The program also makes it easy to design Web pages with cool features like frames, tables, and forms. You can find out more at the Miracle Software Inc. Web site (`www.miracleinc.com/`).

Allaire HomeSite is similar to HTML Web Weaver in that it adds HTML commands to your Web page as you format the contents. The difference is that it's available for Windows 95 and NT computers (not Windows 3.1). Another advantage is that HomeSite comes with Wizards, helpful utilities that guide you through a task such as creating frames or tables. You can find out more about the program at the Allaire Corporation Web site (`www.allaire.com/products/`).

Paint Shop Pro (Windows)

In the More Cool Stuff category. Paint Shop Pro is a shareware graphics viewing and editing tool. A version is available on the CD for Windows 3.1 and Windows 95. Check out `www.jasc.com/pspdl.html` on the World Wide Web for a full description.

Crosswind (Windows)

In the More Cool Stuff category. Two scheduling products from Crosswind Technologies that take advantage of the Internet are included on the CD. CyberScheduler and Synchronize Calendar Server are designed specifically to work with offices that are connected to the Internet or that operate internal intranets. Together, these two programs enable office employees to view and maintain schedules using a Web browser interface.

Synchronize is calendaring and scheduling database server software that is installed on your UNIX or Windows NT office server. CyberScheduler is the Web client software that can be installed on any computer that needs to access the database. Once users install CyberScheduler, on-site and remote employees alike can connect to the office server and update and review schedules using any Web browser, such as Netscape Navigator or Microsoft Internet Explorer.

The versions on the CD are for offices that are on the Net and that use Windows NT to run a network. Versions for UNIX systems are available from the Crosswind Web site (www.crosswind.com).

Anarchie 2.0.1 (Mac OS)

In the FTP category. A great FTP client program for the Macintosh by Peter N. Lewis. As described in Chapter 16, Anarchie acts as a guide as you scour FTP archives around the world for software you can use in the office or just for fun. Anarchie comes with an extensive list of bookmarks that take you to popular software archives on the Internet. The program requires a Macintosh running System 7, MacTCP 1.1, and Open Transport 1.1 or later. If you decide to keep the trial copy of Anarchie included on the CD, you should pay a $10 shareware fee to Peter Lewis. You can find out more about Anarchie at www.stairways.com.

Disinfectant 3.7.1 (Mac OS)

In the More Cool Stuff category. If you're worried about catching a computer virus (and you should be), Disinfectant will go a long way toward making your Internet computing experience worry-free. Disinfectant is a popular, freeware virus protection utility created by John Norstad of Northwestern University. After installing the program, Disinfectant will not only clear out any viruses you might already have, but the program can also watch over your system for any viruses you might encounter when downloading software. You can find out more about Disinfectant at charlotte.at.nwu.edu/jln/progs.ssi.

Eudora Light (Mac OS and Windows)

In the E-mail category. As described in Chapter 7, Eudora by Qualcomm Inc. is one of the most popular Internet e-mail programs for both Macintosh and Windows computers. Eudora is especially good if you want to automate the handling of your incoming e-mail by setting up filters: sets of criteria that enable an e-mail program to recognize particular types of e-mail and automatically file, delete, or otherwise handle them. Of course, Eudora also lets you do basic sending and receiving of e-mail, too. Eudora comes in two versions: Light and Pro. To download a trial copy of Eudora Pro or to find out more about the program, visit the Qualcomm Inc. Web site (www.eudora.com).

Internet Phone (Mac OS and Windows)

In the Real Time Communications category. Internet Phone, by VocalTec Communications, is one of the first and best-known Internet phone programs. Internet Phone lets you contact another computer user and speak to that person using your computer sound card, microphone and speakers. You can save on long-distance phone bills because you only pay to make a local call to your Internet provider in order to connect to the Net. You can find out more about Internet Phone at www.vocaltec.com.

NetPresenz (Mac OS) and WSFTPD (Windows)

In the FTP category. These programs allow you to set up your own File Transfer Protocol (FTP) site on any computer that is connected to the Internet. Once you have your own FTP server, your friends and business colleagues can log in to your computer directly and send you files without having to go through a third party such as an Internet Service Provider. You can also make files available to others by transferring to the FTP directory on your server.

NetPresenz, by Peter N. Lewis, is about the best FTP server software available for the Macintosh. It's easy to set up, and is available for only a $10 shareware fee.

WFTPD stands for *Windows FTP daemon.* (A *daemon* is a program that operates on your computer all the time.) This program, by Alun Jones, is available for a $20 shareware fee. You can find out more about WFTPD and download upgrades to the program at www.io.com/~alun.

Pegasus Mail (Mac OS and Windows)

In the E-mail category. Pegasus Mail is a freeware Internet e-mail program that lets manage your e-mail in sophisticated ways. For instance, you can have Pegasus Mail respond to an incoming message by automatically sending an acknowledgment or other message to the sender. You can download versions of Pegasus Mail for other operating systems at www.pegasus.usa.com/ftp.htm.

PowWow (Windows)

In the Real Time Communications category. Want to conduct a business meeting on the Internet? PowWow, by Tribal Voice, is a program that allows up to nine people to chat, transfer files, and cruise the World-Wide Web together. The program is available for Windows 3.1 and higher. You can find out more at www.tribal.com/powwow.

SLMail (Windows NT and 95)

In the E-mail category. SLMail 2.5 by Seattle Labs is software that lets you create your own mailing list so you can send out information to large numbers of your customers all at once. SLMail works best if you have a direct Internet connection, but it will work with dial-up connections as well. SLMail is a versatile program that provides not only an e-mail server, but mailing list administration and automatic replies to e-mail messages as well. Chapter 7 includes some instructions for getting started with the program. You can find out even more at the Seattle Labs Web site (www.seattlelabs.com/slmail).

Stuffit Expander 4.0.1 (Mac OS)

In the More Cool Stuff category. In order to install and use the software that you have downloaded from the Internet, you need a program that decompresses files that have been compressed or decodes files that have been encoded. One of the best programs you can use is StuffIt Expander by Aladdin Systems Inc. To find out more, visit the Aladdin Systems Web site (www.aladdinsys.com).

WS_FTP LE (Windows)

In the FTP category. WS_FTP by Ipswitch, Inc. is an easy-to-use program that lets you transfer files on the Internet with File Transfer Protocol (FTP). WS_FTP comes in the LE version included on this CD as well as a Pro version with more powerful features. You can download a trial version of WS_FTP Pro at the Ipswitch Web site (www.ipswitch.com).

WinZip 6.3 (Windows)

In the More Cool Stuff category. WinZip is the preeminent program for un-packing archived files on a Windows. A compressed file archive is a single file that contains several different files. It's a convenient format for transferring groups of files at once. You can use WinZip to create as well as unpack archives. It's easy to install and use, and is pretty much indispensable for anyone who uses the Internet extensively. WinZip is so popular that it has its own Web site (www.winzip.com), where you can download more recent versions of the program.

WinGate (Windows)

WinGate is a server that allows several users to access the internet through only one modem (or almost any other type of connection).

To use this software, you will need to got to the WinGate web site, at www.wingate.net/trialkey.htm, and register for a Trial Key. This trial key will allow you to use the WinGate PRO software for 30 days. Then it will revert to a one-user version of WinGate LITE.

If You've Got Problems (Of the CD Kind)

I tried my best to compile programs that work on most computers with the minimum system requirements. Alas, your computer may differ, and some programs may not work properly for some reason.

The two likeliest problems are that you don't have enough memory (RAM) for the programs you want to use, or you have other programs running that are affecting the installation or running of a program. If you get error messages like Not enough memory or Setup cannot continue, try one or more of these methods and then try using the software again:

- ✔ Turn off any anti virus software that you have on your computer. Installers sometimes mimic virus activity and may make your computer incorrectly believe that it is being infected by a virus.

- ✔ Close all running programs. The more programs you're running, the less memory is available to other programs. Installers also typically update files and programs. So if you keep other programs running, installation may not work properly.

- ✔ Have your local computer store add more RAM to your computer. This is, admittedly, a drastic and somewhat expensive step. However, if you have a Windows 95 PC or a Mac OS computer with a PowerPC chip, adding more memory can really help the speed of your computer and enable more programs to run at the same time. This may include closing the CD interface and running a product's installation program from Windows Explorer.

If you still have trouble with installing the items from the CD, please call the IDG Books Worldwide Customer Service phone number: 800-762-2974 (outside the U.S.: 317-596-5430).

Index

(continued)

(continued)

IDG Books Worldwide, Inc., End-User License Agreement

READ THIS. You should carefully read these terms and conditions before opening the software packet(s) included with this book ("Book"). This is a license agreement ("Agreement") between you and IDG Books Worldwide, Inc. ("IDGB"). By opening the accompanying software packet(s), you acknowledge that you have read and accept the following terms and conditions. If you do not agree and do not want to be bound by such terms and conditions, promptly return the Book and the unopened software packet(s) to the place you obtained them for a full refund.

1. **License Grant.** IDGB grants to you (either an individual or entity) a nonexclusive license to use one copy of the enclosed software program(s) (collectively, the "Software") solely for your own personal or business purposes on a single computer (whether a standard computer or a workstation component of a multiuser network). The Software is in use on a computer when it is loaded into temporary memory (RAM) or installed into permanent memory (hard disk, CD-ROM, or other storage device). IDGB reserves all rights not expressly granted herein.

2. **Ownership.** IDGB is the owner of all right, title, and interest, including copyright, in and to the compilation of the Software recorded on the CD-ROM ("Software Media"). Copyright to the individual programs recorded on the Software Media is owned by the author or other authorized copyright owner of each program. Ownership of the Software and all proprietary rights relating thereto remain with IDGB and its licensers.

3. **Restrictions on Use and Transfer.**

   (a) You may only (i) make one copy of the Software for backup or archival purposes, or (ii) transfer the Software to a single hard disk, provided that you keep the original for backup or archival purposes. You may not (i) rent or lease the Software, (ii) copy or reproduce the Software through a LAN or other network system or through any computer subscriber system or bulletin-board system, or (iii) modify, adapt, or create derivative works based on the Software.

   (b) You may not reverse engineer, decompile, or disassemble the Software. You may transfer the Software and user documentation on a permanent basis, provided that the transferee agrees to accept the terms and conditions of this Agreement and you retain no copies. If the Software is an update or has been updated, any transfer must include the most recent update and all prior versions.

4. **Restrictions on Use of Individual Programs.** You must follow the individual requirements and restrictions detailed for each individual program in this Book. These limitations are also contained in the individual license agreements recorded on the Software Media. These limitations may include a requirement that after using the program for a specified period of time, the user must pay a registration fee or discontinue use. By opening the Software packet(s), you will be agreeing to abide by the licenses and restrictions for these individual programs that are detailed in this book and on the Software Media. None of the material on this Software Media or listed in this Book may ever be redistributed, in original or modified form, for commercial purposes.

5. **Limited Warranty.**

   (a) IDGB warrants that the Software and Software Media are free from defects in materials and workmanship under normal use for a period of sixty (60) days from the date of purchase of this Book. If IDGB receives notification within the warranty period of defects in materials or workmanship, IDGB will replace the defective Software Media.

   (b) **IDGB AND THE AUTHOR OF THE BOOK DISCLAIM ALL OTHER WARRANTIES, EXPRESS OR IMPLIED, INCLUDING WITHOUT LIMITATION IMPLIED WARRANTIES OF MER-CHANTABILITY AND FITNESS FOR A PARTICULAR PURPOSE, WITH RESPECT TO THE SOFTWARE, THE PROGRAMS, THE SOURCE CODE CONTAINED THEREIN, AND/OR THE TECHNIQUES DESCRIBED IN THIS BOOK. IDGB DOES NOT WARRANT THAT THE FUNCTIONS CONTAINED IN THE SOFTWARE WILL MEET YOUR REQUIREMENTS OR THAT THE OPERATION OF THE SOFTWARE WILL BE ERROR FREE.**

   (c) This limited warranty gives you specific legal rights, and you may have other rights that vary from jurisdiction to jurisdiction.

6. **Remedies.**

   (a) IDGB's entire liability and your exclusive remedy for defects in materials and workmanship shall be limited to replacement of the Software Media, which may be returned to IDGB with a copy of your receipt at the following address: Software Media Fulfillment Department, Attn.: Small Business Internet For Dummies, IDG Books Worldwide, Inc., 7260 Shadeland Station, Ste. 100, Indianapolis, IN 46256, or call 800-762-2974. Please allow three to four weeks for delivery. This Limited Warranty is void if failure of the Software Media has resulted from accident, abuse, or misapplication. Any replacement Software Media will be warranted for the remainder of the original warranty period or thirty (30) days, whichever is longer.

   (b) In no event shall IDGB or the author be liable for any damages whatsoever (including without limitation damages for loss of business profits, business interruption, loss of business information, or any other pecuniary loss) arising from the use of or inability to use the Book or the Software, even if IDGB has been advised of the possibility of such damages.

   (c) Because some jurisdictions do not allow the exclusion or limitation of liability for conse-quential or incidental damages, the above limitation or exclusion may not apply to you.

7. **U.S. Government Restricted Rights.** Use, duplication, or disclosure of the Software by the U.S. Government is subject to restrictions stated in paragraph (c)(1)(ii) of the Rights in Technical Data and Computer Software clause of DFARS 252.227-7013, and in subparagraphs (a) through (d) of the Commercial Computer–Restricted Rights clause at FAR 52.227-19, and in similar clauses in the NASA FAR supplement, when applicable.

8. **General.** This Agreement constitutes the entire understanding of the parties and revokes and supersedes all prior agreements, oral or written, between them and may not be modified or amended except in a writing signed by both parties hereto that specifically refers to this Agreement. This Agreement shall take precedence over any other documents that may be in conflict herewith. If any one or more provisions contained in this Agreement are held by any court or tribunal to be invalid, illegal, or otherwise unenforceable, each and every other provision shall remain in full force and effect.

Installing the CD-ROM

To use software from *Small Business Internet For Dummies* CD-ROM, insert the CD-ROM into your PC's CD-ROM drive. Start the CD-ROM installation program by running Setup.exe from the first directory of the CD-ROM.

The CD-ROM installation program offers you the product categories that are shown in the following illustration. To see the programs in a product category, click the name of the product category. To install a program from a product category, click the name of the program and follow its on-screen instructions.

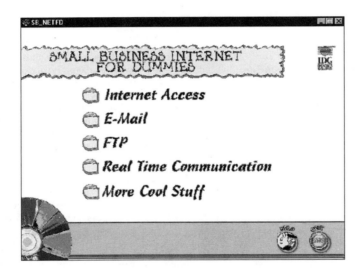